797,885 Books

are available to read at

www.ForgottenBooks.com

Forgotten Books' App
Available for mobile, tablet & eReader

ISBN 978-1-333-86452-1
PIBN 10549184

This book is a reproduction of an important historical work. Forgotten Books uses state-of-the-art technology to digitally reconstruct the work, preserving the original format whilst repairing imperfections present in the aged copy. In rare cases, an imperfection in the original, such as a blemish or missing page, may be replicated in our edition. We do, however, repair the vast majority of imperfections successfully; any imperfections that remain are intentionally left to preserve the state of such historical works.

Forgotten Books is a registered trademark of FB &c Ltd.
Copyright © 2015 FB &c Ltd.
FB &c Ltd, Dalton House, 60 Windsor Avenue, London, SW19 2RR.
Company number 08720141. Registered in England and Wales.

For support please visit www.forgottenbooks.com

1 MONTH OF FREE READING

at

www.ForgottenBooks.com

By purchasing this book you are eligible for one month membership to ForgottenBooks.com, giving you unlimited access to our entire collection of over 700,000 titles via our web site and mobile apps.

To claim your free month visit:
www.forgottenbooks.com/free549184

* Offer is valid for 45 days from date of purchase. Terms and conditions apply.

English
Français
Deutsche
Italiano
Español
Português

www.forgottenbooks.com

Mythology Photography **Fiction** Fishing Christianity **Art** Cooking Essays Buddhism Freemasonry Medicine **Biology** Music **Ancient Egypt** Evolution Carpentry Physics Dance Geology **Mathematics** Fitness Shakespeare **Folklore** Yoga Marketing **Confidence** Immortality Biographies Poetry **Psychology** Witchcraft Electronics Chemistry History **Law** Accounting **Philosophy** Anthropology Alchemy Drama Quantum Mechanics Atheism Sexual Health **Ancient History Entrepreneurship** Languages Sport Paleontology Needlework Islam **Metaphysics** Investment Archaeology Parenting Statistics Criminology **Motivational**

A HISTORY

OF THE

PROTESTANT EPISCOPAL CHURCH

IN

AMERICA.

BY

Wilberforce

SAMUEL, LORD BISHOP OF OXFORD.

NEW-YORK:
STANFORD AND SWORDS, 137, BROADWAY.

1849.

J. R. M'GOWN, PRINTER AND STEREOTYPER,
No. 57 ANN-STREET, NEW-YORK.

PREFACE TO THE AMERICAN EDITION.

To the American Editor of this volume it seems important, that the interesting historical facts contained in this "Church History," should be more extensively known in this country. In answer to the question, How is it that the history of the Church in these United States has been written by a Prelate of the Church in England? We may be answered, that the opportunity afforded in England, to consult the works of the earlier writers upon America and the correspondence of the earlier missionaries to America, has been embraced by the Author and most laboriously improved. He has brought out many facts and selected many very interesting incidents before generally unknown.

This cannot be called a *complete* History of the Church in this country; but it approaches nearer to it than any other work before published. The character of the various Bishops who have, after having ruled over their respective Dioceses, "gone to their rest," is admirably drawn out and perhaps with more impartiality than would have been done, by a clergyman of our own Church. Members of the Church in this country ought to feel under great obligation to the distinguished Prelate, who, amidst so many cares and avocations has found time to compile this valuable work.

E. M. J.

PREFACE.

In giving the following pages to the press, their Author desires, in the first place, to acknowledge the kindness which from many quarters, both in America and England, has supplied him with the materials for their composition. Never can he forget the ready aid which he has received from personal strangers on the other side of the Atlantic. To particularize any, where he cannot enumerate all, he feels to be impossible. He can only express his earnest wish that his volume were more worthy of their several contributions; and his hope that, in stating openly and freely what seem to him to be the defects of the organization or conduct of their body, he shall give no needless pain to any one. Convinced as he is, that to draw a veil over such evils would be disloyalty to their common cause, he has felt under an imperative necessity of speaking openly and fully. But it would most deeply grieve him, were any cause of offence to be found in his words, or anything which could sever those who should be so closely united as the Churchmen of England and America. On the subject to which he here especially refers, namely, the treatment of the colored race, the use of the Church's moral influence in its behalf is that which alone he would claim. And this claim he advances under a humbling sense of the past deficiencies of members of his own communion. Still, in their case it must be urged, that they were afar from the sight, and therefore from the real knowledge, of the evils of colonial life. Those evils would not have been endured, had they been daily submitted to the eyes of the laity and clergy of the English Church.

On one other important point a few words must here be added to the following pages. Throughout their course the Author has felt oppressed by the recurring question, how he ought to deal with those other religious bodies by which the Protestant Episcopal Church in North America is so abundantly surrounded. To have entered into their history would, within the limits of this work, have been absolutely impossible; and yet, to confine himself to the history of one department only of the vast host which bears the Christian name, must of necessity give to his work a narrow and one-sided appearance. To escape this imperfection, he believes to have been unavoidable, and he has therefore submitted to it; writing the history, not of religion, but of the Protestant Episcopal Church. Only would he here protest against being supposed to entertain any intention of contemptuously passing by the many great deeds for Christ's truth wrought in that western world by the members of other societies, or of pronouncing by the way a decisive judgment on any of the intricate questions to which the co-existence of these various bodies must give birth. He has dealt with them only as they directly affect that communion whose history he writes; and in doing so, he has endeavored to treat them honestly and fairly, although, from his limits, it must be slightly and imperfectly.

Amongst those who in this country have assisted him with valuable materials, and to whom he would beg publicly to return his thanks, he may venture to enumerate his father's early friend, Thomas Clarkson: the Rev. H. H. Norris, of Hackney; Petty Vaughan, Esq.; the Lord

Bishop of London,—who most liberally allowed him access to all the MS. treasures of the Fulham library; the Rev. H. Caswall,—whose local knowledge made him able to revise those parts which touch upon existing institutions; and the Rev. Ernest Hawkins, Secretary to the Society for the Propagation of the Gospel in Foreign Parts.

To the labors of that society the following pages repeatedly bear witness. They show on this one stage how, throughout the coldness and negligence of the last century, when, in this land at least, no other body so made head against the general apathy as to think of the foreign advancement of the Gospel as a Christian duty, this venerable society ever followed in the wake of our colonial extension, watched for opportunities of sowing the good seed, labored ever noiselessly and unobserved in this great work, nurtured the faint beginnings of colonial piety, and has been, under God's grace, the one first instrument in preventing the upgrowth of positive infidelity, and in promoting the existence and spread of Christianity throughout those vast districts which make up our colonial empire— the widest empire and the greatest trust which God ever committed to any people.

The Author hopes that this may be, amongst others, one effect of his labor, that, seeing what was attempted, and what was effected, in America by this society, some of his readers may be aroused to consider what are indeed its claims upon their grateful and affectionate support.

CONTENTS.

CHAPTER I.

Interest of general subject—Times of Queen Elizabeth—Influence of the Reformation—Martin Frobisher—His first voyage—A native kidnapped—Second and third voyages—Master Wolfall—Black ore—Sir Humphrey Gilbert—Letters patent—Religious purpose of colonisation—Prospect of its late fulfilment—Gilbert's second voyage—His death—Sir Walter Raleigh—His expeditions—Tobacco—Settlements—Raleigh's troubles; and death—Settlement of Virginia—Robert Hunt—James Town—Captain Smith—Trials of the Settlers—Starving time—Lord Delaware—Master Bucke—Whittaker—Pochahontas---Early Laws 15

CHAPTER II.

FROM 1620 TO 1688.

Virginia Company—Measures of Sir E. Sandys, Nicholas Ferrar, and others—Churches endowed—College founded—Mr. Thorpe—Indian massacre—Indian Conquest—Effects of the massacre—Virginia in the Great Rebellion—Loyalty—Love of the Church—Effects of Puritan rule—King Charles II. proclaimed—Enactments of Legislature in behalf of the Church—Popish plots suspected 34

CHAPTER III.

FROM 1608 TO 1688.

Neighboring colonies—New-York—New-Jersey—Philadelphia—Carolina—Maryland—New-England—Its settlement—Rise of Puritanism in England—Emigration, to Leyden, to New-England—Piety of the early Puritans—Their hatred of Church Principles—Severity---Treatment of Indians...Proselyting spirit towards other communions 43

CHAPTER IV.

FROM 1688 TO 1775.

Spiritual destitution of the colonies—Exertions of the Bishop of London, Hon. Robert Boyle, and others—Drs. Blair and Bray sent as commissaries to Virginia and Maryland—New-York conquered by English—Trinity Church endowed—Progress of the Church in New-England—Boston petition for Episcopal worship—Foundation of the Society for the Propagation of the Gospel—Religious state of the colonies—Labors of the Missionaries of the Venerable Society—Rev. Geo. Keith—Violence of Quakers—Opposition from New-England magistrates—Yale College—Leading Congregationalists join the Church—Progress of the Church at Newtown under Mr. Beach—Violence of Congregationalists—General state of the Church in Virginia—Mr. Whitefield—Spreading dissent—Rise of Anabaptists in Virginia—Resistance to the clergy—Low state of the Church—Its causes—Clergy dependent on their flocks—Want of bishops—Attempts to obtain an American episcopate, in the reign of Charles II, of Queen Anne—Bishop Berkeley opposed by Walpole—Supported by Archbishop Secker—Efforts in the colonies—Zeal of northern colonies—Virginia refuses to join in the attempt—Causes of this refusal 72

CHAPTER V.

FROM 1775 TO 1783-4.

Revolutionary war—Loyalty of the Northern clergy—Persecution—Virginian clergy generally loyal—Treated with Violence—Thomas Jefferson—Zeal of the Anabaptists—Their hatred to the Church—Repeal of all former acts in its favor—Incomes of the clergy stopped—They are stripped even of the glebes and churches—Conduct of the Methodists—John Wesley persuaded to consecrate Dr. Coke—Depressed state of the Church at the end of the war—Religion at a low ebb—The revolutionary war a consequence of the Church not having been planted in America 131

CHAPTER VI.

FROM 1783 TO 1787.

Depression of the Church—Parties—And Opinions—attempted organisation in the south—Mr. White—Conventions in Virginia and Philadelphia—Agreement on common principles—First movements for general union—General voluntary meeting at New-York—Want of episcopate—Movement amongst the eastern clergy—They elect Dr. Seabury Bishop—He sails for England—Disappointed of consecration there—Dr. Berkeley and the Scotch bishops—Dr. Seabury applies to them—Opposition—His consecration—And return—First Convention at Philadelphia—Difference of Opinion—Dr. White—Proposed liturgy—Application to the English prelates for the apostolical succession—Their objections to some changes in the Liturgy—These reconsidered—Drs. White and Provoost embark for England—Are consecrated at Lambeth—Return to America, April 1787 . 142

CHAPTER VII.

Convention assemblies—Case of Dr. Bass—Bishop Seabury joins the Convention—The Liturgy—First and succeeding consecrations—Period of depression—Its causes—Ecclesiastical constitution—Parish—Diocese—Convention—Laity in Convention—Anglo-Saxon usage—Difficulties of true organization in America—Neglect of the mother-country . 166

CHAPTER VIII.

FROM 1801 TO 1811--12.

Death and character of Bishop Seabury—Bishop White—Bishop Provoost—His character—Resigns the episcopal jurisdiction—Nomination and consecration of Bishop Moore—His character—Improvement of the state of the Church—Maryland—Bishop Claggett—Party Spirit —Bishop Claggett applies for a suffragan—Division of convention in 1812—Method of Electing a bishop—The laity negative the nomination of the clergy—Convention of 1813—No attempt at an election made—Dr. Kemp elected suffragan in 1814—Consequent party feuds—Bishop Claggett's death—Dr.

Kemp succeeds—His death—Renewed contests as to the Episcopate Bishop Stone elected—Troubles on his death—The see vacant—State of Delaware—No Bishop—Application to Maryland—Refused—Decay of the Church there—And in Virginia—Issue of the long struggle with the Anabaptists and others—The glebes confiscated—Prostration of the Church . . . 193

CHAPTER IX.

1811, 12.

Death of Bp. Madison—Renewal of diocesan convention—Election of Dr. Bracken to the episcopate—He refuses it—Dr. Moore elected—His early life—Ministerial success—He visits the diocese—Stirs up the spirit of Churchmen—Revival of the Church—Growth of Church principles—Improved canons—Theological seminary founded—And poor scholars fund—Dr. Meade elected suffragan, with a restriction—Conduct of the house of Bishops—Removal of restrictions—Bishop B. Moore of New-York applies for an assistant Bishop—Dr. J. H. Hobart elected—His origin and youth—First ministerial charge in Pennsylvania—Removes to New-York—His studies—Publications—Services in state and general Convention—Controversy with Dr. Mason—Elected Bishop—Opposition—Bishop Provoost's claim to the bishoprick of New-York—Disallowed by the Convention—Bishop White's treatment of Bishop Hobart—and high esteem for him 206

CHAPTER X.

FROM 1810 TO 1820.

Episcopate of Bishop Hobart—First two years of opposition—Rise of Church societies—Effect upon the laity—New tone of feeling and action—Bishop Hobart with his clergy—His language as to the Church of Rome—His visitations—General spread of the Church—Increase of bishopricks—State of "the West"—Need of missionary pastors—Pioneers of the Church—Lay readers—Samuel Gunn—His early years—Labors—Removal to Ohio—Consecration of Bishop Chase—His life—Founds Kenyon College—Its building—Students—Their missionary excursions—How received—Funds for domestic purposes—Jackson Kemper—Bishop Hobart's canon—His labors amongst the Indians—Oneida reserves—Eleazer Williams—His history—The Bishop's visit 228

CHAPTER XI.

FROM 1820 TO 1836.

American education—Temper of American Youth—Jealousy of high education—Absence of theological training—Foundation of the General Theological Seminary—Its success—Bishop Hobart's connexion with it—His death—And character—Bishop B. T. Onderdonk succeeds—Increase of the episcopate—Bishops Ravenscroft and Ives of North Carolina—Bishop Meade of Virginia—And H. U. Onderdonk, assistant bishop of Pennsylvania—Bishop Chase of Ohio—Resigns his bishopric—Consecrations of Bishops M'Ilvaine of Ohio, Hopkins of Vermont. Smith of Kentucky, and Doane of New-Jersey—Change of feeling as to the episcopate—Convention of 1835—Bishop Chase of Illinois—Division of dioceses—New organization of missionary board—The missionary bishop—Bishop Kemper consecrated—Success of the new plan—Subsequent growth of the Church—Bishop White's illness—Death and character 261

CHAPTER XII.

Present influence of the Episcopal Church—Rapid extension—Estimated numbers—Clergy—Extent and population of dioceses—Influence on the moral character of the people—Favorable symptoms—Sects—Revivals—Socinianism—Sober tone of the Church—Duelling—Its character in America—Instance—Church resists duels—Canon—Instance—Unfavorable Symptoms—Divorce—Marriage—Treatment of the colored race—The great sore of America—State of negroes in the South, religious, moral, physical—Slave-breeding states—Internal slave-trade—Duty of the Church to testify—Her silence—Participation—Palliation of these evils—State of the colored population in the North—Insults—Degradation—Caste—Duty of the Church—Her silence—Case of General Theological Seminary—Alexander Crummell—Estimate of her influence—Her small hold on the poor—Architecture and arrangement of churches—Pew-rent system—Prospects of the Church—Danger from indifference to formal truth—Chaplains to Congress—Thomas Jefferson—Romanism—Its schismatical rise in America—Spread in the West—Promises a refuge from the sects—Courts democracy—Main resistance from the Church—How she may be strong—Need of adhering to her own principles—Of a high moral tone—The slave-question—Favorable promise—Higher principles—More care of the poor—Colored race—Gains on the population—Conclusion. 288

AMERICAN CHURCH

THE

AMERICAN CHURCH.

CHAPTER I.

Interest of general subject—Times of Queen Elizabeth—Influence of the Reformation—Martin Frobisher—His first voyage—a native kidnapped—Second and third voyages—Master Wolfall—Black ore—Sir Humphrey Gilbert—Letters patent—Religious purpose of colonisation—Prospect of its late fulfilment—Gilbert's second voyage—His death—Sir Walter Raleigh—His expeditions—Tobacco—Settlements—Raleigh's troubles: and death—Settlement of Virginia—Robert Hunt—James Town—Captain Smith—Trials of the Settlers—Starving time—Lord Delaware—Master Bucke—Whitaker—Pocahontas—Early laws.

FEW subjects can be more full of interest to members of the Church of England than the history of the Church in America. Indeed, the Church in every daughter nation has large claims on the affections of the mother state; and other circumstances here combine to strengthen the strait bands of Christian love. Our long neglect of our bounden duty, followed as it has been by God's merciful acceptance of our latest service, may well call out our affection for this child of our old age. Full of interest is it also to watch the up-growth of such a body amongst institutions so unlike our own; to note its various nourishment and well-proportioned increase in the western wilderness, into which it has been given wings to fly.

Such a narrative is full also of instruction. Many are the grounds for self-upbraiding and humiliation which it brings before us; and rich are its lessons as to the true treatment in religious matters of the dependent colonies of any Chistian people.

The age of Elizabeth, fertile in great men, produced

especially great naval heroes : all the circumstances of the nation favored their production. The fierce hostility of Spain forced upon England especial attention to her navy. The service of the sea had not as yet grown into a separate profession ; to equip and to command a ship became a common practice of ambitious courtiers, and even of independent country gentlemen. The rich plate fleets of Spain often repaid the expense of fitting out an expedition, and not seldom was a goodly inheritance sold to furnish forth the daring adventurer. To this inducement was added the alluring hope of making profitable foreign settlements. The mines of Spanish America glittered before the eyes of many an ardent Englishman ; and he eagerly exchanged his patrimony here for the hope of those golden acres which he expected to possess on the other side of the Atlantic, on the easy terms of paying the Queen the fifth part of all precious metals.

Other causes, moreover, were at work preparing the way for extensive emigration. The reformation of religion had restored to its full vigor the national life of England, which even popery had not been strong enough to stifle utterly ; and one of the first fruits of this revival was, its sending forth its race beyond the narrow limits of their own land. This tendency to wander has always marked the Anglo-Saxon family ; and the formation of a middle class, by the diffusion of wealth and the spread of mercantile adventure, at once set the current into active motion. It was accordingly in the reign of Elizabeth that the first attempt was made to found an English colony on the shores of America.

The first steps which led to the vast undertaking are not a little curious. Among the stirring spirits of the time none adventured more in maritime exploits than Captain Martin Frobisher. He " being persuaded of a new and nearer passage to Cataya* than by Cape de Buona Speranza, which the Portuguese yearly use, determined with himself to go and make full proof thereof."†

---

* *i. e.* China.
† Hackluyt's Collection of Early Voyages, vol. iii. p. 85.

After many delays he accordingly set forth upon the 15th of June, 1576, in two barques of twenty and twenty-five tons burden, provisioned for twelve months, on this dangerous voyage. Deserted by his second barque, this gallant man pushed on in those unknown regions, amidst " cruel storms of snow and haile, great islands of yce, and mighty deere that seemed to be mankinde, which ranne at him so that hardly he escaped with his life :"* until he discovered the straits which bear his name.† Having advanced so far, and finding the cold still increasing, he turned his face homeward ; but first being desirous to bring thence some token of his travel, he wrought what, in the temper of the times, is termed by his biographer " a pretty policy." Knowing that the natives " greatly delighted in toyes and belles, he rang a pretty low bell, making signs that he would give him the same who would come and fetch it : and because they would not come within his danger for feare, he flung one bell unto them, which of purpose he threw short, that it might fall into the sea and be lost ; and to make them more greedy of the matter, he rang a louder bell, so that in the end one of them came neere the ship side to receive the belle, and was taken himself ; for the captain being readily provided, let the bell fall, and caught the man fast, and plucked him with maine force, boat and all, into his barke ; which strange infidell, whose like was never seene, read, nor heard of before, was a sufficient witness of the captains farre and tedious travel."‡

But the native thus cruelly kidnapped was not the only specimen they gathered. They brought home also "some floures, some greene grass, and one a piece of blacke stone, much like to a sea-cole in coloure, which by the weight seemed to be some kind of metall or minerall." This was " a thing of no account at first sight, in the judgment of the captain ;" but after his return " it fortuned a gentlewoman, one of the adventurers wives, to have a

* Hackluyt, vol. iii. pp. 67, 68, 87.
† Frobisher's Straits, lying to the north of Cape Farewell and West Greenland, long. 42 W., lat. 63 N.
‡ Hackluyt, vol. iii. p. 87.

piece thereof, which by chance she threw and burned in the fire so long, that at the length being taken forth and quenched in a little vinegar, it glistered with a bright marquesset of gold;" whereupon, having been adjudged by certain goldfiners in London "to holde golde, and that very nobly for the quantity," it inflamed the public mind with notions of the great wealth of those parts; and in the hope of rivalling the mines of Peru, another expedition was shortly afterwards set forth.

The captain's "special commission" on this voyage was directed to the searching for this golden ore; and so high was expectation raised, that he was admitted, before he sailed, into the Queen's presence; and after "kissing her highness' hand, with gracious countenance and comfortable words, departed towards his charge." He sailed with three ships on May 26th, 1577, hoping to bring home vast spoils of gold from the frozen shores of the *meta incognita*. On reaching this inhospitable coast, these expectations were increased by their finding "spiders, which, as many affirm, are signes of great store of gold,"* and by the assurance that streams flowed into the sea beneath the frozen surface, " by which the earth within is kept warmer, and springs have their recourse, which is the only nutriment of golde and minerals."†

When, therefore, the expedition reached the straits, no new discoveries were attempted; but having, " with five poore miners and the help of a few gentlemen and soldiers," who labored so hard that, by " overstraining, they received hurts not a little dangerous," " reasonably well filled their shippes," they set sail with about 200 tons of ore, " every man therewithal well comforted," and reached home safely on the 23d day of September.

The captain of the returning expedition repaired to Windsor, " to advertise her Majesty of his prosperous proceedings." These were considered of so promising a character, that a larger expedition was soon planned, which was to carry out a " number of chosen soldiers and discreet men, who should be assigned to inhabit there." For this

Hackluyt, vol. iii. pp. 63, 88. † Ibid. p. 64.

purpose forty mariners, thirty miners, and thirty soldiers, besides gentlemen, goldfiners, bakers, carpenters, and other necessary persons, were embarked on board of "fifteen sayle of good ships," which set off from Harwich on the 31st of May.

The name of one other adventurer must not be left unrecorded, since a higher object than the thirst of gold led him to face the dangers of the frozen sea. This was one "Master Wolfall, a learned man, appointed by her Majesty's council to be their minister and preacher, who, being well seated and settled at home in his owne countrey, with a good and large living, having a good honest woman to wife and very towardly children, being of good reputation amongst the best, refused not to take in hand this painfull voyage, for the only care he had to save soules and to reform those infidels, if it were possible, to Christianitie."*

Frobisher again acted as admiral; but the season was less favorable than it had been in former years. The straits were closed; and they were "forced many times to stemme and strike great rocks of yce, and so, as it were, make way through mighty mountaines." The icebergs were so vast, that, under the action of the sun, their tops melted and poured down streams "which made a pretie brooke, able to drive a mill." One bark was struck by such a floating island, and "sunk down therewith in the sight of the whole fleete;" whilst the rest "were faine to submit themselves and their ships to the mercy of the unmercyful yce, strengthening the sides of their ships with juncks of cables, beds, mastes, plankes, and such like, which being hanged overboard, on the sides of their ships, might the better defend them from the outrageous sway and stroke of the said yce."†

"The brunt," however, "of these so great and extreme dangers, the painfull mariners and poore miners overcame," and about the beginning of August, they reached their former harbor in safety; for which "they highly praysed God, and altogether, upon their knees, gave Him due, humble, and heartie thanks." Upon such occasions, "Master Wolfall celebrated a communion upon land, at

---

* Hackluyt, vol. iii. p. 116.   † Hackluyt, vol. iii. p 109, &c.

the partaking whereof was the captaine and many other gentlemen, and souldiers, mariners, and miners, with him. The celebration of the Divine mystery was the first signe, seale, and confirmation of Christ's name, death, and passion ever knowen in these quarters."

But it was soon found that the main object of the expedition must be abandoned. The fear of death from cold and hunger possessed those who were selected to remain, and they threatened a mutiny. In the quaint language of their historian, they did "greatly feare being driven to seek sowre sallets amongst the cold cliffs;" and it was at length resolved that they should defer the intended settlement until another year, and return home, laden with the black ore which promised gold. When this delusion was discovered we are not told; but after this voyage, the "black ore" is never mentioned farther.

Such were the first attempts at forming an English settlement in America; fruitless in themselves, and yet preparing the way for wiser and more successful efforts. Men with nobler aims than finding ore of gold were soon engaged in the work. Sir Humphrey Gilbert, himself a courtier of Queen Elizabeth, and nearly connected with that "prince of courtesy," Sir Walter Raleigh, was "the first of our nation that caused people to erect an habitation and government in these countreys." Instead of seeking to discover mines and acquire great riches suddenly, he desired "to prosecute effectually the full possession of these so ample and pleasant countreys for the crown and people of England." Amidst the motives given for this his so "virtuous and heroical minde," are "the honor of God, compassion of poore infidels captived by the devil (it seeming probable that God hath reserved these Gentiles to be reduced into Christian civility by the English nation), advancement of his honest and well-disposed countrymen willing to accompany him in such honorable actions, and reliefe of sundry people within this realme distressed."

These were great and noble ends, and they were not lightly undertaken; he knew that "the carriage of God's word into those very mighty and vast countreys was a high and excellent matter, likely to excite God's heavy judgments if it were intermeddled in with base purposes."

His preparations were suitable to these convictions. He sacrificed the bulk of his fortune at home, in order to complete the equipment of his ships; and gathered a numercus party of volunteers to settle this new land. The letters patent, which were granted to him by the Queen, proceed upon the supposition, that the spread of the Christian faith amongst the natives justified such settlements. His patent granted him "free power and liberty to discover all such HEATHEN LANDS as were not actually possessed by any Christian prince or people." To his settlers were secured the rights of Englishmen; whilst to himself was assigned the sole jurisdiction, civil and military, of the country within 200 leagues of his settlement, "provided always, that the statutes he devized should be, as near as conveniently might, agreeable to the laws and policy of England; and provided also, that they be not against the true Christian faith professed in the Church of England."

The most marked feature of the whole adventure is this repeated recognition of the making known the faith of Christ as its leading object: and far as after years fell below these early aspirations, and long, therefore, as this blessed end has been deferred, we at least who look across the broad Atlantic to the orderly and happy increase of the daughter Church, are allowed to witness much of its completion. Few sights can call more loudly for deep gratitude to God. Our own peculiar situation must make us watch with an unusual love the welfare of this body; for, as an independent national communion, this is our only offspring; and we are separated more or less from all around us. Old divisions, centuries ago, have parted widely the East from the West; whilst, nearer home, the deep pollutions and schismatical violence of Rome have rudely shivered the visible unity of Christendom; dividing us through our recovered purity of doctrine from all in union with herself, and leading to our separation from the mass of the reformed communions through that want of apostolic order with which the clinging curse of her old corruption has afflicted them. There are few sadder thoughts for painful hearts than those which spring from the consideration of these multiplied divisions. Those who remember that their Lord's last prayer for His disciples was, that "they all might be one," must long earnestly for that time when in visible oneness, "the Holy Church throughout all the world shall acknowledge Him." They must weep for the remembrance of those early ages, when those that believed in Christ in different lands were all seen by the joints of the common episcopate to be of one body and in communion with each other.

How our present divisions can be healed, and the blessing of visible unity again be restored to the Church, the most sanguine speculations cannot forecast. But the first great obstacle which bars all progress towards it is, the fearful error, that the different members of the Church must find their union with each other through union with the see of Rome. For this is, indeed, to deny the presence of Christ with His Church, which is her true glory : since that presence would make her everywhere a centre to herself, and would unite her several parts between themselves by their common union with Him. This, therefore, exalts into the place of Christ that which they fondly name "the Holy See," and makes the Church the representative of an absent, instead of the instrument for conveying to each soul the mysterious presence of an unseen Saviour.

This one delusion must prevent our ever desiring any union with Rome. For it is not merely that her creed is defaced with human additions, or her practice fallen and corrupt on separate points : these we might hope to see one by one abandoned or reformed, until the time might come when we would be again united with her. But this cannot be until this master-deceit is altogether thrown aside; until she shall cease to exalt the Church, as she designates her own communion, into the place of Christ, and to require oneness with it, as the condition of union with her Lord.

Most unlike this was the union of the earliest times ; when, with no professed visible centre of unity, each diocese, under its own bishop, was a free and equal member of the common body ; and all was gathered into unity under one Head—their unseen but present Saviour. The best promise of such a restoration is in the wide-spread and intimate connexion of those branches of the Church which are reformed in doctrine, and apostolical in discipline.

On every ground, therefore, we must needs look with more than common interest upon the daughter-communion of the West. This is "the seed the Lord hath given us;" these are the children of her who was too long barren. In our intercourse with them we may return to the happy condition of primitive times, when the people of Christ, though in various countries and under different rules, made up but one body, and lived in the daily and perpetual interchange of acts of Christian brotherhood. Such a fellowship with distant countries we shall find the best argument against the specious show of Roman unity, and one great safeguard for our people against its allurements.

In this connexion, therefore, it is full of interest to trace back our first national attempts at founding colonies to the spirit of the reformation; to find that we owe, in no slight measure, our maritime supremacy and wide colonial empire to the same true-hearted martyrs who, under God, bequeathed to us, by their witness and their blood, our English Bible and reformed communion.

The first expedition was designed in strict accordance with the royal charter; but when just on the eve of sailing, dissension broke up the band. Nothing daunted, however, the gallant Sir Humphrey still set forth, with a small company of faithful adherents. Of the adventures of this voyage there is scarcely any record. Its issue was unfortunate; mainly, as it is believed, from a conflict with the Spaniards, when, in a "dangerous sea-fight, many of his company were slain, and his ships therewith also sore battered and disabled."*

Five years elapsed before any fresh expedition was fitted out; but in 1585 the approaching expiration of his patent, which was to last but six years unless some settlement was effected, spurred him on to one more effort. The sale of all his landed propery, with the assistance of

---

* Hollinshed's Chronicles, vol. ii. fol. 1586, epist. ded.

other wealthy adventurers, enabled him to fit up two ships and three small barques, with which he set forth to colonise the new world. He sailed with the highest expectations. The haughty Elizabeth, though she would not share in the risk of the undertaking, condescended to bestow on him a golden anchor, in proof of her esteem; and Parmenius, an Hungarian scholar, went with him to chronicle his voyage. He crossed the Atlantic safely; and having reached the harbor of St. John's, Newfoundland—even then a fishing-station where thirty-six sail of all nations were assembled—he took possession of the territory, in spite of opposition, in his sovereign's name. Here a Saxon "mineral man," who formed part of his company, assured him, "on the peril of his life," that an ore he had discovered was nothing else than silver, which "is generally found in cold climates."* But Gilbert was above the low temptations of avarice. His views were of a nobler kind; and, ordering his "mineral man" to guard sacredly the secret, he resolved to prosecute a full examination of the southern coast. Had his success equalled his resolution, he might have been the first settler of the United States; but the weather, the dangers of the coast, and the restless temper of his crews, all conspired against him. Deserted by two of his captains and many of his men, he was obliged to leave one ship behind; and himself commanding one of his barques, the Squirrel, he steered southward with it and two of his remaining ships. They were soon entangled amongst shoals and shallows; and losing one ship with almost all its crew, including the "mineral man" and the Hungarian scholar, Gilbert was forced, most unwillingly, to turn his course homeward. His own little barque was ill suited for the violence of the open sea; but he would not forsake his comrades. On the voyage the storms grew "more dangerous," and he was pressed to come on board the larger vessel. "We are as near to heaven by sea as by land," was the answer of the gallant man. But he could not save the crew he would not leave. That same night, as he led the way, his

* Harris.

companions in the large vessel saw the lights of his barque suddenly extinguished : she had sunk utterly with all on board.

Disappointment could not damp the spirit which was kindled ; and Gilbert found a worthy successor in his half-brother, Sir Walter Raleigh. In the following March (1584) he obtained a patent, and sent forth two well-appointed vessels, which sailed at once to the coast of Carolina. Raleigh was too much engaged at court to lead the expedition ; and his commanders, who seem to have been men of no mark, only landed to take possession of the soil, and then returned to spread abroad in England the fame of the paradise which they had seen.

Charmed with these descriptions, Elizabeth bestowed upon the new country, as a record of herself, the title of Virginia ; and Raleigh sent out, in the following year, seven vessels, manned with more than 100 colonists. But again the incapacity of their commanders disappointed all his hopes. The resources of the expedition were wasted in a fruitless search for mines of gold, until, at length, fifteen men being left behind to guard the island of Roanoke, on the shores of what is now known as North Carolina, the rest of the intended colony returned to England. Amongst these were some who had noted carefully the natural advantages of the country they had visited, and their report kept alive the spirit of adventure. It is not a little curious to review their discoveries. One of them was the value of the tuberous roots of the potato ; and the other is thus stated by Thomas Hariot, "a man of learning, and a very observing person, a domestick of Sir Walter's, and highly in his patron's friendship."—" There is an herb which is sowed apart by itself, and is called by the natives uppowoc. The leaves thereof being dried and brought into powder, they use to take the fume or smoke thereof by sucking it through pipes made of clay, into their stomach or head : from whence it purgeth superflueous fleame, and other grosse humores, and openeth all the pores of the body ; . . . . whereby their bodies are notably preserved in health. This uppowoc is of so precious estimation amongst them, that they thinke their gods are marvellously delighted therewith; whereupon sometime they make hallowed fires, and cast some of the powder thereon for a sacrifice: being in a storme upon the waters, to pacify their gods they caste some therein and into the aire; also, after an escape of danger, they caste some into the aire likewise: but all done with strange gestures, stamping, sometime dancing, clapping of hands, holding up of hands, and staring up into the heavens, uttering therewithall and chattering strange words and noises. We ourselves, during the time we were there, used to sucke it after their manner, as also since our return, and have found many rare and wonderfull experiments of the vertues thereof: of which the relation would require a volume by itself: the use of it by so many of late, men and women of great calling, as els, and some learned physicians also, is sufficient witnesse."*

One result followed from this voyage. Raleigh learned from it to look to agricultural produce as the staple of his intended colony. In the next spring a fleet of transports sailed, carrying out a numerous band of emigrants, who, with their wives and families, adventured themselves to settle in this new world. They landed upon the island of Roanoke, where, as an evil omen, they found nothing but the scattered bones of their unhappy predecessors. There, however, they founded the city of Raleigh; and here was born the first Anglo-American, the grand-daughter of Raleigh's governor; Virginia Dare.†

But America was not as yet to be tenanted by the Anglo-Saxon race. As the summer closed, the colonists looked homeward with anxious longing, and began to fear that they had been forgotten. By passionate entreaties

---

* Hackluyt, vol. iii. p. 331. Hariot. "It is related," says the historian of Virginia, "that a country servant of Sir Walter's bringing him a tankard of ale into his study as he was intently engaged at his book, smoking a pipe of tobacco, the fellow was so frightened at seeing the smoke reek out of his mouth, that he threw the ale into his face in order to extinguish the fire, and ran down stairs alarming the family, and crying out his master was on fire, and, before they could get up, would be burnt to ashes."

† Stith's History of Virginia.

they forced their governor to an unwilling return on their behalf. He found England gathering up her energies to repel the invincible armada. All communication with the new colony was for a season suspended; and when the storm had cleared away, and Raleigh sent again to visit his settlement, no trace of the unhappy settlers could be found. Six times, with decreasing hopes, but with unconquered resolution, did this great man despatch expeditions, on the same errand, till his fortune was expended in the fruitless search. With the accession of King James in 1603, fresh misfortunes crowded upon his declining years. On a charge of intending to change the succession to the crown, he was tried for high treason on most improbable evidence, convicted, and condemned to die. This sentence was not then executed; but for twelve years, in spite of the friendship of Prince Henry, who indignantly declared that " no king but his father would keep such a bird in a cage," he was left to linger in the Tower. In 1616 he was discharged; and, still bent upon his old plans, he sacrificed all his remaining property, even to his plate, to fit out one more expedition to the west. Its issue was altogether disastrous. He lost all that he had adventured; and, far beyond all other losses, he saw his eldest son fall during its course. A letter to his wife after this event strikingly displays his character;—" I was loth to write," he says, " because I know not how to comfort you; and God knows I never knew what sorrow meant till now. All that I can say to you is, that you must obey the will and providence of God, and remember that the Queen's majesty bore the loss of Prince Henry with a magnanimous heart. Comfort your heart, dearest Bess; I shall sorrow for us both; and I shall sorrow the less because I have not long to sorrow, because not long to live. The Lord bless and comfort you, that you may bear patiently the death of your most valiant son."

The prediction which closed this letter did not wait long for its fulfilment. He was arrested immediately on landing, and first accused of exceeding his commission in this voyage. This pretext, however, proved too shallow to justify his execution; and as nothing less would satisfy his enemies, his old sentence was revived, and under that he suffered publicly, October 29, 1618.

But the great work in which he had been a pioneer was now about to be accomplished. The various expeditions he had manned kept up a constant intercourse between America and England; and in 1606, a new company applied for and obtained from James I. a charter for the settling of Virginia. The names of two knights, several gentlemen, and Richard Hackluyt, clerk, prebendary of Westminster, appear in this document.

This design included the establishment of a northern and southern colony; and amidst "the articles, instructions, and orders" of the charter, provision was made for the due carrying out of that which is the highest end of every Christian colony. For it is expressly ordered, that "the said presidents, councils, and ministers should provide that the true word and service of God be preached, planted, and used, according to the rites and doctrine of the Church of England, not only in the said colonies, but also, as much as might be, amongst the savages bordering upon them;" and "that all persons should kindly treat the savage and heathen people in those parts, and use all proper means to draw them to the true service and knowledge of God."*

This expedition sailed upon the 19th of December, 1606, and reached Cape Henry, in Virginia, on the 26th of April, 1607. Their voyage had been tedious and dangerous; and would have been absolutely ruined by internal disagreement, but for the healing influence of the Rev. Robert Hunt, a priest of the English Church, who, as their first chaplain, accompanied the expedition. Happy were they in the choice of this good man, who went forth to the strange land with all the zeal and earnestness of apostolic times. "Six weekes," says one of the party,† "wee were kept in sight of England by unprosperous winds; all which time Mr. Hunt, our preacher, was so weake and sicke that few expected his recoverie: yet although wee were but ten or twelve miles from his habitation (the time wee were in the Downes), and notwithstanding the stormy weather,

* Stith, b. ii. pp. 37, 40.   † Purchas's Pilgrims, p. 1705.

nor the scandalous imputation (of some few, little better than atheists, of the greatest rank amongst us) suggested against him, all this could never force from him so much as a seeming desire to leave the businesse, but preferred the service of God, in so good a voyage, before any affection to contest with his godlesse foes, whose disastrous designs had even then overthrowne the business, had he not, with the water of patience and his godly exhortations (but chiefly by his true devoted example), quenched these flames of envy and dissension."

Fresh troubles broke out in the little band as soon as they arrived, when again his influence alone healed the division; and he had the joy of administering the holy eucharist to the united company upon the 14th of May, 1607, the day after their first landing. Here, on a peninsula, upon the northern shore of James River, was sown the first seed of Englishmen, who were in after years to grow and multiply into the great and numerous American people. It was an omen for good, that almost their first act on reaching land was to offer unto God this appointed " sacrifice of prayer and thanksgiving;" and that amongst the first humble reed-thatched houses in which, under the name of James Town, they found shelter for themselves, they at once erected one to be the church and temple of the rising settlement.

On their first landing, everything smiled around them. They " found a country which might claim the prerogative over the most pleasant places in the known world, for large and majestic navigable rivers; for beautiful mountains, hills, plains, valleys; rivulets and brooks gurgling down and running most pleasantly into a fair bay, encompassed on all sides, except at the mouth, with such fruitful and delightful land. Heaven and earth seemed never to have agreed better to frame a place for man's commodious and delightful habitation, were it fully cultivated and inhabited by industrious people."*

But this bright morning was soon clouded over; and the first years of the colony were, as is commonly the case,

---

* Stith, b. ii. p. 48.

years of discouragement and sorrow. All the forms of suffering pressed on them in turn. Their Indian neighbors slew many by treachery; they were often disunited among themselves; they depended for subsistence on the supplies of food they could obtain from home, and from the neighboring tribes,—so that any failure here (and failures were frequent) threw them at once into the miseries of famine: upon this disease followed hard, until at times almost all the population was mowed down. "Unwholesome water," says George Percy, brother of the Earl of Northumberland, himself one of the sufferers, " was our drink; our lodgings, castles in the air." Within ten days of the ships leaving them, the colonists "fell into such violent sickness that scarce ten amongst them could either go or stand."* Half of those who had been left perished before the setting in of winter.

The fate of the colony seemed to hang upon one man. In spite of the bitterest envy, the merits of Captain Smith raised him to supreme command; and he alone was equal to the great emergencies of every day. His early life† had fitted him for daring deeds. Trained in the war in which the Low Countries fought, for freedom and their faith, against the power of Spain, he had afterwards maintained the borders of Christendom against the Turks in Hungary. Being taken prisoner in a skirmish, he was sold into slavery; sent first to Constantinople, and thence, with a merciful intention, to the Crimea. Here being sorely oppressed by those who were charged to protect him, he escaped after a desperate encounter with his guards, and passed on horseback through the skirts of Russia to his old Hungarian quarters. We find him next in northern Africa, whence he returned to England in time to cast himself into the current which was then sweeping the most daring spirits to the unknown regions of the New World. In the sufferings and dangers of this expedition his courage never failed. He made excursions amongst the neighboring tribes of Indians; he obtained supplies of food; defeated hostile attacks; sunk, or threatened to sink,

---

* Stith, b. ii. p. 47. † Bancroft's America.

the barque in which the trembling handful of remaining colonists would otherwise have attempted a shameful and impossible return; and was the great instrument of planting the English race in that reluctant but at length prolific soil.

In all his trials he was supported by the zealous aid of the admirable Hunt, whose patient meekness disarmed all opposition, while his cheerful faith was a bright example to the colony. Amid its severest sufferings, it is cheering to find the minister of Christ in that far land repeating those lessons by which his forerunners in the holy office had so often kept alive the first faint sparks of social life. With unwearied patience he maintained the sinking spirits of his flock by the mighty influence of Christian truth, of which he gave a bright example in his own active faith and cheerful patience. Thus when, in a fire which destroyed their rising town, "the good Mr. Hunt lost all his library, with every thing else that he had, except the clothes on his back, yet no one ever heard him murmur or repine at it."* He seems to have entered on the work as one which, in the language of the first royal charter, "may, by the providence of Almighty God, hereafter tend to the glory of His divine Majesty, in propagating the Christian religion to such people as yet live in darkness and miserable ignorance of the true knowledge and worship of God."† When this good man died, we know not; it is merely recorded that he left his bones in that land of England's after-inheritance. But amongst the earliest settlers his mantle fell on others of like spirit. In the year 1610, after a period of the sorest famine, "remembered for many years by the name of THE STARVING TIME,"‡ the few whom hunger and disease had spared resolved to quit for ever this unpropitious country. They embarked with all they had in four small vessels,—"none dropped a tear, for none had enjoyed one day of happiness;" and had already fallen down the river with the tide, when

---

* Stith, b. ii. p. 59.
† Hazard's State Papers, quoted in Hawks's Virginia, p. 19.
‡ Stith, b. iii. p. 117.

they descried the long-boat of Lord Delaware, who, with three ships, and a new commission, had arrived at that precise moment for their rescue.

He carried back the fainting settlers to their abandoned town, and again took possession of the land with the offices of our holy faith. Hunt was no more: but the new governor was happily attended by a chaplain; and his were the first services called for by Lord Delaware. "He cast anchor," says one of the new-comers, "before James Towne, where we landed; and our much grieved governor, first visiting the church, caused the bell to be rung; at which all such as were able to come forth of their houses repayred to church, which was neatly trimmed with the wild flowers of the country, where our minister, Master Bucke, made a zealous and sorrowful prayer, finding all things so contrary to our expectations, and full of misery and misgovernment."*

Bucke was fixed at James Town, and when, after a few years, the colony had so far taken root as to have spread itself into the neighboring town of Henrico, he was joined by Mr. Whitaker, (son of the celebrated Dr. W. Whitaker, master of St. John's College, Cambridge,) who was established "in a handsome church,"† which, through the zeal of the settlers, was one of the first buildings raised. Whitaker was no unworthy successor of Hunt. By the saint-like Nicholas Ferrar, his contemporary, he was honored with the title of "apostle of Virginia." "I hereby let all men know," writes W. Crashaw,‡ in 1613, "that a scholar, a graduate, a preacher, well borne and friended in England; not in debt nor disgrace, but competently provided for, and liked and loved where he lived; not in want, but (for a scholar as these days be) rich in possessions, and more in possibility, of himself, without any persuation (but God's and his own heart's,) did voluntarily leave his warm nest, and, to the wonder of his kindred, and amazement of them that knew him undertake this hard, but, in my judgment, heroicall resolution

---

* Purchas's Pilgrims, b. ix. c. 6.   † Hawks's Virginia, p. 28.
‡ Quoted in Hawks's Virginia, p. 28.

to go to Virginia, and helpe to beare the name of God unto the Gentiles."

With the name of Whitaker is joined the romantic story of the first Indian convert, whom he baptised into the Church of Christ. Pocahontas, the favorite daughter of Powhatan, the most powerful Indian chieftain of those parts, then a girl of twelve years old, saved from barbarous murder Captain Smith, the early hero of this colony, whilst a prisoner at her father's court. For years she remained the white man's constant friend and advocate; and even dared to visit, on more than one errand of mercy, the new settlement of James Town. After Captain Smith's removal from Virginia, Pocahontas was ensnared by treachery, and brought a prisoner to the English fort. But her captivity was turned into a blessing. She received the faith of Christ, and was not only the first, but one of the most hopeful of the whole band of native converts. Her after-life was strange. She formed a marriage of mutual affection with an English settler of good birth; who, after a time, visited his native land, taking with him to its shores his Indian wife and child. She was received with due respect in England; visited the English court (where her husband bore the frowns of the royal pedant James I. for having dared to intermarry with a princess;) and, after winning the goodwill of all, just on the eve of her return, died at Gravesend, aged 22, in the faith of Jesus. "What would have been the emotions," well asks the ecclesiastical historian of Virginia, "of the devoted missionary, when he admitted Pocahontas to baptism, could he have foreseen that, after the lapse of more than two hundred years, the blood of this noble-hearted Indian maiden would be flowing in the veins of some of the most distinguished members of that Church, the foundations of which he was then laying!"*

But though thus happy in her early clergy, it must not be supposed that the infant Church of Virginia flourished without many a drawback. The mass of those who flock to such a settlement will ever be, like David's followers in

---

* Dr. Hawks's Memorials of the Church in Virginia, p. 28.

the desert, men of broken fortunes and ungoverned habits; the bonds of society are loose; strong temptations abound; and there will be much that must rebel not only against morals and religion, but even against civil rule. So it was in this case; and to such a pitch, at one time, had this insubordination risen, that but for the governor's proclaiming martial law, the whole society had perished through internal strife.

This code of law may still be seen; and, as is implied in its title—" Lawes divine, morall, and martiall, for Virginia"—it enforced obedience to the faith of Christ, as the foundation of all relative obligations. There can be little doubt that, in that stage of society, these laws (the harsh penalties attached to which were never enforced) proved a great blessing to the colony, and prepared it for better days.

CHAPTER II.

FROM 1620 TO 1688.

Virginian Company—Measures of Sir E. Sandys, Nicholas Ferrar, and others—Churches endowed—College founded—Mr. Thorpe—Indian massacre—Indian conquest—Effects of the massacre—Virginia in the Great Rebellion—Loyalty—Love of the Church—Effects of Puritan rule—King Charles II. proclaimed—Enactments of Legislature in behalf of the Church—Popish plots suspected.

It was the great happiness of Virginia, that the company who managed its affairs contained at this time men who looked far beyond direct commercial profit. Amongst these should be especially remembered the names of Sir Edwin Sandys, son of the Archbishop of York, and pupil of Richard Hooker, and of Mr. Nicholas Ferrar;* who composed all their letters and instructions to their servants. These, and the rest who acted with them, earnestly desired to make the rising colony indeed an outpost of the faith.

For this end, they endeavored to raise its internal character; and many were their schemes with this intent. Their first care was to provide a more settled population, by promoting female emigration and colonial marriages. They laid the foundation of a college for the reception both of the English and Indian youth; they set apart 10,000 acres for its permanent support, and collected large sums of money, both by a king's letter and from private charity, to furnish endowments for a body of professors; and in a new charter which they now sent out, they provided for the settled maintenance of the colonial clergy. Nor were the settlers backward in the like endeavors. In

---

*See Walton's Life of R. Hooker: and Memoir of Nicholas Ferrar, by Rev. T. M. Macdonough.

the year 1619, when Sir Thomas Yeardley entered on the government, he called together the first representative legislature of Virginia. One of the early enactments of this body fixed the payment of their clergy at £200 worth of corn and tobacco,* their principal productions. One hundred acres were marked off for glebes in every borough, for each of which the company at home provided six tenants at the public cost. They applied to the Bishop of London to find for them a body of "pious, learned, and painful ministers;"— a charitable work in which he readily engaged,

Many large-hearted Christians helped on these good beginnings. The Bishop of London† raised £1000 towards the expenses of their infant college; an unknown benefactor sent £500 more, to be laid out in instructing the young Indians in the faith of Christ. Money to be spent in building churches, and providing communion-plate for those already built, flowed in from other quarters. An exemplary zeal appears in all the dealings of the company. They impressed upon their governors that they "should take into their especial regard the service of Almighty God, and the observance of His divine laws; and that the people should be trained up in true religion and virtue." They urged them "to employ their utmost care to advance all things appertaining to the order and administration of divine service according to the form and discipline of the Church of England, carefully avoiding all factious and needless novelties, which only tend to the disturbance of peace and unity."

They besought them "to use all probable means of bringing over the natives to the knowledge of God and His true religion; to which purpose, the example given by the English in their own persons and families will be of singular and chief moment." They suggest to them that "it will be proper to draw the best disposed amongst the Indians to converse and labor with our people for a convenient reward, that thereby, being reconciled to a civil way of life, and brought to a sense of God and reli-

---

* Stith, b. iii. p. 173.   † Bp. King.

gion, they might afterwards become instruments in the general conversion of their countrymen, so much desired; that each town, borough, and hundred, ought to procure, by just means, a certain number of children to be brought up; that the most towardly of these should be fitted for the college. In all which pious work they earnestly require help and furtherance, not doubting the particular blessing of God upon the colony."*

All these good beginnings were advancing in the settlement. The headship of the college was accepted by an exemplary man, Mr. George Thorpe, of good parts and breeding, (he had been of the king's bedchamber in England,) from an earnest desire of helping-on the conversion of the Indians. His heart was given to this work, and he sought to farther it in every way. He visited the Indian chiefs at their own haunts, to win them over to the faith of Christ; and he was ever watching in the colony to remove every ground of quarrel or offence.

The general treatment of the Indian race was mild and friendly. The settlers' houses and tables were open to them; they often slept under the white men's roofs, and freely used the boats which they had built upon the various creeks and rivers. The two races promised to blend peaceably together; whilst Mr. Thorpe and his Christian coadjutors looked gladly forward to the day when, by these Indian tribes, the knowledge of salvation should be spread through all the Western world.

Yet in the midst of this apparent calm there was secretly arising one of those fearful hurricanes to which the neighborhood of Indian life has always been exposed. The red tribes, whose extreme simplicity and seeming mildness had led the English to lay aside the commonest precautions, were forming secretly a wide-spread plot to rid their land at one blow of the strangers, whose increasing numbers seemed to make immediate action needful.

With that deliberate stillness of preparation which aggravates so fearfully the murderous onset of savage warfare, the Indians sprang at once upon the whole slumber-

* Stith, b. iv. pp. 194, 195.

ing colony. Neither age nor sex, character nor station, acts of kindness past or present, turned aside m a single instance the knife or hatchet of the savage. Mr. Thorpe was slain and mangled in the midst of his confiding labors; and within an hour, 347 men, women, and children, were left bleeding and dismembered corpses. Yet, terrible as this blow was, it would have been far more fatal but for the conduct of one Indian convert. His chief sent to him the general order, bidding him slay upon the morrow his unsuspecting master; but obedience to the laws of clanship yielded, in the heart of the Christian Indian, to a higher obligation. As soon as the messenger, his own brother, had departed, he rose and warned his master of the meditated treachery; thus enabling him not only to preserve his own house, but to prepare the inhabitants of James Town to expect and to resist the blow. The Indians, finding their attack suspected, retreated from the town, and the great mass of colonists escaped. The conversion of one native man had saved the English settlement.

Yet their miseries were not over. The affrighted colonists fled to the shelter of James Town, where famine soon visited their crowded ranks. When the storm had passed away, the whole face of the settlement was changed. Of "eighty plantations which were advancing to completion, eight only remained; and of twenty-nine hundred and sixty inhabitants, eighteen hundred were all that were left.*"

Still the blow had been averted; the colony was saved; and its loss was soon repaired by reinforcements from the mother country. But lasting evil had been done; a spirit of deadly hostility sprang up between the white men and the Indians. To overawe all whom they did not exterminate was now their settled policy; and all thoughts of the college, with its promise of mercy, was wholly laid aside for years.

Some of the first records of the reviving colony are of a happier character. The first seven laws (amongst thirty-

* Hawks's Virginia, b. iv. p. 1.

five) passed two years afterwards, provide for the interests of religion. They require the erection of a house of worship, and the separation of a burial-ground, on every plantation; they enforce the attendance of the colonists at public worship; provide for uniformity of faith and worship with the English Church; prescribe the observance of her holydays, and of a yearly fast upon the anniversary of the massacre; and enjoin respectful treatment and the payment of a settled stipend to the colonial clergy.

This was almost the last act of the legislature of Virginia whilst it continued under its early charters. Two years afterwards (in 1624) the crown resumed its grant, and the settlement became a royal colony. Although this change, which transferred the management of its affairs from the hands of Sandys and Ferrar to the interested courtiers of King James, had no doubt an influence upon the spiritual interests of the colony, and especially upon its missionary character, yet it produced no direct alteration in religious matters. The laws of the succeeding period continued to enforce the observance of the same duties; and though their distance saved the colonists from that full severity of rule with which matters were administered at home by the Court of High Commission, yet its decisions were acknowledged as authority, and the harsh tone which was now unhappily assumed in England was felt even in Virginia. At the same time, the temper of the colony was far different from that which was spreading at home. Without much warmth of religion, the attachment of the people to their fathers' Church was general and decided. An attempt made from without to gather a congregation of the Independent character, met with but small support, and was easily suppressed by the authorities.* The Puritan writers complain, in their peculiar language, that the governor was " a courtier, and very malignant to the way of the Churches;" but the whole temper of the colony was with him; and when the humors of the mother-country broke out into the great rebellion, Virginia continued loyal.

* Leah and Rachell, or the two fruitful Sisters of Virginia and Maryland. 1656. Quoted by Dr. Hawks.

In dissenting New England, all were fully satisfied that the battles which Cromwell had fought at home were the battles of the Lord; and "the spirits of the brethren were carried forth in faithful and affectionate prayers in his behalf."* But with this state of feeling Virginia had no sympathy. The expatriated cavalier fled to her as a refuge; and with a population now multiplied to 20,000, she resisted Cromwell's arms. The terms on which she at length capitulated to superior numbers show the true grounds of her resolute fidelity; for she stipulates for "the use of the Booke of Common Prayer for one yeare ensuing, the continuance of ministers in their places, and the payment of their accustomed dues and agreements."† Nor did the success of the Puritans alter these leading features, though it raised one of their body to the seat of governor, and spread a few of his adherents through the land. The chief evil which flowed from it was the growth of unconcern about religion. "Many places" became "destitute of ministers, through the people ceasing to pay their accustomed dues, and manifesting great negligence in procuring religious instruction."‡

But the Independent form of worship found no favor in the colony. It is described by a contemporary as "bearing a great love to the stated constitutions of the Church of England, in her government and public worship, which gave us (who went thither under the late persecutions of it) the advantage of liberty to use it constantly amongst them, after the naval force had reduced the colony under the power (but never to the obedience) of the usurpers."§

Through the whole period of the great rebellion such remained the temper of Virginia. Eight years after his deposition, Sir W. Berkeley, the ex-governor, was still lingering in the colony, and opening "his purse and his house to all the royal party, who made Virginia their re-

---

* Bancroft's United States, vol. i. p. 445.
† Hening's Virginia,—Statutes at large, p. 362.
‡ Ibid. p. 378.
§ Virginia's Cure, p. 22, quoted by Dr. Hawks.

fuge."* When a felon convict,† who had escaped from justice, was employed by Cromwell, in the neighboring state of Maryland, "in the holy work of rooting out the abominations of popery and prelacy," Virginia fearlessly sheltered his victims, in defiance of the usurper's censure of "the presumption and impiety of her interference." Sixteen months before the king was restored at home, he was proclaimed in Virginia;‡ and amongst the earliest business brought before the colonial legislature, when it reassembled under the royal commission, was the revival of the Church. This had already suffered greatly: of fifty parishes, into which the colony was now divided, the greater number wanted alike glebe, parsonage, church, and minister, as there were not above ten clergymen remaining. The first article in the instructions furnished to Sir W. Berkeley, the royal governor, recommended "the duties of religion, the use of the Book of Common Prayer, the decent repairs of churches, and a competent provision for conforming ministers."§ These suggestions were acted on at once by the colonial legislature. Provision was made for the building and due furniture of churches; for the canonical performance of the Liturgy; for the ministration of God's word; for a due observance of the Sunday; for the baptism and Christian education of the young. "These," says the Virginian Statute Book,‖ "among many other blessings, God Almighty hath vouchsafed to increase" into "a very numerous generation of Christian children born in Virginia, who naturally are of beautiful and comely persons, and generally of more ingenious spirits than those of England."¶

With these provisions the Church and religious matters were again established on their ancient basis, and proceeded as before; though in the next few years, the general outlines of ecclesiastical affairs at home may be traced by their reproduction in the colony.

* Churchill's Journal of Norwood, in Voyages, vol. vi.
† 2 Burk, 113, by the same. ‡ Ibid. p. 118.
§ 2 Burk, 124, in Hawks's Virginia, p. 65.
‖ Hening, vol. i. p. 336.
¶ Virginia's Cure, p. 5, quoted in Bancroft's United States.

Strict enactments against non-conformists, then deemed necessary to prevent political disturbance, marked its beginning; and were followed, under James II., by fears of Popish innovation. The Papists and the Indians were believed to be in secret league against the colony; and, in spite of all her loyalty, Virginia hailed, with no less joy than eager Protestants at home, the accession of King William and Queen Mary.

CHAPTER III.

FROM 1608 TO 1688.

Neighboring colonies—New-York—New Jersey—Philadelphia—Carolina—Maryland—New England—Its settlement—Rise of Puritanism in England—Emigration to Leyden, to New England—Piety of the early Puritans—Their hatred of Church-principles—Severity—Treatment of Indians—Proselyting spirit towards other communions.

HITHERTO the thread of our history has run along almost entirely with that of the single colony of Virginia. But from this time we must include in our notice many of her sister settlements: and for this purpose it will be convenient to survey their religious posture at this time, and from their first beginning.

Very different now was the condition of that great western continent from its state when the first settlers in Virginia landed on its shores. Then, in all the great wilderness around them, the Lord of heaven was an unknown God. The echoes of its vast forests had never yet awoke to the name of Christ; the whole expanse was only dotted here and there by the scattered wigwams and hunting-lodges of the savage Indians. But now, along the whole coast, and continually more and more inland, a busy swarming people, bearing the Christian name, were overspreading all its extent, and driving back before them the retiring wave of Indian life.

Some of these settlements had been formed but little later than Virginia, though under a widely-different religious influence.

Thus the district of Pennsylvania had been settled in 1608, one year after Virginia, by the Dutch. Whilst about 1627, some Swedish emigrants seated themselves at

New-York and New Jersey, and long held possession of them. For, though the English laid claim, as first discoverers, to the whole northern continent, it was not till 1664 that the Dutch governor surrendered to the summons of Sir R. Cave, and transferred to English rule the city of New Amsterdam, which, with its change of rulers, changed also its name, and became thenceforth New-York. Here, therefore, were established the religious rites and usages of the Dutch and Swedish presbyterian worship.

In 1683 a different element was largely introduced, when Newcastle Town, with twelve miles of the surrounding country, was sold by the Duke of York, to whom it had been granted by the crown, to William Penn, who built the town of Philadelphia, and peopled it with quakers.

Thirteen years before (in 1670), Carolina had been granted by King Charles II. to Lord Berkeley and others, who established there a constitution, drawn up by the famous John Locke; which, with many more peculiarities, professed to establish perfect religious equality amongst all sects, only requiring that each stripling of seventeen should select one for himself, and publicly enroll himself amongst its members.

Bordering directly on Virginia, Maryland was settled, in 1633, by about two hundred English families, of Roman Catholic tenets, under the direction of Lord Baltimore, and soon grew into a flourishing community: in which, whilst all who professed the faith of Jesus Christ were allowed the free exercise of their religion, Romanism was long the dominant belief. So fully had the unhappy religious feuds of Christendom been borne across the Atlantic, to seed with fresh divisions the new world which lay outspread before the Christian settlers.

But of all these colonies, the most important, under every aspect, were those which had peopled the extensive district known, from their occupation, by the title of New England. This was the great seed-plot of division in religion; and the history of its foundation will, therefore, require a more detailed and particular account.

Its first settlement was the consequence of religious troubles at home. The curse of popery had long lain heavy upon England; and had eaten out in great measure the very life of Christianity amongst us. It was " as with the people, so with the priest;" or rather, the evil had begun with the priest, and had gone down to the people. When we look into the religious history of that period, we should almost conclude that, with some few noble exceptions, in which the absolute deadness of the system in which he was set forced the saint out of all system into a direct commerce with the unseen world, Christianity had, in the mass of cases, become a great scheme of formality. The withholding of God's word from the people, the denial of the master truth of our being justified by faith only, and, above all, the robbing men of the presence of their only Saviour, by putting in His place those outward institutions which were intended to be signs and means of His true nearness to them,—all this had wrought fearfully amongst us; and though, through God's goodness, there was doubtless underneath this frozen surface some hidden life kept here and there in being, yet, for the most part, formality had chilled it utterly. There was no dealing with the consciences of men; no treating them as individual souls, each one with the great mystery of spiritual life within, which was to be nurtured and perfected; but empty outward forms were all; and when once that divinely appointed organization, which, as the channel of God's living grace, was intended to quicken as much as to direct the soul of man, was itself thus changed into a set of lifeless observances, it could maintain any power at all, only by suspending within each of its victims the true energies of his own inner being. This, therefore, became the object of those worldly-minded men, who sought to use Christ's Church as an instrument for working out their own earthly ends. And so long as men's consciences could be wholly sent to sleep, this scheme was perfect of its kind; for it stilled the cravings of man's soul by the opiate of insensibility; passing over to the priest and the system, that care about his own inner self, which is indeed the charge of each reasonable being. So long, too, as men could be kept in gross ignorance, the fearful starts to which a sleeping conscience is subject could be set again at rest. There were penances, and indulgences, and remissions, and the showy jugglery of outward devotion, all specially directed to this end. And so for years had it been in England; prayers in which the heart or even the reason of the worshipper could take little or no part, had been, for the mass of the people, the only allowed attempt at approaching God. Formalities and shows, which, at the best, addressed themselves to the sensitive faculties, these had been the food provided for the deep and wonderful spiritual life; and the reason had been abased, until it received the lying legends of the day, instead of that word of God which "giveth light unto the eyes."

But so could it be no more after the time of Wickliffe. He had spoken words over these slumberers which had broken their charmed sleep. He spoke of God, of their need of Him, of the Mediator between Him and them, of their own inner being; and conscience had awoke, as the words reached their understandings. A multitude of men began to perceive that they were men; that they had souls, for which they must themselves care; as to them, above all, they were precious beyond price. They began to feel the need of personal religion. Strange and often ill-directed were their first efforts after it, as are the actions of men who are roused suddenly from a deep sleep; greatly did they need the soothing voice and guiding hand of their appointed pastors. But the religious system of the papacy could not guide their efforts and satisfy their new-born wants. Its whole desire was to crush them. This it soon found to be impossible; for to each one of these Lollards there was now revealed a truth, which he held as a reality, and which reached down to the very centre of his soul. It could not be torn from him; he must be slain first. He could not be made to cease believing, or cease feeling. The knowledge of his own humanity had flashed upon him; he could not forget it; and it must be dreadful to him, until he could find out its true healer. Hence popery strove in vain with those who were once infected with this new disorder; and, finding this strife to be hopeless, it soon set itself to prevent its spreading, by marking out for death or sufferings each one who yielded himself up to it.

This strife went on long before its being was proclaimed. Just as knowledge increased, so far spread the awakening of conscience; and whenever this awoke, the struggle followed between him in whom it woke, and those who sought to keep it sleeping. From which there followed always this evil consequence, that the man in whom personal religion was but beginning to reveal itself found the Church-system under which he lived the great enemy of that religion. The priests, who should have nourished, instructed, and perfected it, he knew only as those who hated, reviled, and endeavored to extinguish it. The religious sympathies, which should have clung to the Church-system, and by it been raised to a goodly maturity, finding in it no sure stay, cast forth their tendrils upon strange supports; thus becoming themselves entangled with evil, and separating the personal religion of the man from the unity and blessedness of the Church. In such a state men soon chose wilfully for themselves, as a part of their religion. They rejected ignorantly the greatest truths, from their dread of the errors with which they had been mixed. There was no blessed truth of Christ's gospel to which some deadly delusion had not been wedded; and the just-opening eye, which saw men as trees walking, could not nicely distinguish between truth and falsehood; whilst it had been made to loathe as its worst enemies those who should have been its guides.

For more than one hundred and fifty years this leaven had been working widely amongst the people, when the outbreak of the Reformation spread the ferment through the nation. For a time all went on prosperously. The vexed and angry minds of men were well satisfied as long as the work of demolition proceeded. The obstacles which it received in the latter part of Henry's reign came rather from the king than the clergy. The bishops were still reformers; all at least whom the people looked to as bishops indeed. Accordingly, when Edward the Sixth became king, the work proceeded apace. The reformed part of the nation seemed to be united: much was yet to be done before religion would be purified; but upon doing this they were agreed amongst themselves. Then came the sharp check of Mary's reign, and the strife burnt more fiercely than ever; but still the reformed were all gathered on one side, and the popish on the other.

So it continued while she lived; but with the accession of Elizabeth the whole aspect of the field was changed. The Reformation was established; and immediately the evil seed sown heretofore sprung up and multiplied. Now was seen the true curse with which popery had cursed us, in divorcing the religious sympathies of men from that external organisation which had been framed by the Lord specially to foster them; in making men judges and teachers, because the very love of truth within them had made them fear to be learners and the taught. The reformed began to divide amongst themselves. The Reformation had lifted up the cover which the seal of mystery had heretofore secured, and from the opened vessel there issued a spirit, vast, undefined, and fearful, on which men looked and trembled; marvelling how it had been held before in such a narrow compass, seeing that never again could it be charmed into its former quietness. The principle of obedience had been unawares dissolved. Their former long separation from Roman errors, in spite of authority, had tainted the spirit of many of the best of our people, and made them self-choosing schismatics. Each was to judge for himself. The authority of the early Church was nothing; for it was confounded with the vile tradition which for so long a time had cheated their souls. The succession of the priesthood was a lie; for the lying priests of old had claimed it for themselves. The deep need of support and sympathy, for which God has graciously made provision in the communion of saints, and for which the heart of man craves, was wholly forgotten in the first fever-heat which waited upon the discovery of individual responsibility and individual salvation; and the great twin truths which had been wedded together in primitive times, which the hollowness of the popish system had severed by seeking to destroy individual religion, were henceforth, it seemed, to strive for the mastery,—as if man's peace lay in one destroying the other, and not in the perfect harmony of both.

In such a state was the nation. The spasms of convulsion had followed in due course upon the numbness of lethargy. All through the reign of Elizabeth, society was convulsed by these struggles. The party which began to be known every where under the title of the Puritans professed to aim at a more perfect or entire reformation of religion. The work, they thought, had been left half done. They were many of them men of true and deep piety, whose errors were the natural consequence of the unhappy influence under which their minds had grown and ripened. Their unsettled and unquiet spirits were the legacy which popery bequeathed us ; " tearing us" when it " hardly departed from us." They strove with all the earnestness of men who had a great reality at stake ; it was, as it seemed to them, for the very life of their own souls, and of their children's souls, that they contended. Yet they strove in ignorance : in seeking to do away the errors which had crept over them, they would fain have overthrown the institutions of Christ Himself. Those who saw this were bound to withhold from them that for which they longed. And so the old feelings of hostility, which the abuses of her Roman garb had kindled, fastened now upon the Church reformed. It became again an open struggle. Law was on the side of those who were defending the existing institutions ; and by the law the rights of truth were enforced. In such a temper of society it was hard to draw the line at all times between persecution and a due resistance to the spread of error. The limits of toleration had been ascertained by neither party ; and it is no great admission to allow that they were now sometimes transgressed by the defenders of the Church. Every thing, indeed, tended to lead them into such a course ; they were maintaining what had clearly stood from the first spread of Christianity. The attacks now made on this must in their eyes have been manifest impiety. They were led on, moreover, by another influence. The Puritans were made bad subjects by the very same qualities which made them bad Churchmen.

The secular arm, therefore, was ready to strike in its own quarrel, and glad to take advantage of the first whisper of the cause of religion. It was not now for toleration simply that the Puritans were striving. During their exile in the reign of Mary, they had learned all the lessons taught by Calvin and John Knox. Their consciences compelled them, not only to practice themselves what they deemed right, but, at all hazards, to enforce this practice upon others also. "The Puritans of this age," says the gentle Fuller,* " were divided into two ranks : some mild and moderate, contented to enjoy their own conscience ; others fierce and fiery, to the disturbance of the Church and State ;" " accounting every thing from Rome which was not from Geneva, they endeavored to conform the government of the English Church to the presbyterian reformation."

It was Elizabeth's maxim, that the first of these classes should be conciliated to the uttermost. And hence Cartwright, Travers, and all the great leaders of the party, were at this time allowed to act as beneficed or licensed preachers.

But when " causes of conscience exceed their bounds, and grow to be matters of faction," to use the words of Sir F. Walsingham,† " the queen judged them to 'lose their nature,' and become such that they should be distinctly punished, though colored with the pretences of conscience and religion." How completely this limit had been reached may easily be seen. Five hundred Puritans, " all beneficed in the Church of England," and styled by themselves " useful preachers," resolved, in 1586, " that since the magistrate could not be induced to reform the discipline of the Church, that therefore, after so many years waiting, it was lawful to act without him, and introduce a reformation in the best manner they could."

The language of their ruder partisans may yet be read in the pages of Martin Mar-prelate and his fellows. They do not speak the tone of men trembling and groaning under dominant oppression : " Our bishops," says they, " and

---

* Church Hist. book ix. p. 76. † Burnet's Hist. Reform. vol. ii.

proud, popish, presumptuous, paltry, pestilent, and pernicious prelates, are usurpers. They are cogging and cozening knaves. The bishops will lie like dogs; impudent, shameless, wainscot-faced bishops. Your fat places are anti-christian; they are limbs of anti-christ,"* &c. "Our lord bishops, as John of Canterbury, with the rest of such swinish rabble, are petty anti-christs, petty popes, proud prelates, enemies to the Gospel, and most covetous, wretched priests."† And the aim of this reviling was openly declared · "The Puritan preachers would have all the remnants and relics of anti-christ banished out of the Church, and not so much as a lord bishop (no, not his grace himself,) dumb minister, (no, not dumb John of London himself,) non-resident, archdeacon, abbey-lubber, or any such loiterer, tolerated in our ministry."

This is not the language of men seeking toleration under religious scruples, but of coarse and open assailants of existing institutions.

Nor was this the mere vulgarity of uneducated ribaldry. It is true that there were many better men amongst the Puritans; but it was such tempers as these against which the ruling powers were forced to take up arms. And these were not the lowest of their faction. Martin Mar-prelate, it was known, came from their leaders' pens; and that great intellect and station could not heal the bitterness of faction, may be seen somewhat later in the prose works of John Milton himself. With less coarseness of tongue, but certainly with no less rancor, he dooms the bishops of the English Church, "after a shameful life in this world, to the darkest and deepest gulf of hell; where, under the despiteful control, the trample and spurn, of all the other damned, who in the anguish of their torture shall have no other ease than to exercise a raving and bestial tyranny over them, as their slaves and negroes, they shall remain in that plight for ever, the basest, the lowermost, the most dejected, most underfoot, and down-trodden vassals of perdition."‡

* Strype's Whitgift, vol. i. p. 570.
† Ibid, p. 353.
‡ Conclusion of Milton's treatise on Reformation, i. 274.

It is not, therefore, wonderful if Churchmen, who, on their part, had a strong perception of the contrary truth, let the arm of law fall heavily upon those who numbered in the ranks of their supporters such troublesome disputants. The true source of the evil was in that former unfaithfulness of those who should have been the watchmen and stewards of the Lord, which had made the Church hateful, not to infidels, because they abhorred religion, but to earnest believers, because they loved it, and the memory of which made many good men still her enemies, though she was now wholly in the right. The points for which she contended were the very guards and instruments of the truth; they could have wounded no sound conscience. But "oppression, which maketh a wise man mad," had held a long rule; men's consciences had become festered and angry, and could not bear the light touch of lawful authority. The time for the full working of this evil was not indeed yet come; but all through the reign of Elizabeth it was gathering strength, and injuring more and more the hearts of those whom it infected. In the following reign it was scarcely repressed by the timid watchfulness of James; and in his son's time it burst forth for a while triumphant. Puritanism was then seen in its maturity; and its violence and persecution far exceeded any excess of rigor which could be charged to the adherents of the contrary side. If some meeting-houses had been heretofore suppressed, we know not of one which, like our cathedrals, was made a stall for horses. If hatred to Puritanism sharpened the edge of that sentence which, for a malicious libel on the queen, deprived Prynne of his ears,* Puritanism could not slake its vengeance till it beheaded Laud. If Puritans were forced by Queen Elizabeth to be present in their parish-church, the Parliament of 1645 sentenced to one year's imprisonment any one who for the third time made use, publicly or privately, of the Book of Common Prayer. But the earlier stages of the struggle are those with which

---

* Prynne himself confessed afterwards, that if, when Charles took his ears, he had taken his head, he had given him no more than his due.

we have to do. In the reigns of Elizabeth, and James the First, the Puritans strove for the mastery in vain; the law enforced conformity; they must attend their parish-church. The ministrations of their chosen teachers were impeded.. The cause of truth, of Christ's Gospel, and of their souls, seemed to them in peril; they looked this way and that for deliverance; they could not rest as they were; they believed that it was unlawful to submit to " the base and beggarly ceremonies"* (as they did not fear to term them) of the Church of England, and were therefore bent on bringing in a "reformation cut or shapen after the manner of Embden or Geneva."†

However mistaken was their zeal, they gave abundant proof of its sincerity. Finding it impossible to follow out their own convictions in their native land, they were content to forsake it rather than violate what they deemed the dictates of conscience. They resolved, therefore, on a voluntary expatriation; and cast their eyes first on Holland, which favored their peculiar views, as the land of their pilgrimage. But this step could not easily be taken; the consent of the civil magistrate was then necessary for such an emigration, and this they were not likely to obtain. Accordingly they endeavored to fly the country secretly. In Lincolnshire especially, a numerous band gathering together their goods and families, in places which they thought likely to escape notice, embarked on board a foreign transport they had hired. They were, however, watched, and their embarkation was prevented; nor was it till after various attempts and many hardships, that " at length they all got over; some at one time, and some at another; some in one place, and some in another." Being " come into the Low Countries," they settled first at Amsterdam; though " they mette together againe with no small rejoicing," yet had they still much to endure. They found there " fortified cities strongly walled; they heard a strange and uncouth language, and beheld the different manners of the

* MS. History of the Plantation of Plymouth, &c.,—in the Fulham Library.
† Ibid.

people with their strange fashions and attires, all so much differing from that of their plain country where they were bred, and so long lived." Before long, moreover, they saw " the grim and grisly face of povertie coming upon them like an armed man with whom they must buckle and encounter." Under the prudent guidance of Mr. Robinson, a man of great parts, who came with them as their first pastor, they surmounted these difficulties, and were soon established in tolerable comfort at Leyden. There they remained twelve years; but many things prevented their taking root amongst the Dutch. Though their industry and honesty, with the interest which attached to their position, had secured for them sufficient employment to provide for their absolute necessities, yet in that shrewd and populous nation they found themselves continually forestalled by the natives of the country. They had been led to take a part in the religious controversies which divided that people; and the skill and readiness in debate, which gained for Mr. Robinson the highest applauses from Polyander and the Calvinists, must have equally displeased the friends of Episcopius, the champion of the opposite side. The truce also, which had now lasted twelve years, between the Netherlands and Spain, was just expiring; and if they remained at Leyden, they knew not how soon they might be involved in all the miseries of war.

Other motives were supplied by their peculiar religious views. Although, in the main, the congregations round them were formed upon their own model, yet there were many things with which they were not satisfied. The Puritans enforced the duty of observing the Lord's day with the formal strictness of the Jewish Sabbath, and they feared the effect upon their children of the opposite example of the Dutch. Already the strictness of their parental rule had been relaxed through the necessity of their position. " Many of their children (by the great licentiousness of youth in that country and the manifold temptations of the place) were drawn away into extravagant and evil courses, getting the reigns off their necks so that they saw their posteritie would be in danger to degenerate and be corrupted."*

* Fulham MS. History.

They longed, too, for something more than toleration; they desired to set up churches after their own model of perfection, and to watch their growth and progress.

The temper of the times naturally turned their thoughts to the new world; already many adventurers had emigrated thither. There they might unfold their present small beginning into a strong people and a pure communion. Who could be more fitted to encounter the necessary hardship of such an enterprise? Already they were "well weaned from the delicate milk of their mother country, and enured to the difficulties of a strange and hard land, which yet in good part they had by patience overcome."* The example of Abraham seemed set before them as a model; and at length, after many misgivings, they resolved upon crossing the Atlantic. Their thoughts were first turned to Virginia, and they opened a negotiation with the company which then governed that colony. Several letters passed upon the subject; and in Sir Edwin Sandys they found one who, whilst he firmly upheld what he believed to be the truth of Christ, was ready to befriend their persons, and to concede a full license to their weak consciences. They acknowledge, in "their owne and their churches name, his singular love in this weighty business," and trust themselves "to the care of his love and the counsel of his wisdom." Difficulties still interposed: the king could not "be wrought upon" to grant them a charter under his seal, though he was willing "to connive at them, and not molest them, provided they carried themselves peaceably." This caused for a time "a damp in the business, and some distraction;" but at length they comforted themselves with the thought, that even if they had obtained their charter, yet if "afterwards there should be a purpose or desire to wrong them, though they had a seale as broad as the house-floor, it would not serve their turn, for there would be means found to recall or reverse it." On this persuasion they at length resolved on settling in the neighborhood of the Virginian colony, under a patent granted by that colony. It was also determined that a part only of their

---

* Fulham MS. History.

body should proceed at once, leaving its weaker members to follow when the settlement was formed.

About the 22d July, 1620, all was ready. They had one ship of near sixty tons, to transport them to England, where they were to join another of 180 tons, and proceed at once to America. Before setting sail they had a day of "solemn humiliation, their pastor taking his text from Ezra viii. 21, upon which he spent a good part of the day." They were afterwards "accompanied with most of their brethren out of the city unto Delft Haven, where the ship lay ready to receive them;" "so they left," says one of their party, "the goodly and pleasante citie which had been their resting-place nere twelve years; but they knew that they were pilgrimes, and looked not much on those things, but lift up their eyes to the heavens, their dearest countrie, and quieted their spirits." It was an affecting parting between these world-pilgrims and their brethren left behind, and even drew "tears from sundry of the Dutch strangers that stood on the key as spectators;" "but the tide (which stays for no man) calling them away that were thus loath to depart, their reverend pastor falling downe on his knees, (and they all with him,) with waterie cheeks commended them, with most fervente prayers, to the Lord and His blessing; and then, with mutual embraces and many tears, they tooke their leaves one of another, which proved to be the last leave to many of them."*

They had a prosperous voyage to London; but many more troubles were yet before them. On the 5th of August the two ships sailed in company, but as they dropped down the Channel the smaller ship leaked so greatly, that they were forced to put in to Dartmouth to refit. After losing much time there in the necessary repairs, they again set sail; but after proceeding about "a hundred leagues without the Land's End," the same cause sent them back to Plymouth. Here, after consultation, they determined to leave behind, for the present year, the faulty ship and part of their company. There were many willing to be left, some "out of feare and discontent, others as unfite, in re-

* Fulham MS. History.

gard of their owne weakness and charge of many yonge children, to bear the brunte of this hard adventure." Thus, says their chronicler, "like Gedions armie this small number was devided; as if the Lord, by this worke of His Providence, thought these few too many for the great worke He had to doe." The letter of one of the leaders in the expedition, written whilst they lay at Dartmouth, gives a lively picture of one of those who stayed willingly behind at Plymouth, out of the "feare he had conceived of the ill success of the voiage." "Our pinass will not cease leaking, els I thinke we had been halfe waye at Virginia: our viage hither hath been as full of crosses as ourselves have been of crokedness. We put in here to trimme her; and I thinke if we had stayed at sea but three or four houres more, shee would have sunke right downe. Shee is as open and leakie as a seive; there was a borde a man might have pulled off with his fingers, two foote longe, where the water came in as at a molehole. Our victuals will be halfe eaten up, I thinke, before wee go from the coast of England. I see not how we shall escape even the gasping of hunger-starved persons. Poore W. King and myselfe doe strive dayly who shall be meate first for the fishes."

All this does not bespeak in its writer the bold heart which such an adventure needed, especially when we learn that the fear of the party had been practised on by artful men as to the apparent danger of the lesser vessel. But there were amongst them some braver spirits; and, after a fatiguing voyage, one ship's company landed on the 9th of November, wearied and exhausted, on Cape Cod. The record of this landing is still kept alive in an engraving on the certificate of membership, as used at this day by the "Pilgrim Society" of Plymouth.* They had been brought thus far to the north by the treachery of their captain,† who had been bribed by their Dutch neighbors to leave the more promising banks of the Hudson open for an intended colony of their own. On this inhospitable shore winter soon set in upon them with extreme severity. In the depths

---

* Buckingham's America, vol. iii. p. 566.
† Cotton Mather's Magnalia, book i. p. 7.

of its frosts, however, they explored enough of the coast to fix upon another site for their intended settlement; and finding a commodious harbor at the bottom of the bay, they all removed thither, and laid the first foundation of the future town of Plymouth. Here their first winter was spent in the endurance of hardships which wore away "more than half their whole company," so that scarcely fifty lived to the ensuing spring. The spot where the dead were laid still maintains the name of Burial Hill. It was ploughed up and sowed by the earliest colonists, lest its graves should make their fearful losses known, and so invite the hostile violence of the surrounding Indians.

In the course of the next year their numbers were increased by a new detachment of their friends from Holland; but their supplies were yet scanty, and their perils extreme. Still, however, they held to their purpose, and a stir was now made for them at home. In 1624, several leading Puritans were interested in their undertaking. In 1627 they had purchased for them from the company, in whom title to the land was vested by the crown, "that part of New England which lyes between a great river called Merrimack, and a certain other river there called Charles River, in the bottom of the Massachusetts Bay." And in the following year a royal charter was granted to them, with power to elect yearly their own magistrates; and the intention was openly avowed of "letting the non conformists, with the grace and leave of the king, make a peaceable secession, and enjoy the liberty and the exercise of their own persuasions about the worship of the Lord Jesus Christ."

The grant of this charter greatly helped on their cause; and for the next twelve years "many very deserving persons transplanted themselves and their families to New England,"* amongst whom were "gentlemen of ancient and worshipful families, and ministers of the Gospel then of great fame at home, and merchants, husbandmen, and artificers, to the number of some thousands." It was reckoned that 198 ships were employed, at a cost of

---

* Cotton Mather's Magnalia, book i.

192,000*l*., to carry over these emigrants, who for these "twelve years kept sometimes *dropping*, and sometimes *flocking* into New England." In the spring and summer of 1630, Winthrop, who must be considered as the founder of New England, arrived with a fleet of seventeen vessels, and about 1500 men, some of whom, like himself, were persons of condition, education, and fortune. Without this reinforcement, to all human appearance, the settlement at Plymouth* would have proved abortive. By the year 1640, the settlers were supposed to have amounted to 4000 persons, who are said in fifty years to have multiplied into 100,000. As their numbers increased, they branched out into the surrounding country, until, in 1637, the neighboring territory of Connecticut was occupied by men of the same sentiments; and, "along the seacoasts of that pleasant bay" began another colony, which soon "surprised the sight with several notable towns," and even extended itself to Long Island, following strictly in religious matters the "use of Massachusetts." To the north, also, and east, New Hampshire and the state of Maine began to receive some straggling settlers, who adopted almost the same model in religious matters.

Many trials waited on these little bands, which, "toiling through thickets of ragged bushes, and clambering over crossed trees, made their way along Indian paths" to the new sites on which they fixed. "The suffering settlers burrowed for their first shelter under a hill-side. Tearing up roots and bushes, from the ground, they subdued the stubborn soil with the hoe, glad to gain even a lean crop from the wearisome and imperfect culture. The cattle sickened on the wild fodder; sheep and swine were destroyed by wolves; there was no flesh but game. The long rains poured through the insufficient roofs of their smoky cottages, and troubled even the time for sleep; yet the men labored willingly, for they had their wives and little ones about them; the forest rung with their psalms, and, 'the poorest people of God in the whole world, they

---

* Plymouth and Massachusetts remained separate colonies, till, on the accession of William and Mary, a new charter was granted, which included Plymouth as a part of the province of Massachusetts.

were resolved to excel in holiness.' Such was the infancy of a New-England village."*

Thus, then, were these wide districts first settled, and with their very earliest texture were thus interwoven the threads of congregational dissent. The name of Independents they eschewed.† Their especial features were a rejection of episcopacy, of the use of "common prayer," and of the ceremonies of the Church. Each congregation of worshippers, united by a willing bond or covenant, submitting themselves to a pastor of their own choice, and exercising discipline, through certain ruling elders, according to what they quaintly termed "the scriptural platform," formed a separate "church," which could have no alliance, save that of friendly alliance, with other "churches," nor own any submission except to their common Lord. For this, which they esteemed a more perfect reformation, they had left their native land, and become settlers in the wilderness.

It is pleasant to believe that there were amongst them many whose whole hearts were governed by a strong personal religion; whilst it is as plain that their consciences were often scrupulous, and their self-will in religion great. Of their earnest piety abundant records are preserved. It was their first care, when they settled in the west, to join themselves together in "a covenant with God," and according to their forms, "to constitute themselves a Christian Church." The lives and writings of their early magistrates and governors are full of proofs of personal religion. Nothing but conscious uprightness could have enabled a father to write to a grown-up son as John Winthrop, governor of Massachusetts, wrote to his son, who filled afterwards the same office in Connecticut. "You are the chief of two families. I had by your mother three sons and three daughters, and I had with her a large portion of outward estate. These now are all gone. . You only are left to see the vanity of these temporal things, and to learn wisdom thereby; which may be of more use to you, through

---

* Bancroft's United States, vol. i. p. 382.
† Cotton Mather's Magnalia.

the Lord's blessing, than all that inheritance which might have befallen you. . . . My son, the Lord knows how dear thou art to me, and that my love has been more for thee than for myself. But I know that thy prosperity depends not on my care, nor on thy own, but upon the blessing of our heavenly Father : neither doth it on the things of this world, but on the light of God's countenance, through the merit and mediation of our Lord Jesus Christ. But if you weigh things aright, and sum up all the turnings of divine Providence together, you shall find great advantage. The Lord hath brought us to a good land ; a land where we enjoy outward peace and liberty, and, above all, the blessings of the Gospel, without the burden of imposition in matters of religion. Many thousands there are who would give great estates to enjoy our condition. Labor, therefore, my son, to increase our thankfulness to God for all His mercies to thee, especially for that He hath revealed His everlasting good will to thee in Jesus Christ, and joined thee to the visible body of His Church in the fellowship of His people, and hath saved thee in all thy travels abroad from being infected with the vices of those countries where thou hast been (a mercy vouchsafed but unto few young gentlemen travellers.) Let Him have the honor of it who kept thee. And therefore I would have you to love Him again, and serve Him, and trust Him for the time to come. Love and prize that word of truth which only makes known to you the precious and eternal thoughts of the Light inaccessible. Deny your own wisdom, that you may find His ; and esteem it the greatest honor to lie under the simplicity of the Gospel of Christ crucified. . . . In all the exercise of your gifts and improvement of your talents, have an eye to your Master's end more than your own, and to the day of account, that you may then have your *quietus est*,—even ' Well done, good and faithful servant.' My last request unto you is, that you be careful to have your children brought up in the knowledge and fear of God, and in the faith of our Lord Jesus Christ. This will give you the best comfort of them, and keep them free from any want or miscarriage ; and when you part from them, it will be no small joy to your soul that you shall meet them again in heaven."*

Such a spirit as this, carried out, as it seems to have been, for ten years of renewed elective government over the tottering feebleness of the infant colony of Massachusetts, might well earn for Winthrop the title which, in the manner of his times, old Mather bestows upon him, of the " New-English Nehemiah." Yet amidst this early promise we may find traces of those evils which multiplied at home so rankly in the great rebellion; as if to show how short-lived and uncertain is the growth of personal religion, when taken from the shelter and protection of the Church. There are many proofs that these New-England settlers were amongst the very movers in those after-troubles. The notorious Hugh Peters (who preached afterwards in England in favor of the murder of the king) was a pastor at Boston; and there seems no good reason for doubting that Sir Arthur Haselrig, Mr. Hampden, and Cromwell himself, were intercepted on the Thames embarking for these colonies: Sir Henry Vane the younger, touching there in 1636, was immediately elected governor of Massachusetts; and at the close of the rebellion no fewer than three of the regicides found shelter in New-England.

Neither here, indeed, nor in England had the Puritans as yet worked out all the consequences of their tenets. At Massachusetts they at first declared that they " were not separatists—that they did not separate from the Church of England;"† and when some who joined them thought to recommend themselves by "holding forth a profession of separation from the Church of England,"‡ they were "stopped forthwith" by the New-England pastors. But this was only the coyness of early schism. They were, in truth, most hostile to her; holding the "composition of common-prayer and ceremonies to be a sinful violation of the worship of God;"§ "and archbishops, bishops, archdeacons, officials, and the like, to be *humane creatures*, mere inventions of man, to the great dishonor of Christ

---

* Cotton Mather's Magnalia, book ii. cap. 11.
† C. Mather, book i. c. 4.   ‡ Ib. c. iii.
§ Ib. ut supra.

Jesus; plants not of the Lord's planting, which all should certainly be rooted up and cast forth."* Some, indeed, went farther still. The fundamental principles of the Newhaven settlement declared, "that all vicars, rectors, deans, priests, and bishops, are of the devil; are wolves, petty popes, and anti-christian tyrants."† "It is a heinous sin," they declared, "to be present when prayers are read out of a book by a vicar or bishop:" nay, they go on to say, " that the lovers of Zion had better put their ears to the mouth of hell, and learn from the whispers of the devils, than read the bishops' books."‡ When the overthrow of the Church of England was made known in the colonies, their exultation broke forth in such rhapsodies as these: " This is the Lord's doing, and ought to be marvellous in our eyes. I have snared thee, and thou art taken, O Babylon, *i. e.* bishops. . . . . These proud Anakims are throwne downe, and their glory laid in the dust. The tiranous bishops are expelled, their courts dissolved, their canons forceless, their service cashiered, their ceremonies useless and despised; and the proud and profane supporters and cruel defenders of these, marvellouslie overthrowne and are not these greate things? who can deny it?"§ So strong, indeed, were their principles, that even their zealous Puritan eulogist avows his " fear that the leaven of that rigid thing they call Brownism has prevailed sometimes a little of the farthest in the administrations of this pious people;"‖ and complains of " religion being like to die at Plymouth, through a libertine and Brownistic¶ spirit prevailing amongst the people."**

The want of the appointed band of unity was already broadly seen in the religious state of the settlements. The

---

* A Platform of Church Discipline, agreed upon at the synod at Cambridge, New England, cap. vii., 1649.
† History of Connecticut, 1781.   ‡ Ibid.
§ Fulham MSS.   ‖ Magn. b. ii. c. 2.
¶ Robert Browne was the founder of the "Independent" Dissenters, who long bore the name of Brownists from him. He is described by Neal (i. 375, 376), the dissenting historian, as being a " fiery, hot-headed young man;" " idle and dissolute" in middle life; and in old age, " poor, proud, and very passionate." He died in 1630.
** Magn. b. i. c. 3.

Puritan magistrates watched with terror the working out of their own opinions in the unlimited divisions of the people. Even in their judgment "the cracks and flaws of the new building portended a fall."* On the other side they were reproached as being "priest-ridden magistrates,"† under "a covenant of works." The Presbyterian ministers were greeted with the same epithets which had been bestowed upon the clergy at home; they were "the ushers of persecution,"‡ "popish factors," and the like. In action also their own principles were turned against them. Roger Williams, a "zealous young minister, with precious gifts," headed the opposition of a faction to the "control over opinion," which his brethren attempted to maintain. He was willing to die for his opinion, that "none be accounted a delinquent for doctrine." It was in vain that he was driven out to become the founder of Rhode Island; his wildest opinions were enlarged by Anne Hutchinson, "a woman of such admirable understanding and 'profitable and sober carriage,' that she won a powerful party in the country."§ She not only "weakened the hands and hearts of the people towards the ministers,"‖ but set aside all fixed forms of faith and laws of conduct, with the pretence of being guided by "a new rule of practice, by immediate revelations."¶ This she explained to mean, not a special revelation "in the way of miracle," but merely that the impression of his own mind was to every one the true rule both of belief and practice. She was succeeded by Gordon, who, with his followers, openly inveighed against the whole body of colonial ministers, and in his dreamy reveries, proclaimed that there was no heaven save in the hearts of the good, nor any hell but in the mind. The Quakers also soon sprung up in this congenial soil; and as she wandered about "to build up their friends in the faith," Mary Dyar proclaimed against the New-England pastors her "woe is me for you, ye are disobedient and deceived."

* Shepherd's Lamentation, quoted by Bancroft.
† Coddington, in ditto. ‡ Ditto.
§ Bancroft.
‖ Winthrop, in Hutch., quoted by Bancroft.
¶ Welde, in Bancroft, cap. ix.

It was in vain that the whole civil power attempted to check the growth of these multiplying sects; it was in vain that the puritan magistrates used without scruple the very arms of which at home they had made the loudest complaints. Like the Independents in England, they had learned from their own sufferings no lesson of toleration towards others. "To say that men ought to have liberty of conscience," affirms one of their great authorities, "is impious ignorance."* "Religion admits of no eccentric notions." Banishment was their first and favorite remedy. "For the security of the flock we pen up the wolf; but a door is purposely left open, whereby he may depart at his pleasure."† This was enforced on all who differed from the reigning sect.

Two brothers, Church-of-England men, a lawyer and a merchant, who had joined unawares the settlement of Salem, finding how matters stood, ventured to "uphold" in their own house, "for such as would resort unto them, the Common-Prayer worship."‡ But such an enormity they were not long suffered to continue; for "a disturbance arising amongst the people upon this occasion," the brothers were called before the magistrates, and "so handled as to be induced to leave the colony forthwith." Nor was it Churchmen alone of whom they thus rid themselves. They dealt the like measure to all sectaries who were not of their own persuasion. "No food," runs one of their brief laws, "and lodgings shall be allowed a Quaker, Adamite, or other heretic."§ It was judged sufficient reason to expel a household from the town of Salem, that its head was by confession "a dam-ned Quaker." Where banishment failed of effecting its purpose, they were not slow in using other methods. Fines, imprisonments, stripes, and even death itself, were amongst their remedies; for "God forbid," say they, "that our love of truth should be so cold that we should tolerate errors." Convicted Anabaptists were fined twenty pounds, or "whipped unmercifully;" "absence from the ministry of the word" was treated in

---

* Ward, quoted by Bancroft, cap. x.   † Norton in Bancroft.
‡ Magn. b. i. c. 4.   § Blue Code, No. 13.

like manner by men whose main complaint in England had been, that they were compelled to be present at their parish church. But of all sects, the Quakers were the most severely handled. Of them Cotton Mather gravely writes, when treating of the troublers of the land: "There have been found amongst us some unhappy sectaries— namely, Quakers and Seekers, and such other energumens."* As such they were treated. Fines were levied on any who harbored the "accursed sect;"† whilst "Friends" themselves were sentenced, after the first conviction, to lose one ear; after the second, another; and after the third, to have the tongue bored through with a red-hot iron. "If any person," say the Puritan laws. "turns Quaker, he shall be banished, and not suffered to return on pain of death."‡ Nor was this an inoperative statute. Many Quakers in New England were put to death for the profession of their faith, until an order from King Charles II. brought this violence to a close.§

Such was the religious liberty of Presbyterian New-England twenty years after the true doctrine of toleration had been carried out in Maryland. But this tone of harshness pervaded the Puritan character. It dictated the "Blue Code" of Connecticut‖ (so named, according to probable conjecture, by the inhabitants of the neighboring settlements from its being written, as it were, in blood), which amongst other things enjoins, that "no one shall run on the Sabbath-day, or walk in his garden, or elsewhere, except reverently to and from meeting;" which makes it criminal in a mother to kiss her infant on the Sabbath-day; which strictly forbids the "reading of the Common-Prayer, keeping Christmas-day or saint's-day, making mince-pies, or playing on any instrument of music, except the drum, the trumpet, and the Jews'-harp." The same code enforced attendance at the established Puritan worship, under

---

* *Energumens*—persons possessed with evil spirits.
† Bancroft, i. 463.   ‡ Blue Code, No. 13.
§ Neale's Puritans, vol. i. p. 334.
‖ History of Connecticut, 1781. Captain Marryat's Diary, Blue Code. A copy of which, through the kindness of the last-named gentleman, lies before me.

the penalty of a money-fine for every time of absence.* Indeed, bare toleration of different forms of worship was condemned amongst them as unquestionable sin. "If," says one of their writers in 1647, "after men continue in obstinate rebellion against the light, the civil magistrate shall still walk towards them in soft and gentle commiseration, his softness and gentleness is excessive large to foxes and wolves, but his bowels are miserably straitened and hardened against the poor sheep and lambs of Christ. Nor is it frustrating the end of Christ's coming, but a direct advancing it, to *destroy the bodies* of those wolves who seek to destroy the souls of those for whom Christ died."†

The same spirit runs through all the dealings of the "pilgrim fathers" with the unhappy Indians whom they dispossessed. It seems scarcely to have crossed their minds, that these devoted tribes were part of the great human family. "By this prodigious pestilence," says their historian, himself evidently a man of a gentle temper, "the woods were cleared of those pernicious creatures, to make room for a better growth."‡ These, again, are his speculations on the mode by which the American continent was first peopled: "We may guess that probably the devil decoyed those miserable salvages hither in hopes that the Gospel of the Lord Jesus Christ would never come here to destroy or disturb his absolute empire over them."§ "Tawny pagans," "rabid wolves," "grim salvages," "bloody salvages," are the usual terms he gives them, unless, when rising into fervor, he boldly declares them to be "so many devils." As such they were treated. These "pilgrims," who left their fathers' land, believing that the "God of heaven had served a summons upon the spirits of His people, stirring them up to go over a terrible ocean into a more terrible desert, for the pure enjoyment of all His ordinances ... to carry the Gospel into those parts, and raise a bulwark against antichrist,"—they thought nothing, on a mere rumor of intended mischief, of "pretending to trade with the Indians," that they might more safely, "with prodigi-

* Cotton's Bloody Tenet washed White. See also Belknap's History of New-Hampshire, c. iii. p. 44.
† C. Mather, Magnalia, i. 7.   ‡ Ib.   § Magn. b. iii. p. 190.

ous resolution, kill divers of their chiefs ;" or of " vigorously discharging their muskets upon the salvages," and so " astonishing them with the strange effects of such dead doing things as powder and shot." Nor was this unconnected with the character of their religion. The Churchmen of Virginia, until they were provoked to retaliate by the attempted massacre of their whole colony, had treated all the Indian tribes with kindness. There were amongst them, from the first, men who devoted all their energies to spread the faith of Christ amongst their heathen neighbors. But the stern and exclusive creed of the New-England Puritans did not favor such attempts. Many of the Puritans, accustomed to regard themselves exclusively as the chosen of God, habitually applied to these poor heathens the denunciations of the Pentateuch against the old inhabitants of Canaan. Not perceiving that they had no direct charge, like the famine or the pestilence, to execute the long-delayed vengeance of the Almighty against a people " whose iniquity was full," they deemed themselves commissioned, like Joshua of old, to a work of blood; and thinking that the sword of God's vengeance was committed to their hands, they rejoiced with enthusiastic triumph at the approaching extermination of these tribes of idol-worshippers. The same fanatical delusions troubled even the more gentle spirits of their band, and kept them from exertion for their Indian brethren.* Even amongst their own countrymen, we are assured by a contemporary Presbyterian writer, who quotes authorities for all his assertions, that three out of four were driven by the rigors of their system from community with any church; and as a necessary consequence, their peculiar views,† he continues, " exceedingly hindered the conversion of the poor pagans. God, in great mercy, having opened a door in these last times to a new world of reasonable creatures, for this end above all, that the Gospel might be preached to them, for the enlargement of the kingdom of Christ,—the principles and practice of the Independents doth cross this blessed hope. What have they

---

* Bishop Berkeley's Sermon before the Society for the Propagation of the Gospel, 1731, pp. 246, 247.

† R. Baylie's Errours of the Time, p. 60. 1646.

to do with those that are without? Their pastors preach not for conversion .... Of all that ever crossed the American seas, they are noted as most neglectful of this work I have read of none of them that seem to have minded this matter."*

It was not till the very year in which this reproach was penned that any efforts were made to remove it from the Christians of New England. In that year, John Eliot, a man of primitive piety, zeal, and mortification, broke through the bondage of the system round him, and treated the red men, whose lands "the pilgrims" now so largely occupied, as having, like themselves, souls for which Christ died. He was one of those whom the unhappy humors of the time drove out of that Church at home, of which he should have been a stay and ornament. But God overruled his loss to the blessing of these heathen. From a complete education at the English University of Cambridge, he was lured over the Atlantic to become the apostle of the Indians. He stood at first alone. "I cannot find," says his Puritan chronicler,† "that any besides the Holy Spirit of God first moved him to the blessed work of evangelising these perishing Indians." "The thought," however, he continues, "may have been suggested to him by the declaration of the royal charter, that to win and incite the natives of that country to the knowledge and obedience of the only true God and Saviour of mankind, and the Christian faith, in our royal intention and the adventurers' free profession, is the principal end of the plantation."

In this spirit Eliot entered on his work, and thenceforth his name has been identified with self-denying and successful efforts to spread the Gospel of our Lord amongst the heathen of North America. He prepared himself for his task with unexampled diligence. One great obstacle to be surmounted was the difficulty of mastering the Indian language. The peculiar feature which pervades its dialects is, the habit of clustering together, into one prolonged word, the separate ideas which, in our language, occupy

---

* R. Baylie's Errours of the Time, p. 60.
† C. Mather, book iii. p. 190.

many distinct words. This made its acquisition seem almost impossible to the contemporaries and even the successors of Eliot. "Its words," says Cotton Mather,* "are long enough to tire the patience of any scholar in the world; one would think they had been growing ever since Babel unto the dimensions to which they are now extended." Further on, he gravely tells us that, "once finding the dæmons in a possessed young woman understood the Latin, Greek, and Hebrew languages, curiosity led me to make trial of this Indian language, and the dæmons did seem as if they did not understand it." These difficulties Eliot's patience overcame; and he was hereby able to render the most effective service to the cause to which his life was given. For the support of these missions, parochial collections to a large amount had been made in Cromwell's time. These had been invested in the purchase of land; and, after the Restoration, Clarendon's influence maintained the proper application of the fund so created. The honorable Robert Boyle, a name never to be mentioned without honor, was placed at the head of the trust; the funds of which, at this time, were mainly expended in printing the Bible and other religious works, of Eliot's translating, in the Indian tongue.† So much had his resolute perseverance effected in this laborious work. Mightier difficulties than these were levelled before him. The fast-closed darkened hearts of these Indians opened before his words, and many converts were gathered by him into the Christian fold. Nobly did he spend himself in these blessed labors. Nor was his example without fruit. At his first engaging in the work, "all the good men in the country were glad of his undertaking: the ministers especially encouraged him." Others soon trod in his footsteps; and, forty-one years after his going forth to these Gentiles, there were reckoned "six churches of baptised Indians in New-England, and eighteen assemblies of catechumens professing the name of Christ; of the Indians, there are twenty-four who are preachers of the word of God, and, besides these, there are four English

---

* Magnalia, book iii. part iii.
† Life of Richard Baxter, book i. part ii. p. 290.

ministers who preach the Gospel in the Indian tongue."*
This flourishing report is not unquestioned by contemporary
writers; but whether it be exaggerated or not, there is no
doubt as to the early indifference of all the Puritans to such
exertions; and it is a striking proof of the fierce and exclusive temper which their peculiarities had nurtured, that,
in a settlement which owed its origin to zeal about religion, for six-and-twenty years of constant intercourse, in
peace and war, with their Pagan brethren, the desire of
their conversion to the faith seems never to have visited a
single breast; no one had so much as thought of attempting to convey to these unhappy tribes around them the
blessed message of salvation. With an apathy made more
portentous by the very language of their charter, they never
thought of them as men partaking of redemption. They
seized without scruple on the lands possessed of old times
by the Indians, "voting themselves to be the children of
God, and that the wilderness in the utmost parts of the
earth was given to them :"† and it is calculated‡ that upwards of 180,000 of the aboriginal inhabitants were slaughtered by them in Massachusetts Bay and Connecticut alone.

With this indifference towards the heathen was combined a restless proselyting spirit towards their brethren.
Early in their history, they attempted to plant the standard
of division amongst the Churchmen of Virginia; and when
once their sect had been established there, New-England
was ever ready to send forth her succors to the founders or
fomenters of religious difference.

* Letter of Increase—Mather's, July 12, 1687. Magnalia, book iii. p. 111.
† History of Connecticut, 1781.   ‡ Ibid. p. 112.

CHAPTER IV.

FROM 1688 TO 1775.

Spiritual destitution of the colonies—Exertions of the Bishop of London, Hon. Robert Boyle, and others—Drs. Blair and Bray sent as commissaries to Virginia and Maryland—New-York conquered by English—Trinity Church endowed—Progress of the Church in New-England—Boston petition for episcopal worship—Foundation of the Society for the Propagation of the Gospel—Religious state of the colonies—Labors of the missionaries of the Venerable Society—Rev. George Keith—Violence of Quakers—Opposition from New-England magistrates—Yale College—Leading Congregationalists join the Church—Progress of the Church at Newtown under Mr. Beach—Violence of Congregationalists—General state of the Church in Virginia—Mr. Whitefield—Spreading dissent—Rise of Anabaptists in Virginia—Resistance to the clergy—Low state of the Church—Its causes—Clergy dependent on their flocks—Want of Bishops—Attempts to obtain an American episcopate, in the reign of Charles II., of Queen Anne—Bishop Berkeley opposed by Walpole—Supported by Archbishop Secker—Efforts in the colonies—Zeal of northern colonies—Virginia refuses to join in the attempt—Causes of this refusal.

To those who have learned to value rightly the importance of Christian unity, it will be no matter of surprise to hear, that in this divided land the Church of Christ could not flourish. So plain, in truth, had become the features of moral and religious evil in our Transatlantic colonies at the close of the seventeenth century, that the slightest observation of them at once startled good men at home, and led them to immediate action. Amongst the first of these were Sir Leoline Jenkins and the Hon. Robert Boyle; the first of whom left by will a foundation for two fellowships at Jesus College, Oxford, to be held by persons in holy orders who should be willing to take upon them the cure of souls in our foreign plantations; and the other, after undertaking to conduct a company in 1661, for the propagation of the

Gospel amongst the heathen natives of New England, left an annual sum to support the lectures which to this day bear his name, that, "being dead," he might "still speak" to all succeeding generations of this great duty of converting infidels to the true faith of Christ.

From these beginnings other efforts followed. In the year 1685, the Bishop of London persuaded Dr. Blair to go as his commissary to Virginia. For fifty-three years he held this office, and zealously discharged its duties. By him the long-neglected project of training for the ministry the English and Indian youth was happily revived, and through his unwearied labors brought at last to a successful close in the establishment of the college of "William and Mary."

The appointment of Dr. Blair was shortly followed by the nomination of Dr. Bray as commissary in Maryland.

This colony, as has been said, was originally founded by settlers of the Roman Catholic persuasion, but with the free allowance of all other forms of worship; and it is well worthy of remark, that at the very time when Puritan Massachusetts was persecuting to the death all who disagreed with the dominant sect, the governors of Maryland were bound by an annual oath, not "by themselves, or indirectly, to trouble, molest, or discountenance any person professing to believe in Jesus Christ, for or in respect of religion; and if any such were so molested, to protect the person molested, and punish the offender."* On this basis things continued until the time of the Great Rebellion. Settlers of various views in matters of religion had been received and protected in the colony. But as soon as the government was wrested from the hands of the Lord Baltimore by the adherents of the parliament, and the Independents thereby made its masters, they repealed these laws of universal toleration, and proscribed entirely "popery and prelacy." It is not a little striking, that the first enactment in the statute-book of Maryland, which forbade to any one the free exercise of that which he believed to be the true form of Christian worship, should have been introduced by

---

* Chalmers, 235; quoted by Dr. Hawks.

such fierce pretenders to religious liberty as the Independents.

So, however, it was; and such the law continued until the fall of Cromwell's party. With the Restoration, Lord Baltimore regained his rights as owner of the colony, and for a season all proceeded on its former plan. But a shock had been given to the old constitution; and the troubles which from time to time disturbed society at home, soon extended to the colony, and took there the same direction. The mass of the population were by this time Protestant; and as during the reigns of Charles and James II., fears of popery were the mainsprings of disturbances in England, Maryland, now brought anew under the rule of a Roman Catholic proprietor, was a favorable theatre for such commotions. Accordingly, the accession of William and Mary to the English throne was, after some preparatory troubles, followed by the overthrow of Lord Baltimore's authority, and the substitution in his stead of a royal governor. This change was succeeded by an act of assembly, which, in 1692, established the Church of England as the religion of the colony; divided its territory into parishes; and endowed its clergy with an income to be derived from the payment of forty pounds of tobacco by every taxable person in the province. To the operation of this law, the opponents of the Church created various hindrances. The Romanists and Quakers,—who abounded in the colony, and both looked on such a law as most injurious to themselves,—united in their opposition to it; and sometimes by colonial resistance, sometimes by misrepresentation to the government at home, they long delayed its execution.

At this critical period, the clergy, feeling their weakness, and seeing that it was in great part owing to that want of union, of which the presence of their proper head is so great a spring and safeguard, besought the Bishop of London to send them at least a commissary, clothed with such power as should "capacitate him to redress what is amiss, and supply what is wanting, in the Church." The bishop assented to their wishes; and most happy was his choice. Dr. Thomas Bray, his first commissary in Maryland, was a man of rare devotion, joined to an invincible energy in action. He abandoned willingly the prospect of large English preferment, to nourish the infant Church in the spiritual wastes of Maryland. No sooner had he accepted the appointment than he set himself to contrive means for fulfilling all its duties. His first care was to find pious and useful ministers, whom he could persuade to settle with him on the other side of the Atlantic; and in this he so far prospered as to increase the number laboring there from three to sixteen clergymen. He began also the formation of colonial libraries; and in the course of his exertion in this work, was led on to still greater efforts. He perceived the need and the fitness of the co-operation of all ranks of Churchmen in such attempts; and having once conceived this idea, he rested not until he had laid the foundation of the Society for Promoting Christian Knowledge, and that for the Propagation of the Gospel in Foreign Parts.

In all these labors he was indefatigable. No difficulties daunted him. Finding, in the course of his preparations, that he required the personal consent of the king to some proposed arrangements, he undertook at once, and at his own expense, a voyage to Holland, where the monarch then was. In a like spirit he acted throughout; for some years he continued patiently completing his preparations in England, though his salary as commissary did not begin until he sailed for Maryland. At length, on the 12th of March, 1700, after a tedious voyage, he reached the land of his adoption. Here he soon displayed the like activity. He assembled the clergy at visitations—instructed them by charges—and enforced discipline, to the utmost of his means, against any of bad lives.

On one notoriously corrupt he enforced, before the other clergy, the aggravations of his crime. First, "that it is done by a person in holy orders. Secondly, by a *missionary* (which, by the way, my brethren, should be a consideration of no small weight with all of us.) Thirdly, as to time, that this scandal is given at a juncture when our Church here is weakest, and our friends seem to be fewest, and our enemies strongest. And, lastly, as to place, it so happens that you are seated in the midst of papists; and,

I am credibly informed, there have been more perversions made to popery since your crime has been the talk of the country, than in all the time it has been an English colony. These considerations, sir, do make it necessary that all possible expedition, which is consistent with common justice, should be made in this affair, so as to acquit you or condemn you."*

What the results of such zeal might have been, if, instead of being a delegated representative of a distant prelate, Dr. Bray had himself, been appointed bishop in Maryland, it is impossible to calculate. As it was, the efforts, which depended wholly on his individual zeal, instead of springing ever fresh out of the system of the Church, scarcely outlived his own stay in Maryland. This was necessarily short. The opposition made to the established rights of the colonial clergy called for his presence at head-quarters, where the Quakers and Romanists were active and united; and he returned to England to maintain the cause of his afflicted community. Upon his departure religion comparatively languished, from the weakness of its imperfect planting, and the uncorrected evil lives of some among the clergy Still, in spite of all hindrances, the Church gained some ground; and a majority of the colony, now increased to 30,000, were accounted of her communion.

Nor was this rising energy confined to Maryland. There was a stir also in the other provinces. New Amsterdam, or New-York, as it was termed after its conquest by the English, was finally ceded by the Dutch, at the treaty of Breda, in 1667. This change of masters transferred at once the garrison-chapel to the use of the Church of England. Within these narrow walls it was limited for many years, until, in 1696, another church was built under the name of "Trinity," and endowed temporarily by Governor Fletcher, and in perpetuity by his successor the Lord Cornbury, with the freehold of a neighboring property, known hitherto as the "King's Farm." Even in New-England, in spite of penal laws, which rigidly prohibited any "ministry or Church administration, in any town or plantation

---

* Hawks's Eccles Con. vol. ii. p. 102.

of the colony, separate from that which is openly observed and dispensed by the approved minister of the place," a movement began towards the long-despised Church of England.

In 1679 a petition, from a large body of persons in their chief town of Boston, was presented to King Charles II., praying " that a church might be allowed in that city for the exercise of religion according to the Church of England." This request was granted, and a church erected for the purpose, bearing the name of " the King's Chapel." Far more considerable matters followed the inquiry which this step occasioned. It was found, that throughout all that populous district there were but four who called themselves ministers of the Church of England ; and but two of these who had been regularly sent forth to the work. This was a state of things which could not be endured ; and by a happy movement, of which Dr. Bray was in great measure the suggestor, the bishops of the Church set themselves to find some means for its correction. They determined to associate themselves into a body for this purpose, with such devout members of the laity and clergy as God should incline to join them in their work of mercy. They issued their address to the community, and were joined by ready hearts on all sides ; so that, having applied for and obtained a charter of incorporation, they met for despatch of business, as the Society for the Propagation of the Gospel, in June, 1701, under the Archbishop of Canterbury as their president. Many great names in the English Church appear in the catalogue of their first and warmest supporters, amongst the chief of whom were Bishop Beveridge, Archbishops Wake and Sharp, and Bishops Gibson and Berkeley.

Funds soon flowed in upon them from every quarter; but the want to be relieved was greater than the worst returns had stated. England, it was found, had been indeed peopling the new world with colonies of heathens. " There is at this day," is Bishop Berkeley's declaration somewhat later, " but little sense of religion, and a most notorious corruption of manners, in the English colonies settled on the continent of America."* Nor will this language appear overstrained, if it is compared with the numerical returns which the inquiries of the day called forth. For from these it appeared that in " South Carolina there were 7,000 souls, besides negroes and Indians, living without any minister of the Church . . . and above half the people living regardless of any religion. In North Carolina above 5,000 souls without any minister, any administrations used ; no public worship celebrated ; neither the children baptised, nor the dead buried, in any Christian form. Virginia contained above 40,000 souls, divided into 40 parishes, but wanting near half the number of clergymen requisite. Maryland contained above 25,000, divided into 26 parishes, but wanting near half the number of ministers requisite. In Pennsylvania (says Col. Heathcote) there are at least 20,000 souls, of which not above 700 frequent the church, and there are not more than 250 communicants. In New York government we have 30,000 souls at least, of which about 1,200 frequent the church, and we have about 450 communicants. In Connecticut there are about 30,800 souls ; of which, when they have a minister among them, about 150 frequent the church, and there are 35 communicants. In Rhode Island and Narraganset there are about 10,000 souls, of which about 150 frequent the church, and there are 30 communicants. In Boston and Piscataway there are about 80,000 souls, of which about 600 frequent the church, and 120 the sacrament. This is the true, though melancholy state of our Church in North America."†

Nor are these merely the accounts of Episcopalian writers. Cotton Mather describes the state of Rhode Island colony in 1695, as " a colluvies of Antinomians, Familists, Anabapists, Antisabbatarians, Arminians, Socinians, Quakers, Ranters, and everything but Roman

---

* A "Proposal for better supplying of Churches in our Foreign Plantations," published in 1725.

† Humphrey's History of the Society for the Propagation of the Gospel, p. 41, &c. These figures, however, it must be borne in mind, give the numbers of the Church of England; not of the whole Christian population.

Catholics and true Christians; *bonna terra mala gens.*"*
Such was, within little more than fifty years, the fruit of
founding a people on the specious attempt of making " no
man a delinquent for doctrine :" not in its true sense, of
abandoning all hope of forcing men to trust in Christ by
penalties and statutes, but in its most false sense, of treating them as if they were not themselves indeed responsible
for their belief; of maintaing no external system of faith,
but counting that as true to every man which he was
pleased to gather for himself in the boundless waste of un-
authorized opinion ; of resting truth upon the shifting sand-
bank of opinion, and not on the sure rock of revelation.

How far such a population could act as an outpost of
the faith may be easily conceived. What their influence
had been amongst their Indian neighbors we are told by
Bishop Berkeley, when he says that these, who " formerly
were in the compass of one colony many thousands, do not
at present amount to one, including every age and sex ;
and these are all servants of the English, who have contributed more to destroy their bodies by the use of strong
liquors, than by any means to improve their minds or save
their souls. This slow poison, jointly operating with the
small-pox and their wars (but much more destructive than
both) have consumed the Indians not only in our colonies,
but also far and wide upon our confines. It must be
owned, our reformed planters, with respect to the natives
and their slaves, might learn from those of the Church of
Rome how it is their interest and duty to behave. Both
the French and Spaniards . . . take care to instruct both
the natives and their negroes in the Popish religion, to the
reproach of those who profess a better."†

To supply the spiritual necessities of these our sons and
daughters, the society addressed itself with zeal. And
much, under God's blessing, they accomplished in various
quarters. Their choice was guided to many fit and zealous instruments for the performance of this holy work.
They sent out clergy, fixed and itinerating, to all the dis-

---

* Magnalia, b. vii. c. 3, p. 20.
† Bishop Berkeley's Sermon before the Society for the Propagation of the Gospel, 1731.

tricts except Virginia and Maryland, which were in some degree supplied already through the influence of their old endowments. Many a soul had cause to bless God for the labors of these men; who,—whether they went into the total darkness which had settled down on many districts, or preached to the "Foxian Quakers," who in their zeal for the "teaching of the inward light," were fast losing all remains of Christianity; or amongst the New-Englanders, who "consisted chiefly of sectaries of many denominations too many of whom had worn off a serious sense of all religion,"*—alike gathered in some converts to the fold. They were indeed in labors abundant. Thus amongst the first was George Keith, who had been himself a Quaker, but was now in English holy orders, and travelled for two years, between 1702 and 1705, through all the governments of England, between North Carolina and Piscataway river in New-England, preaching twice on Sundays and week-days; offering up public prayers; disputing with the Quakers; and establishing the Church. "He has done," says a letter of the day, "great service to the Church wherever he has been, by preaching and disputing publicly and from house to house; he has confuted many, especially the Anabaptists, by labor and travail night and day, by writing and printing of books, mostly at his own cost and charge, giving them out freely, which has been very expensive to him. By these means people are much awakened, and their eyes opened to see the good old way; and they are very well pleased to find the Church at last take such care of her children." Two hundred "Quakers or Quakerly-affected" converts he himself baptised with his own hand, besides "divers other dissenters also in Pennsylvania, West and East Jersey, and New-York."

These successes were not gained without a sharp conflict. Bitter and grievous are the charges with which the Quakers assailed him. He who sees this sect only in the calm into which it has long since subsided can scarcely conceive the storm and fury with which its early enthusi-

---

* Bishop Berkeley's Sermon before the Society for the Propagation of the Gospel.

asm raged. Yet these their old writers everywhere exhibit. The very index to the life of Fox thus disposes of the English Clergy: "They sell the Scriptures—pray by form—are hirelings, tithe-takers, robbers of the people—not ministers of the gospel—plead for sin—dread the man in leathern breeches—are miserable comforters—reproved in the streets—one pleads for adultery—beats friends—are oppressors—persecutors—the devil's counsellors and lawyers."

Men of such a temper as these extracts indicate would not easily yield up their past predominance, and there was no extremity of calumny with which they did not visit Keith. They would not hear of granting to Episcopalians the most ordinary toleration. Thus when Dr. Bray endeavored to stir up the voluntary zeal of Christians at home to make some adequate provision for religion in the colonies, his memorial was met by furious invectives from the famous Joseph Wyeth, who declares his object to be "to prevent, if I may, the setting up and establishing a power of persecuting and imposition in the colonies, which would be to the discouragement of the industrious planter," &c.* Yet, in spite of all assaults, the truth steadily prevailed. "In Pennsylvania"—was his concluding report—"where there was but one Church-of-England congregation, to wit, at Pennsylvania, of few years' standing, there are now five. At Burlington, in New Jersey, a settled congregation; at Frankfort, in Pennsylvania, the Quakers' meeting is turned into a church; and within these two years thirteen ministers are planted in the nothern parts of America."† These, and all save the settled clergy of Virginia and Maryland, were the missionaries of the Society, then newly formed, for the Propagation of the Gospel in Foreign Parts. To the labors of that venerable body, throughout a long season of sluggish inactivity and wintry darkness, the colonies of England are indebted for all the spiritual care bestowed upon them by the mother-country. Well did its ministers deserve the honored name of Christian Missionaries. Theirs were toils too often unrequited, carried on in the face of

---

* Remarks on Bray's Memorial by J. Wyeth, 1701.
† Narrative of the Rev. George Keith, &c.

dangers, loss, and extreme hardships. The hardly settled country was still liable to Indian incursion. The homesteads of the settlers lay far apart from one another, severed by woods, wastes, and morasses, across which, in many places, no better roads were yet carried than an Indian path, with all its uncertainty and danger. Day by day these must be passed by those who discharged in that land the office of the ministry. "In many places also there were great rivers, from one, two, to six, twelve, and fifteen miles over, with no ferry. He that would answer the end of his mission must not only have a good horse, but a good boat and a couple of experienced watermen."* In such a country he often had to minister at "places above sixty and seventy miles distant, and found it a very laborious mission."† How laborious it was, may be learned from the following sketch of his mission, sent from North Carolina to the Society of 1722. "The first Sunday I preach, going by land and water some few miles, at Esquire Duckenfield's house, large enough to hold a great congregation, till we have built a church, which is hereafter to be called Society Church. The second Sunday I take a journey up to a place called Maheim, about forty miles off, where there are abundance of inhabitants. Third Sunday, as the first. Fourth, I go up to a place called Meaon, about thirty miles journey. Fifth, I cross the sound to Eden Town. Sixth, to the chapel on the south shore, about twelve miles by water; and so, the seventh, begin as above, except once every quarter I go up to a place called Roanoke, about eighty miles journey; and the five last Sundays of the year the vestries do give me, that I may go my rounds and visit the remote parts of the country, where the inhabitants live some 150 miles off; people who will scarce ever have the oppurtunity of hearing me, or having their children baptised, unless I go to them . . . "‡ These were their labors; for which they had no other recompense than such as have at all times animated martyrs

---

* MS. letters of the S. P. G., quoted in "Early Colonial Church," No. iv., by Rev. E. Hawkins.
† Ibid. xvi. p. 92.
‡ MS. Letters in "Early Colonial Church," xvi. p. 92.

and confessors; fifty pounds a year from the Society, and, sometimes at least, but " thirty pounds paid during five years in depreciated paper," was the stipend of such laborers. Their mode of living embraced no luxuries. "The water," says one, describing what he saw around him, " was brackish and muddy; their ordinary food was salt pork, but sometimes beef; their bread, of Indian corn, which they are forced, for want of mills, to beat." "My lodging," adds another, " was an old tobacco-house, exposed even in my bed to the injuries and violences of bad weather."* These were not their severest trials; long neglect had hardened the settlers' hearts against the truth; the dying sparks of religion had to be fanned into a flame amidst abounding opposition; the people were "barbarous and disorderly," they impiously profaned the holiest rites, and heaped upon these messengers of peace " abuses and contumely." The sectarians, who had been suffered to forestall them, were " very numerous, extremely ignorant, insufferably proud, ambitious, and consequently ungovernable."†

It can cause no surprise to find that some turned back in hopeless despondency from such a task; and that others, whose first care was "so to acquit themselves, in that troublesome and unsettled country, as to be able to give a comfortable account of their stewardship at that dreadful tribunal where the secrets of all hearts shall be disclosed," soon sunk under their exhausting labors.‡ Some good no doubt they did; some wanderers in that distant wilderness shall one day rise up and call them blessed. Their record is on high. Even here they were not always without witness. "We shall ever bless Providence," says the vestry of Carotuch of one who in that great day shall rise out of his distant grave in Carolina, "that placed him amongst us, and should be very unjust to his character if we did not give him the testimony of a pious and painful pastor, whose sweetness of temper, diligence in his calling, and

---

* MS. Letters in " Early Colonial Church," ix. p. 273; iv. p. 105.
† Letters, *ut supra*.
‡ Of one (the Rev. Clement Hall) we read, " It is no excessive computation, that this good and most laborious missionary baptised ten thousand persons." *S. P. G. Report*, 1760.

soundness of doctrine, hath so much conduced to promote the great end of his mission, that we hope the good seed God hath enabled him to sow will bear fruit upwards."* But for such efforts as these, the very name of Christ's Gospel would have perished out of that land, and, shameful as it is to England that she made no better provision for her colonies, blessed was their work, and great, doubtless, will one day be their reward who devised and carried out these unrequited labors.

In New-England also the Church was rooted amidst storms and opposition. Wherever the missionaries came, "the ministers and magistrates of the Independents were remarkably industrious, going from house to house persuading the people from hearing them, and threatening those who would attend with imprisonment and punishment."† At one place a magistrate with officers came to the preacher's lodgings, and in the hearing of the people read a paper, declaring that "in coming among them to establish a new way of worship, he had done an illegal thing, and was now forewarned against preaching any more." Yet here too the good seed was not sown in vain; for in many spots throughout the country devout and abiding congregations of the faithful were gathered under apostolic order.

The movement began, in spite of all precautions, within the walls of Yale College,‡ the stronghold of the Independents. So carefully had this been fenced from such attempts, that its fundamental law prescribed that no student should be allowed instruction in any other system of divinity than such as the trustees appointed; and every one was forced to learn the Assembly's Catechism, and other books of puritanical authority.

For a time the dry metaphysics of this school excluded all healthier learning. But about the year 1711, the agent of the colony in England sent over 800 volumes, amongst which were many of the standard works of the divines of the English Church. These books were eagerly devoured

---

* MS. Letters, *ut supra*.

† Humphrey's History of the Society for the Propagation of the Gospel, p. 339.

‡ Life of Dr. Johnson, by Chandler, p. 24, &c.

by the hungry students; and amongst the first whom they affected were the rector of the college, Dr. Cutler, and two of its leading tutors, Messrs. Johnson and Brown. They were amongst the most distinguished of the Puritan divines; and their humble adoption of the Church's teaching, their abandonment of their endowments in the college, laying down the ministry which without due warrant they had hitherto discharged, and setting out for England to receive ordination at the bishop's hands,—drew general attention to the subject. Brown fell a victim to the small-pox in England; Cutler suffered severely from the same disease, but recovering, was, with Johnson, ordained to the priesthood, and with him returned, in 1723, to the colony,* where their influence ere long was widely felt. Cutler was settled at Boston, and, amidst unceasing persecutions, maintained to the last the standard of the faith. For fifty years of patient toil Johnson labored earnestly at Stratford.

His answers to the queries issued by the Bishop of London will follow up this history of his ministry, amongst " a people" whom he found " low and poor in fortune, yet very serious and well minded, and ready to entertain any instructions that may forward them in the paths of virtue and truth and godliness."

"Q. How long is it since you went over to the plantations as a missionary?

"A. I arrived upon my charge November 1st, 1723.

"Q. Have you had any other church before you came to that which you now possess; and if you had, what church was it, and how long have you been removed?

"A. I was a teacher in the Presbyterian method at West Haven, about ten miles off from this town; but never was in the service of the Established Church till the honorable society admitted me into their service as missionary.

"Q. Have you been duly licensed by the Bishop of London to officiate as a missionary in the government where you now are?

"A. I was licensed by your Lordship to officiate as a missionary in this colony of Connecticut.

* Life of Dr. Johnson, p. 36.

"Q. How long have you been inducted into your living?

"A. I was admitted into the honorable society's service in the beginning of January, 1722-3.

"Q. Are you ordinarily resident in the parish to which you have been inducted?

"A. I am constantly resident at Stratford, excepting the time that I am riding about to preach in the neighboring towns that are destitute of ministers.

"Q. Of what extent is your parish, and how many families are there in it?

"A. The town is nigh ten miles square, and has about 250 or 300 families in it, nigh 50 of which are of the Established Church. But indeed the Episcopal people of all the towns adjacent esteem themselves my parishioners; as at Fairfield about 30 families, the like number at New Town, at West Haven about 10, and sundry in other places.

"Q. Are there any infidels, bond or free, within your parish; and what means are used for their conversion?

"A. There are nigh 200 Indians in the bounds of the town, for whose conversion there are no means used, and the like in many other towns; and many negroes that are slaves in particular families, some of which go to church, but most of them to meeting.

"Q. How oft is divine service performed in your church; and what proportion of the parishioners attend it?

"A. Service is performed only on Sundays and holydays, and many times 100 or 150 people attend it, but sometimes not half so many, and sometimes twice that number, especially upon the three great festivals; and when I preach at the neighboring towns, especially at Fairfield and New Town, I have a very numerous audience; which places, as they very much want, so they might be readily supplied with ministers from among ourselves, and those the best that are educated here, if there was but a bishop to ordain them.

"Q. How oft is the sacrament of the Lord's supper administered? and what is the usual number of communicants?

"A. I administer the holy eucharist on the first Sunday of every month, to about thirty and sometimes forty communicants; and upon the three great festivals, to about sixty. But there are nigh one hundred communicants here and in the towns adjacent, to whom I administer as often as I can attend them.

"Q. At what times do you catechise the youth of your parish?

"A. I catechise every Lord's day, immediately after evening service, and explain the catechism to them.

"Q. Are all things duly disposed and provided in the church for the decent and orderly performance of divine service?

"A. We have no church; have begun to build one; but such is the poverty of the people, that we get along but very slowly. Neither have we any furniture for the communion, save that which Narraganset people lay claim to; concerning which I have written to your lordship by my churchwarden.

"Q. Of what value is your living in sterling money, and how does it arise?

"A. I have 60*l*. sterling settled on me by the honorable society, and receive but very little from my poor people, save now and then a few small presents.

"Q. Have you a house and glebe? Is your glebe in lease, or let by the year, or is it occupied by yourself?

"A. I have neither house nor glebe.

"Q. Have you more cures than one? If you have, what are they? and in what manner served?

"A. There are Fairfield, eight miles off; New Town, twenty; Repton, eight; West Haven, ten; and New London, seventy miles off; to all which places I ride, and preach, and administer the sacrament, as often as I can; but have no assistance, save that one Dr. Laborie, an ingenious gentleman, does gratis explain the catechism at Fairfield; but all these places want ministers extremely.

"Q. Have you in your parish any public school for the instruction of youth? If you have, is it endowed? and who is the master?

"A. The Independents have one or two poor schools among them, but there are no schools of the Church of

England in the town nor colony; for which reason I have recommended my churchwarden to your lordship and the honorable society.

"Q. Have you a parochial library? If you have, are the books preserved, and kept in good condition? Have you any particular rules and orders for the preserving of them? Are those rules and orders duly observed?

"A. We have no library save the 10*l*. worth which the honorable society gave, which I keep carefully by themselves in my study, in the same condition as I keep my own."*

These inroads on their undisturbed sway were ill endured by the sturdy Congregationalists. They claimed, and endeavored to exercise, powers rarely wielded by any established national communion. They called together synods, in which, but for the direct interposition of the civil arm, they would have enacted canons wherewith to bind men of all opinions in the colonies. They assumed the right of taxing all for the support of their ministers and meeting-houses; and wherever they could gain over the local governor to their persuasion, proceeded to enforce their claim with signal violence. "With melancholy hearts," the members of a "young church" at Wallingford, Connecticut, wrote home to complain, ".have divers of us been imprisoned, and our goods from year to year distrained, for taxes levied for the building and supporting meeting-houses; and when we have petitioned our governor for redress, notifying to him the repugnance of such actions to the laws of England, he hath proved a strong opponent to us; but when the other party hath applied to him for advice how to proceed against us, he hath given sentence to enlarge the gaol, and fill it with *them, i. e.* the Church "† From words and taunts they often passed to actual violence. As late as 1750, an old man, who had been long a member of the Church, was whipped publicly for not attending meeting. They fined heavily, in the same year, an episcopal clergyman of English birth and education, on the pretence that he had broken the Sabbath by walking home too fast from church;

---

*. July 2, 1729 : Fulham MSS.   † Fulham MSS.

and at Hartford one of the judges of the county court, assisted by the mob, pulled down a rising church, and with the stones built a mansion for his son.*

This spirit was continually breaking out. "We are oppressed," writes Mr. Johnson, "and despised as the filth of the world, and the off-scouring of all things, unto this day. The Independents boast themselves as an establishment, and look down upon the poor Church of England with contempt, as a despicable, schismatical, and popish communion. Their charter is the foundation of all their insolence. . . . . . I cannot but think it very hard that that Church, of which our most gracious king is the nursing father, should not, in any part of his dominions, be at least upon a level with the dissenters, and free from any oppressions from them. Another instance is this. All persons that shall come to inhabit in this colony, or are born here, have, by the charter, all the liberties and immunities of free and natural subjects, as if they were born within the realm of England. Notwithstanding which, they have made laws to prevent strangers from settling among them. As soon as any stranger, though an Englishman, comes into town, he is, according to their laws, immediately warned to go out,† which they always do if he is a Churchman. And it is in the breast of the select men of the town whether they will accept of any bondsmen for him; neither can he purchase any lands without their leave; and unless they see cause to allow him to stay, they can by their laws whip him out of town, if he otherwise refuses to depart. By this means several professors of our Church, for no other crime but their profession, have been prevented from settling here. A very worthy man, who had not before been of any religion, but was, by God's blessing on my endeavors, induced to become a very serious conformist to our Church, came here to set up a considerable trade; but for want of men to carry on his business, (occasioned by the forementioned practices,) and by reason of the discouragement he every way meets with from them, he is forced to

---

* History of Connecticut, 1781.

† This was done under the general provisions of the poor-law, to prevent strangers gaining a settlement *sub silentio*.

break up and depart, to his unspeakable damage; and the Church has lost a very worthy friend and benefactor."*

Such assumed powers they continued to exert, although it was shown them that the lords justices in 1725 had expressly declared, "that there was no regular establishment of any national or provincial Church in these plantations." But they were not soon daunted; and even when these continued exactions had led the sufferers to obtain a fresh opinion from the law-officers of the crown, which distinctly declared that no such colonial rules could be enforced on Churchmen, they endeavored to evade its power, by passing an act which exempted members of the Church from future payments, but at the same time declared, that all who lived at more than a mile from any church were not to be esteemed as Churchmen. "It were too long and tragical,"† writes another New-England clergyman after the passing of this law, "to repeat the several difficulties, and severities, and affronts, which our hearers are harassed with in many parts of this colony, by rigorous persecutions and arbitrary pecuniary demands, inflicted on the conscientious members of our Church by domineering Presbyterians, the old implacable enemies of our Sion's prosperity. Here your sons are imprisoned, arrested, and non-suited with prodigious cost, contrary to the laws of God and man. All professors of the Church of England, over whom there is not a particular missionary appointed, are obliged to support Presbyterian teachers and their meeting-houses—a cruelty, injustice, and usurpation, imposed on no other society."

In the midst of these difficulties from without, the injury inflicted on the Church by its imperfect spiritual organization was felt with the greatest bitterness. "The Independents, or Congregationalists"‡ they complain, "here in New-England, especially in Massachusetts and Connectient, without any regard to the king's supremacy, have established themselves by law, and so are pleased to con-

---

* Fulham MSS. A respectable bookseller at Boston was convicted of a libel for publishing Leslie's "Short Method with the Deists."— *Waterland's Letters to Jno. Loveday, Esq.* vol. xi. 441.

† Fulham MSS. ‡ Fulham MSS.

sider and treat us of the Church as dissenters. . . . The Presbyterians chiefly obtain in the south-western colonies, especially in those of New-York, Jersey, and Pennsylvania, where they have flourishing Presbyteries and synods in full vigor; while the poor Church of England in all these colonies is in a low, depressed, and very imperfect state, for want of her pure primitive episcopal form of Church government. We do not envy our neighbors, nor in the least desire to disquiet them in their several ways ; we only desire to be at least upon as good a footing as they, and as perfect in our kind as they imagine themselves in theirs. And this we think we have a right to, both as the Episcopal government was the only form at first universally established by the apostles, and is, moreover, the form established by law in our mother country. We therefore cannot but think ourselves extremely injured, and in a state little short of persecution, while our candidates are forced, at a great expense both of lives and fortunes, to go a thousand leagues for every ordination, and we are destitute of confirmation and a regular government. So that, unless we can have bishops, especially at this juncture, the Church, and with it the interest of true religion, must dwindle and greatly decay, while we suffer the contempt and triumph of our neighbors, who even plume themselves with the hopes (as from the lukewarmness and indifference of this miserably apostatising age I doubt they have too much occasion to do) that the Episcopate is more likely to be abolished at home than established abroad ; and, indeed, they are vain enough to think that the civil government at home is itself really better affected to them than to the Church, and even disaffected to that ; otherwise, say they, it would doubtless establish episcopacy."

Yet, in spite of all hindrances, the persecuted body grew and multiplied. Sometimes a wealthy resident would build a church upon his own estate ; sometimes the movement rose amongst the mass of poorer persons. " I have lately,"* says one of these reports, been preaching at New-Haven, where the college is, and had a considerable

* Fulham MSS.

congregation, and among them several of the scholars, who are very inquisitive about the principle of our Church; and after sermon ten of the members of the Church there subscribed 100*l*. towards the building a church in that town, and are zealously engaged about undertaking it; and I hope in a few years there will be a large congregation there." "It is with great pleasure," says another, "that we see the success of our labors in the frequent conversions of dissenting teachers in this country, and the good disposition towards the excellent constitution of our Church growing amongst the people wherever the honorable society have settled their missions. Sundry others of their teachers are likely to appear for the Church; and two very honest and ingenious men have declared themselves this winter.

We are persuaded that it is from a serious and impartial examination of things, and the sincere love of truth and sense of duty, that they have come over to our communion."

What was the character of the ministry which some faithful men were, under all discouragements, enabled to maintain, may be gathered from the following letter :*—

"Being by the favorable providence of God arrived in New-England, in obedience to your lordship's commands, I make bold to lay before you the state of this colony of Connecticut, to which your lordship has licensed me. The people here are generally rigid Independents, and have an inveterate enmity against the established Church; but of late the eyes of great multitudes are opened to see the great error of such an uncharitable, and therefore unchristian spirit. This is come to pass chiefly in six or seven towns, whereof this of Stratford, where I reside, is the principal; and though I am unworthy and unmeet to be entrusted with such a charge, yet there is not one clergyman of the Church of England besides myself in this whole colony; and I am obliged, in a great measure, to neglect my cure at Stratford (where yet there is business enough for one minister) to ride about to the other towns, (some ten, some twenty miles off,) where in each of them there is as much

---

* Mr. Johnson to the Bishop of London. Fulham MSS.

need of a resident minister as there is at Stratford, especially at Newtown and Fairfield. So that the case of these destitute places, as well as of myself, who have this excess of business, is extremely unhappy and compassionable.

"Now, at the same time, there are a considerable number of very promising young gentlemen—five or six I am sure of—and those the best that are educated among us, who might be instrumental to do a great deal of good to the souls of men, were they ordained; but for want of episcopal ordination decline the ministry, and go into secular business; being partly from themselves, and partly through the influence of their friends, unwilling to expose themselves to the danger of the seas and distempers,—so terrifying has been the unhappy fate of Mr. Brown.* So that the fountain of all our misery is the want of a bishop, for whom there are many thousands of souls in this country who do impatiently long and pray, and for want do extremely suffer.

"Permit me to remember the concern you were pleased to express for sending a suffragan into this country when we were before you, which gave me the greater pleasure, because I have the satisfaction to know that, so great is your deserved interest with his most sacred majesty King George (whom God long preserve), that you might very probably be the first, under God and the king, in effecting for us so great a blessing.

"And suffer me farther to say, that there is not one Jacobite or disaffected person in this colony, nor above two or three, that I know of, in America. But, for want of a loyal and orthodox bishop to inspect us, we lie open to be misled into the wretched maxims of that abandoned set of men, as well as a great many other perverse principles.

"May God, therefore, direct your thoughts, and second your pious endeavors, for effecting this or any other good work, that may contribute to the advancement or enlargement of His Church; and may I have an interest in your

---

* See page 85.

compassionate prayers and benedictions in the great task that lies upon me."*

It will be useful to trace out more fully the rise of one of these churches in the New-England district."† At Newtown, in Connecticut, a young and zealous Independent teacher, Beach by name, was at this time settled over a flourishing Congregational society. His ministry had been unusually successful, and he was himself the idol of his flock. Once in three months the Rev. Mr. Johnson visited five episcopalian families then settled in the place: frequent meetings and earnest discussions between the two teachers resulted from these visits; until Mr. Beach began at length to doubt the soundness of his former principles. Slowly and cautiously did he make up his mind. The first serious alarm was suggested to his flock, after two or three years of patient meditation had passed over him, by his frequently employing the Lord's Prayer in public worship, and even proceeding to read to them whole chapters of the word of God. Then he ventured to condemn a custom common in their meetings, of rising to bow to the preacher as he came in amongst them; instead of which, he begged them to kneel down and worship God. This, in the language of the day, they declared to be "rank popery," and no slight presumption that Mr. Beach would one day "turn Churchman; as did all people," said an experienced matron of their body, "who kept on reading the Church books." In this, at least, they were not deceived; for in about a year Mr. Beach, whose mind was now thoroughly convinced, told the people from the pulpit, that, "from a serious and prayerful examination of the Scriptures, and of the writers of the earliest ages of the Church, and from the universal acknowledgment of episcopal government for 1500 years, compared with the recent establishment of Presbyterian and Congregational discipline, he was fully convinced of the invalidity of his ordination, and of the unscriptural method of organising and governing congregations, and of admitting

* Dated "Stratford in Connecticut, New England, Jan. 18, 1723-4."

† This account is taken from a series of original papers, which appeared in 1822-23 in the Churchman's Magazine, Hartford, U. S.

persons to the privileges of church-membership, as by them practised; and farther, that extempore prayer in Christian assemblies was a novelty in the Christian Church." He therefore, "in the face of Almighty God, had made up his mind to conform to the Church of England, as being apostolic in her ministry and discipline, orthodox in her doctrine, and primitive in her worship." He "affectionately exhorted them to weigh the subject well; engaged to provide for the due administration of the sacraments while he was absent from them, and spoke of his intended return to them from England in holy orders."

So greatly was he beloved, that a large proportion of his people seemed ready to acquiesce in his determination. But such a threatened defection the Congregational teachers of the neighborhood could not see with unconcern. They set themselves at once to stir up the embers of intestine strife against their awakening brother, and at length assembled at Newtown, in 1732, and in spite of Mr. Beach's remonstrances, proceeded to depose him from the ministry. From this sprang up a printed discussion between Mr. Beach and his deposers; carried on with kindness, sobriety, and force of reasoning on his part, and with no little harshness of invective upon theirs.

Thus, in one of these attacks, after many charges against Mr. Beach, the author closes with a general condemnation of the English Church, as an "illegitimate daughter of the harlot of Babylon;" and describes her bishops as "the most vile and wretched set of beings that ever disgraced human nature."

Nor was this all. Under the auspices of the Society for the Propagation of the Gospel, Mr. Beach had opened a mission to a small tribe of native Indians. God had blessed his labors, and amongst these despised men a little flock was being gathered into Christ's true fold. This the Congregational teachers could not endure. The Indians were shrewd enough to meet their occasional attempts at conversion with the plea of their own multiform divisions. "We value not your gospel, which shows so many roads to Kicktang (God): some of them must be crooked, and lead to holbamockow" (the evil spirit). But the sectarian teachers could not endure that Episcopalians should convert these heathens to the truth. They sent, therefore, an agent amongst Mr. Beach's flock, with ribald ballads, suited to the native taste, decrying him and all his efforts. And when the good man next visited his native flock, instead of receiving from the Sachem the calumet of peace, and finding a circle of attentive listeners, eager to drink in his words, he was met by the taunts and derision which the heathens had been too industriously taught.

These violent proceedings defeated in great measure their intended purpose. The claims of the Church became the subject of general discussion. The eyes of many were opened; and from the first a small but growing company clave to Mr. Beach. Soon after, he set sail for England, bearing with him the following testimonial from his brethren in Connecticut.

"Mr. Beach," it says, "had his education at Yale College, where he made uncommon proficiency in learning, and hath, since he left it, taken care to improve himself in divinity and other useful studies, and when he entered into the dissenting ministry (which was indeed almost the unavoidable consequence of his education and want of proper books) he was thought the most proper person to oppose the growth of the Church in Newtown, on account of the good opinion that every one had of his learning and piety, and was accordingly placed there,—though he never did anything to the Church's prejudice. But having since, by his neighborhood to some of us, had the advantage of better books and information, he hath found it his duty to quit their service and come over to our communion, whereby he hath done great service to the Church in these parts, and we doubt not will always be an honor to it, if your lordship shall think fit to ordain him, and the honorable society to admit him into their service. And as we are well assured his labors will be of great use here, so we beg leave to assure your lordship of his firm attachment to the present government as established in the illustrious house of Hanover. Upon the whole, therefore, we humbly hope your lordship and the honorable society will think fit to empower and employ him, who for the peace of his conscience hath left the possessions he enjoyed, and now taken a long and dangerous voyage, melancholy in itself, but rendered more so by his leaving his wife and children."

The prayer of his brethren was granted, and he returned in holy orders to Connecticut. In a little while a church was built for him; in which, and in the neighboring town of Reading, he ministered as a missionary of the Society for the Propagation of the Gospel, to a faithful and devoted flock.

In this state things continued till the time of Mr. Whitefield's visit to New-England. Here, as elsewhere, his preaching produced wonderful effects. He found the flame of piety already burning low amongst the Independent congregations; for in the institutions of no separatist from the Church has the gift of enduring spiritual vitality been found. He boldly charged them with having left "the platform" of their ancient doctrines, and reviled them in his sermons under the unwelcome titles of "hirelings and dumb dogs, half beasts and half devils." He endeavored to revive the ancient spirit by a series of violent excitements. The Independent teachers betook themselves to penal inflictions, subjecting itinerants to heavy penalties, and excluding them from the protection of the laws. But the flame only burned the fiercer for this opposition. Fanaticism in its maddest forms triumphed for a while; introducing new divisions in its train, and leading many into the open profession of Antinomian tenets. These scenes are thus described in the letter of an eye-witness:*

"The duties and labors of my mission are exceedingly increased by the surprising enthusiasm, or what is worse, that rages among us: the centre of which is the place of my residence. Since Mr. Whitefield was in this country there have been a great number of vagrant preachers, the most remarkable of whom is Mr. Davenport, of Long Island, who came to New London in July, pronounced their ministers unconverted, and by his boisterous behaviour and vehement crying, 'Come to Christ,' many were *struck*, as the phrase is, and made the most terrible and affecting

---

* To the Bishop of London. Fulham mss.

noise, that was heard a mile from the place. He came to this society, acted in the same manner five days, and was followed by great numbers; some could not endure the house, saying that it seemed to them more like the infernal regions than the place of worshipping the God of heaven. Many, after the amazing horror and distress that seized them, received *comfort* (as they term it); and five or six of these young men in this society are continually going about, especially in the night, converting, as they call it, their fellow-men. Two of them, as their minister and they affirm, converted above two hundred in an Irish town about twenty miles back in the country. Their meetings are almost every night in this and the neighboring parishes; and the most astonishing effects attend them,—screechings, faintings, convulsions, visions, apparent death for twenty or thirty hours, actual possessions with evil spirits, as they own themselves; this spirit in all is remarkably bitter against the Church of England. Two, who were struck, and proceeded in this way of exhorting and praying, until they were actually possessed, came to me and asked the questions they all do: Are you born again? Have you the witness of the Spirit? They used the same texts of Scripture as the rest, taught the same doctrines, called me Beelzebub the prince of devils, and during their possession burnt a large amount of property. They have since both been to me, asked my forgiveness, and bless God that He has restored them to the spirit of a sound mind.

"There are at least twenty or thirty of these lay holders-forth within ten miles of my house, who hold their meetings every night in the week in some place or other, excepting Saturday night; and incredible pains are taken to seduce and draw away the members of my church; but, blessed be God, we still rather increase."*

The result of this sudden excitement was by no means favorable to the ruling sect. "The Independents or Congregationalists," Mr. Johnson reports, "are miserably harassed with controversies amongst themselves, at the same time that they unite against the Church. One great cause

* Fulham MSS.

of their quarrels is the Arminian, Calvinistic, Antinomian, and enthusiastic controversies, which run high amongst them, and create great feuds and factions; and these chiefly occasion the great increase of the Church, as they put thinking and serious persons upon coming over to it, from no other motive than the love of truth and order, and a sense of duty; at which they are much enraged, though they themselves are the chief occasion of it."* "When I came here there were not a hundred adult persons of the Church in this whole colony,† whereas now there are considerably more than two thousand, and at least five or six thousand young and old; and since the progress of this strange spirit of enthusiasm, it seems daily very much increasing."‡

From such fierce divisions many learned to value the peaceful and holy shelter of the Church; and Mr. Beach received so large an accession to his charge, that his church would not hold two-thirds of those who joined him. Not a few of these were of the first families within the colony, and a new and spacious building was soon erected for him. The same causes led to the building of eight other churches within different neighboring towns, and to the best amongst the Independent teachers joining his communion and receiving holy orders.

Here was plainly the finger of God. In the violent divisions of those times, as well as in the deadness which preceded them, were the elements of that Socinian leaven which has since worked so fatally throughout those parts; leading in 1821 to the choice of the chaplain to the national legislature from the ranks of that most unhappy sect. Yet, in establishing the Church, these very evils were so overruled by God as to furnish their own antidote.

In Connecticut her roots took a deeper hold in the soil, from the action of the storms amongst which she had grown up. In no part of America was her communion so pure and apostolical as here. Her clergy were, for the most

---

* Letter of the Rev. S. Johnson to the Bishop of London. Fulham MSS.
† Stratford, in New-England.
‡ Fulham MSS.

part, natives—men of earnest piety, of settled character, and well established in Church principles; and so greatly did she flourish, that at the outbreak of the troubles which ended in the separation of the colonies and mother country, there was every reason for believing that another term of twenty years' prosperity, such as she had last enjoyed, would have brought full half the population of the state within her bosom.

A contemporary writer, professing himself "unable to recollect the names of the multifarious religious sects" then existing in Connecticut, adds the following list "of a few of the most considerable."

	Congregations.
Episcopalians	73
Scotch Presbyterians	1
Sandemanians	1
Sandemanians Bastard	1
Lutherans	1
Baptists	6
Seven-day do.	1
Quakers	4
Davisonians	1
Separatists	40
Rogereens	1
Bowlists	1
Old Lights	80
New Lights	87

So greatly had the Church gained upon the sects around her, through the zeal and piety which here adorned her members.

But this is far the brightest spot in the whole picture. Here and there, indeed, throughout the continent individual zeal imparted life and warmth to separate congregations. But altogether there are few of the marks of the Church Catholic impressed in that age upon the English branch of it settled in America. Seldom, if ever, was she zealous and full of love and holy union inwardly, and to those without "terrible as an army with banners." There was a general languor of devotion; sects and divisions multiplied and often gained upon the Church; her own sons grew careless or apostates, and scarcely anything was done to bring the Indian tribes around her to the knowledge of her Lord. All this may be traced most easily in the history of Virginia, where from different causes it was most signally developed. A hasty sketch of such a painful subject will be all that is required.

From a contemporary writer* it appears, that in the year 1722 there were in Virginia not fewer than seventy churches, with dwelling-houses and glebes for the incumbent in almost every parish. Dissent was scarcely known; since it is still a matter of dispute, whether there were in the whole country three meetings of Quakers and one of Presbyterians, or whether one of Quakers stood alone. "For one hundred and fifty years," Dr. Hawks complains, "the Church had been fixed in Virginia, and yet the state of religion was deplorably low." "Many of the clergy were unfitted for their stations;" and the laity, from "loose principles and immoral practices, were often a scandal to their country and religion." Here and there a light sprung up, as in the case of Morgan Morgan, a humble and zealous layman, through whose labors the faith was planted in the newer western settlements, amongst a population composed chiefly of Presbyterian emigrants from Ireland. It was in the year 1740 that he erected the first church on the south side of the Potomac, in the valley of Virginia. But such men were rare; while for the most part all was lethargy.

In this state Mr. Whitefield found religion in the colony. As an English clergyman he was readily received, and at the desire of Dr. Blair, then commissary for the bishop of London, he preached at the seat of government and elsewhere. He was here far more restrained, and proportionably useful, than amidst the wild sectarian wastes of the New-England colonies. His efforts kindled some zeal amongst a lukewarm people; but his addresses, which were made too exclusively to the mere emotions of his hearers, and not sufficiently directed to the general revival of a

---

* Present State of Virginia, by Rev. Hugh Jones.

drooping Church, laid few or no foundations for a really permanent result. The feelings of the moment passed away with the passing voice which had awakened them; and left, it must be feared, the hearts which they had ineffectually visited even colder than they were before. No lasting blessings seem to have followed from these labors. Soon after his visit, earnest but irregular attempts for the diffusion of religion were made throughout the eastern districts by a pious layman of the name of Morris. These, after a little, led to the settlement in various parts of Presbyterian teachers from New-England. At first the local government objected to their entrance; but under the provisions of the act of toleration they made good their footing, and by a more apparent earnestness drew away many from the Church. With them the Anabaptists, a few of whom had come long since from England, now rose into notice. They had recently been strengthened by allies from Maryland; and they now appeared in force, ready to join with any adversary of the Church.

The time of their appearance was propitious for their purpose. The endowment of the clergy of the colony, from very early times, consisted of a certain fixed weight of tobacco, the staple produce of the land. Some years before this time, a failing harvest had so greatly raised its price, as to make this mode of payment burdensome, and a fixed money-payment had been substituted for it until the scarcity was over. To this expedient another threatened failure of the crop shortly afterwards again inclined the colonial legislature. But the act was disallowed at home, and the clergy disputed its authority by legal process. The courts of law decided in their favor; but when damages came to be assessed, the jury, predisposed by popular impression, and wrought on by a sudden burst of eloquence from the opposing counsel, awarded such as were merely nominal. The court, under the same influence, refused another trial; and the clergy lost alike their rights and the little which remained to them of the affections of the people. So rapid at this time was the progress of dissent, that a few years later it claimed, as belonging to its ranks, two-thirds of all the population. All things, indeed, were out of joint. In a country containing not less than half a million souls (all of them professing the Christian religion, and a majority of them members of the Church of England, living under British govenment and laws, and in general thriving, if not opulent), there was yet not a single college, and only one school with an endowment adequate to the maintenance of even a common mechanic * Two-thirds of all the little education of the colony was given by indented servants or transported felons.

The causes of this state of things are well worth examination. Some of them were evidently peculiar to Virginia, in which and in Maryland alone such questions on the rights of property could have arisen. But in other parts matters were not, on the whole, much better. Nowhere was the Church flourishing and spreading. Everywhere division multiplied. Baptists, Presbyterians, Moravians, Methodists, Tunkers, Shakers, Quakers, Socinians, and Infidels, grew daily in importance, and shed on every side of them the fruitful seed of farther subdivision. In 1729, Berkeley found at Newport, in Rhode Island, " a mixed kind of inhabitants, consisting of many sects and subdivisions of sects; four sorts of Anabaptists, besides Presbyterians, Quakers, Independents, and many of no profession at all."† To the northward and eastward of Maryland there were but eighty parochial clergymen; and all of these, except in the towns of Boston and Newport, New-York and Philadelphia, were missionaries sent out from England by the Society for the Propagation of the Gospel.

The best calculation of the numbers of the white population, and of the various religious persuasions on the continent of North America, transmitted to the Bishop of London,‡ in 1761, gave the following results:—

* Boucher's American Revolution, pp. 183, 184.
† Berkeley's Letters, p. xxxvii.
‡ Fulham MSS.

North American Continent.	Whites.	Church People.	Presbyterians and Independents.	Quakers German & Dutch of various sects, Jews, Papists, &c.
Newfoundland and Nova Scotia.	25,000	13,000	6,000	6,000
Four New-England Colonies				
New Hampshire . 30,000				
Msssachusetts 250,000				
Rhode Island . 35,000				
Connecticut . 120,000				
	435,000	40,000	250,000	145,000
New-York	100,000	25,000	20,000	55,000
New Jersey	100,000	16,000	40,000	44,000
Pennsylvania . . .	280,000	65,000*	45,000	170,000†
Maryland	60,000	36,000	6,000	18,000‡
Virginia	80,000	60,000	10,000	10,000
North Carolina . . .	36,000	18,000	9,000	9,000
South Carolina . . .	22,000 }	20,000	5,000	3,000
Georgia .	6,000 }			
Total . .	1,144,000	293,000	391,000	460,000

* This includes 40,000 Swedes and German Lutherans, who reckon their service, &c. the same as that of the Church.
† About a third of these are Quakers, about 10,000 Papists, the rest Germans of various sects.
‡ Chiefly Papists.

Some general cause there must have been for such a state of things. The power of Christ's truth could not be worn out. That church which had hitherto subdued all people, rude or polished, against whom she had gone forth, had she lost her empire over men's hearts? She who had conquered the conquerors of the great Roman empire, and gathered one and another of the hordes of Gothic and Teutonic blood, who had invaded her dominion, into the faith and hope of the people whom they conquered,—she seemed in the West not only to have lost her subduing might, but to be powerless even to retain her hold upon her own.

It is not very difficult to find the cause for this great difference. Her planting in America had been after a new and unknown manner. Heretofore the great aim of her founders, in any country, had been to make her truly indigenous—to reproduce her out of the people amongst whom she had come. For this end she was sent forth complete,

—a living germ, with all the powers of reproduction in herself. To this, as the greatest work of Christians, the boldest and truest hearts were summoned; and he who won and held a band of converts to her Lord, was consecrated bishop of the Church amongst them, if he went not out in that holy character. Thus he could at once ordain new pastors and evangelists from amongst his native converts. Through them he could extend his influence; at their mouths the truths he taught, coming to the hearers in the beloved tongue of their fathers' land, were listened to with new readiness. Their blood, if persecution arose, was at once the seed of new converts: the Church was perfect and complete, and she went on conquering and to conquer. Such was the equipment of Pothinus of old, when with Irenæus as his deacon, he went from Asia to sow amongst the Gauls the seed of the kingdom; and the Church of Lyons was his glorious harvest. So Boniface went forth from this land of ours, to become "the apostle of Germany." But wholly unlike this was our equipment of the Church in America. We sent out individual teachers, with no common bond of visible unity, no directing head, no power of ordaining; we maintained them there like the garrison of a foreign Church; and the consequence was, what might have been foretold, the Church languished and almost passed away. To this fault the religious evils of that land may be distinctly traced. Throughout the northern colonies the scattered missionaries, whom the venerable society sent out and paid,—who had no connexion with each other, no common head, and no co-operation in their work,—were the representatives of the body of foreigners across the ocean who supported and directed them. And even in the southern colonies, where the Church was established with provincial endowments, the want of bishops produced the same effect. There was no power of obtaining ordination in America: hence any young Americans, who desired to enter the ministry, must cross the Atlantic to receive holy orders. This was both costly and perilous. One in five, it has been calculated, of all who set out returned no more.* Hence in a new country,

* The small-pox was exceedingly fatal to Americans who visited

where every sort of employment abounded, few parents devoted their children to the work of the ministry. The earliest bent was given in a contrary direction. The native candidates were therefore few; whilst of those who were sent out from England, some, in spite of every care at home, would be those whose characters were most unfit for such a post,—who proposed themselves for that peculiar service because they desired to escape the vigilance of Episcopal control. This brought a reproach upon the priesthood; and the proper check on clerical unfitness being thus wanting, the people began to substitute another. Upon any vacancy, the governor and commissary recommended a successor to a Virginian benefice. The vestry received the minister so sent, and he then officiated in their church. If they chose, they might present him for induction to the governor; and when inducted, he had full and legal possession of the benefice. But the common practice was to receive the minister, and give him in possession the fruits of the benefice, without presenting him for due induction; and then the vestry could dismiss him when they chose. This seems to have been meant at first to guard the people from unworthy pastors. From the nature of the case, there could be scarcely any other check on such men. The Bishop of London, indeed, had his commissaries in America; but their limited power and derived authority could do little when their principal was on the other side of the Atlantic. Nor was the power of the Bishop of London himself over those distant provinces certain or well defined. Whence it had first sprung is exceedingly uncertain. The most probable account attributes it to the hearty concurrence of the then Bishop of London in the earliest schemes of the Virginian Company for establishing the Church amongst their settlers. This led to his being requested to find and appoint their first clergy; and from this practice there gradually grew up a notion that there were in some way in his diocese. Thus, Bishop Compton wrote, in

England. Within a very few years, seven candidates for orders from the northern colonies died during their absence from America. Amongst these was the son of Dr. Johnson, mentioned above, p. 85, who sunk under the small-pox.

March 1676, "As the care of your churches, with the rest of the plantations, lies upon me as your diocesan, so to discharge that trust, I shall omit no occasions of promoting their good and interest."*

Such the practice continued until the appointment of Bishop Gibson to the see of London. Upon inquiring into the source of his authority, he was told, that, though no strict ecclesiastical title could be found, yet by an order in council in the reign of Charles the Second, the colonies were made a part of the see of London. For this order he, being a careful man, caused a diligent search to be made, when he discovered that none such existed. Finding, therefore, no ground whatever on which to rest his claim of jurisdiction, he declined even to appoint a commissary. Thus the colonies were separated from all Episcopal control. But after a while, having obtained a special commission from the crown, committing this charge to him, and thinking it better, under all the circumstances of the case, to act under this authority than to abandon them entirely, he began to discharge it with his usual fidelity. Yet even then he felt that his hold upon those distant parts was little what it should be, if he were indeed to deem himself their bishop. Every line of his first address to them† breathes this spirit.

"Being called," he tells them, "by the providence of God to the government and administration of the diocese of London, by which the care of the churches in the foreign plantations is also devolved upon me, I think it my duty to use all proper means of attaining a competent knowledge of the places, persons, and matters entrusted to my care. And as the plantations, and the constitutions of the churches there, are at a far greater distance, and much less known to me, than the affairs of my diocese here at home, so it is the more necessary for me to have recourse to the best and most effectual methods of coming to a right knowledge of the state and condition of them. Which knowledge I shall not fail, by the grace of God, faithfully to employ to the service of piety and religion, and to the maintenance of

---

* Fulham MSS. † Dated Nov. 2, 1723.

order and regularity in the Church." He then furnishes a paper of inquiries, and promises his "best advice and assistance, in order to the successful and comfortable discharge of their ministerial function."

This authority, shadowy as it was, expired with the life of Bishop Gibson; since the commission under which he acted was granted only to himself personally, and not to his successors.* How little it sufficed to maintain any form of discipline was shown in the fearful laxity of conduct which was visible on every side. Thus, at this very time, the marriage-licenses, which, by a first stretch of principle, had been granted to any "Protestant minister," instead of the authorized clergy, were now "expounded to intend a justice of the peace, as being a *minister* of justice, and a Protestant by religion;"† and they accordingly took upon them to marry all applicants at their own pleasure. No one felt this want of discipline more keenly than the Bishop of London. But it was beyond his power to remedy the evil; and, as is commonly the case where the true safeguard provided by the Church is carelessly neglected, men began to invent others for themselves. Thus, in the state of Maryland, where the scandal of ill-living clergymen had risen to a fearful height, acts were passed by the provincial assemblies subjecting the clergy to the jurisdiction of a board of laymen, or mingled laymen and clergymen. It was in vain that men of the highest character amongst the clergy exclaimed against a proposal so utterly at variance with all ecclesiastical principle. The pressing evil was keenly felt; and in the absence of the true Church-remedy, they sought another for themselves. This law they would have carried into operation, if it had not been defeated by the opposition of the governor on grounds of state-policy.

* Bishop Sherlock, in 1749, tells Dr. Johnson that he will appoint a commissary "as soon as I take a proper authority from the king, which I have hitherto delayed, in hopes of seeing another and better settlement of ecclesiastical affairs in the country...... I am persuaded that no bishop residing in England ought to have, or will willingly undertake the province."—*Life of Dr. Johnson.* pp. 131-2.

† Fulham MSS.

So also it was in Virginia. To secure that which lawful authority should have provided for them, the vestries at first desired to try their pastors before they confirmed their full appointment. And this, as was natural, soon grew into a great abuse. The vestries were now the masters of the clergy. On the most paltry or unworthy grounds they changed their minister. If he testified with boldness against any prevalent iniquity, the people whom his zeal offended soon rid themselves of so disagreeable a monitor. Hence ecclesiastical appointments in the colony grew into disrepute. Few would accept such uncertain stations; and those few were led to do so by necessity. Thus the clergy declined both in numbers and character. From this sprang another evil. The lack of clergy led to a general employment of lay readers. These lay readers were naturally taken from a lower class than the ordained clergy; they were also natives. It was not difficult for them to insinuate themselves into the regard of the congregations which they served; and it happened frequently that the benefice was kept unfilled in order to prolong the more acceptable services of the unordained reader.

Thus at every hand the Church was weakened. The laity were robbed of the sacraments, and led to choose their pastors on unworthy grounds. The clergy who came out were those least fitted for a work which, far more than that of ordinary stations, required the highest gifts of holy zeal and knowledge. For in Virginia causes of moral and social corruption were at work which nothing but the holy faith in its utmost vigor could counteract. From an early time the curse of slavery had rested upon Virginian society. Conditional servitude, under covenants, had been coeval with the first settlement of the colony. The emigrant was bound to render to his master the full cost of his transportation. This led to a species of traffic in those who could be persuaded to embark. The speculation proved so lucrative that numbers soon took part in it; since men might be imported at a cost of eight pounds, who would afterwards be sold in the colony for forty pounds.* So

---

* Smith, i. 105. Bullock's Virginia, p. 14, quoted by Bancroft.

established became this evil, that white men were purchased on shipboard as horses are bought at a fair.* This under the rule of the Parliament, was the fate of the royalist prisoners of the battle of Worcester. To this was added in 1620 negro slavery, which differed from indented serviture in being perpetual instead of for a term of years, and in the degradations which the distinctive features of the race of Ham soon associated with it. Marriage was early forbidden, under ignominious penalties, between the races of the master and the slave ;† and the grievous social evils which follow the dishonor of humanity sprung up freely around. "All servants,"‡ was the enactment of 1670, "not being Christians, imported into this country by shipping, shall be slaves ;" yet it was added, "conversion to the Christian faith doth not make free." The death of a slave from extremity of correction was not accounted felony ; and it was made lawful for "persons pursuing fugitive colored slaves to wound or even to kill them."

The evils which such laws attest and aggravate were yet more exasperated by the whole character of the first centuries of Virginian life. Whilst the New-England settlers were early gathered into villages, and even towns, the Virginian landowners dwelt apart from one another, each one a petty despot over his indented servants and his slaves. Bridle-ways were their roads ;§ bridges were unknown ; and the widely scattered population met at most but once on the Lord's Day for worship, and often not at all ; while the remoter families could rarely find their way through the mighty forests to the distant walls of their church. Education was almost neglected. "Every man," said the governor, in 1671,‖ "instructs his children according to his ability ;" and what this instruction was, may be gathered from another of his sayings ; " I thank God there are no free-schools nor printers ; and I hope we shall not have them these hundred years."

In such a state of things religion could not flourish,

Bancroft, i. 177. † Henry, i. 146. quoted by Bancroft.
‡ Bancroft, ii. 193. § Ib. p. 212, &c. ‖ Ib. p. 192.

and a ministry already depressed was sure to sink into absolute debasement. The Church was best served by those ministers, as we have seen, whom she had gained over in New England from the ranks of Congregational dissent; for these were natives of the land, trained to the work, and men of earnest zeal and self-denying love of truth. But here, too, the want of bishops and the whole Church-system was lamentably felt. The sectaries around them possessed each their own system, such as it was, in perfection: they could appoint and send out teachers; gather in the young and active to the work; hold their synods and conventions; act, in short, as a living and organised body. "It is hard," was the complaint of Churchmen at the time, "that these large and increasing dispersions of the true Protestant English Church should not be provided with bishops, when our enemies, the Roman Catholics of France and Spain, find their account in it to provide them for theirs. Even Canada, which is scarce bigger than some of our provinces, has her bishop; not to mention the little whimsical sect of Moravians, who also have theirs."* "The poor Church of America is worse off in this respect than any of her adversaries. The Presbyterians have come a great way to lay hands on one another (though, after all, they had as good stay at home, for the good they do); the Independents are called by their sovereign lord the people; the Anabaptists and Quakers pretend to the Spirit: but the poor Church has nobody upon the spot to comfort or confirm her children, —nobody to ordain such as are willing to serve; therefore they fall back into the hands of the dissenters."† These complaints were but too well founded. Only that communion which clave close to the apostolic model was on all sides cramped and weakened: without the centre of visible unity—without the direction of common efforts— without the power of confirming the young, whilst it taught the young that there was a blessing in the very rite which it withheld from them—without the power of ordination, whilst it maintained that it was needful for a

* Fulham MSS.   † Fulham MSS.

true succession of the priesthood,—declaring, by its own teaching, its maimed and imperfect condition, and feeling it practically at every turn.

"There is a dispute amongst our clergy," says Mr. Johnson,* applying for directions from the Bishop of London, "relating to the exhortation after baptism to the godfather, to bring the child to the bishop to be confirmed. Some wholly omit this exhortation, because it is impracticable; others insert the words 'if there be opportunity,' because our adversaries object it as a mere jest to order the godfather to bring the child to the bishop when there is not one within a thousand leagues of us, which is a reproach that we cannot answer."

At any time, and under any circumstances, such a state of things must have been widely and fatally pernicious. But in this case the injury was even more than usually great. Many causes had been in operation, from the era of the Reformation, which tended to make the bishops the only external centres of vigorous and united action in the English Church. From changes in the body politic, from the weakening of her synods and councils, and from the loneliness of her condition, almost every element of outward strength and visible unity was now centred in the episcopal office. The clergy, therefore, of such a Church, when set down in the far West, without a bishop nearer than the see of London, were at once reduced to the utmost extremity of weakness. They had no other lines of strength upon which to fall back to rally and re-form their broken ranks; and they became thus single-handed combatants, instead of marching in combined phalanx against a common scattered foe. Deeply was this felt by the most earnest and spiritual amongst them; and moving, oftentimes, were their entreaties to the Church, which had thus put them forth unfitted for their charge, to send them over the succession of the apostolical episcopate.

Year after year their lamentations and entreaties crossed the Atlantic. "We beg,"† they write at one time to the Bishop of London, "your fatherly compassion on

* Fulham MSS.
† From New-London in Connecticut. Fulham MSS.

our truly pitiable circumstances; we are forty-four miles from the nearest Church of England to us . . the incumbent of which hath visited us four times a year. There have been several adults and infants baptised amongst us, ... and a church raised, which we hope to have finished by the next fall. We have never, since our first settlement, had the Gospel of Christ, or its comfortable sacraments, regularly administered to us by any episcopal minister; whereby sundry persons bred up in the Church of England at home, others that have been baptised here and become conformists, and a greater number still strongly inclined to conformity, do labor under that last and most grievous unhappiness of being left ourselves and leaving our posterity in this wilderness, excluded as wild uncultivated trees, from the saving benefits of a transplantation into your soundest part of the Holy Catholic Church."

Similar appeals were sent from all parts of the Continent. "The Church," they say, "is daily languishing for want of bishops." "Some that were born of the English have never heard the name of Christ, and many others who were baptised into his name have fallen away to heathenism, quakerism, and atheism, for want of confirmation."* "It seems the strangest thing in the world, and it is thought history cannot parallel it, that any place which has received the Word of God so many years should still remain altogether in the wilderness as sheep without a shepherd." "There never was so large a tract of the earth overspread with Christians without so much as one bishop, nor ever a country wherein bishops were more wanted."† "We have several countries, islands, and provinces, which have hardly an orthodox minister among them, which might have been supplied, had we been so happy as to see a bishop *apud Americanos*." "Above all things, we need a bishop for the confirming the baptised, and giving orders to such as are willing and well qualified to receive them; there being a considerable number of actual preachers and others, of New England education, well disposed to serve in the ministry."‡ "We have been deprived

* S. P. G. MSS.   † Fulham MSS.   ‡ 1705. S. P. G. MSS.

of the advantages that might have been received of some Presbyterian and Independent ministers that formerly were, and of others that are still, willing to conform and receive the holy character, for want of a bishop to give it." "Last year* there went out, bachelors of arts, near twenty young men from the college, all or most of whom would gladly have accepted episcopal ordination, if we had been so happy as to have had a bishop of America, from whom they might have received it; but being discouraged at the trouble and charge of coming to England, they accepted of authorities from the dissenting ministers, and are all dispersed in that way."

The pressing sense of these necessities forced them often to a passionate earnestness of entreaty. "We pray God," they write,† "to inspire the government with compassion towards this country, to the taking away our reproach amongst the adversaries of our Church." "We speak the wish of great multitudes of souls in this land, and the necessities of a vast many more who perish for lack of supervision." In "the miserable case of the country from this want," they "would be glad that a true episcopate might obtain amongst them in any shape." Thus one of them suggests to the Bishop of London, "whether one or other of the youngest and ablest of the bishops of the smaller dioceses might not be disposed to have a commission to visit these parts of the world, and spend a year or two among us; and so from time to time, once in about seven years, till a settlement could be had, duty being in the mean time done for the absent bishop by one of the neighboring bishops. This might answer many good ends, if nothing else could be done." "The presence and assistance of a bishop is most needful; the baptised want to be confirmed; his presence is necessary in the councils of these provinces, to prevent the inconveniences which the Church labors under by the influence which seditious men's councils have upon the public administration, and the opposition which they make to the good inclinations

---

* Rev. G. Thoms, 1705: S,P G. MSS.
† From New-Haven, 1724: Fulham MSS.

of well-affected persons. He is wanted not only to govern and direct us, but to cover us from the malignant effects of those misrepresentations that have been made by some persons."* "We have great need of a bishop here, to visit all the Churches, to ordain some, to confirm others, and bless all."†

Letters and memorials from the colonies supply, for a whole century, a connected chain of such expostulations; yet still the mother country was deaf to their entreaties. At home they were re-echoed from many quarters. Succeeding archbishops pressed them on successive administrations; and the Society for the propagation of the Gospel, during almost every year, made some effort in the same cause. The records of these memorials show how earnestly and with what strength of argument it pressed this great cause upon the notice of the government.

It may well seem strange that these prayers were never granted. England stood alone in not establishing her Church in all its perfectness amongst her colonies. In Spanish America, whilst the crown had carefully excluded the power of the pope, securing to itself the appointment to all benefices, and not allowing any papal bull to be published which had not first been sanctioned by the royal council of the Indies, the greatest care was taken to set up amongst the colonists that form of faith and worship which, debased as it was, the mother country believed to be alone consistent with the truth. Thus a monastery had been established in New Spain within five years from its first settlement. And in 1619, about 120 years later, Davila estimates the staff of the Spanish Church in America to have been—"1 patriarch, 6 archbishops, 32 bishops, 316 prebends, 2 abbotts, 5 royal chaplains, 840 convents." Besides these, there were a vast number of inferior clergy, secular as well as regulars, who were arranged in a threefold division; "curas," or parish priests, amongst the emigrants from Spain, and their descendants: "doctrineros," to whom were entrusted the Indians who had submitted to the rule of Spain; whilst for the fiercer tribes, to whom

---

* Nov. 1705: S. P. G. mss. † From New-York, 1702.

the civil arm had not yet reached, there were bands of "missioneros," who labored to reduce their untamed spirits to the faith.

In these institutions, as Bishop Berkeley endeavored to enforce upon the nation, was a strong condemnation of the supineness of a people who held a purer faith, and did not in like manner exert themselves to spread it. For whatever was deemed needful for the Church's strength at home, that, as a Christian people, we are manifestly bound to give her in our colonies, where, upon the outskirts and borders of christendom, she needed arms for every service, and defence from every enemy. Yet, even from their earliest establishment, circumstances had led to this neglect. The first episcopal colonies were settled by private adventurers; their beginnings were feeble and uncertain; they proceeded on no general and matured plan, and their continued existence was long doubtful. They had no sooner gained some strength than the king resumed the charter he had given, by which they were removed from the control of those who valued their religious interests, and fell into the hands of the courtiers of James I., who were then under Spanish influence, and therefore hostile to the extension of the English Church. Then followed the troubles of King Charles's reign, and the triumph of Dissenters in the great rebellion, ending in the overthrow of throne and altar, both at home and in our colonies. After the restoration, the subject was not wholly overlooked. Lord Clarendon perceived its importance, and prevailed on Charles II. to appoint a Bishop of Virginia, with a general charge over the other provinces.*
Dr. Alexander Murray, a sharer in the royal exile, was selected for the office; and a patent was made out for his appointment by Sir Orlando Bridgeman, who was lord keeper from 1667 to 1672. But a change of ministers cut short the scheme.† The king, a concealed papist,

---

* McVickar's Life of Hobart, pp. 177-218.
† Archbishop Secker says, in his letter to Horace Walpole, it fell to the ground because the tax to support it was to be laid on the customs. Dr. Jonathan Boucher states that it was through the King's death. *American Revolution*, p. 92.

could have had no warm affection for it; and the reins of government which Clarendon relinquished fell into far different hands.

His successors set themselves against all measures planned by him, and to this the Virginian bishoprick was not likely to form an exception; since of the five men who now absolutely ruled the state, two were infidels, two papists, and the fifth a Presbyterian.*

During the life of Charles, therefore, the scheme was dropped; and James II. certainly would not resume it. Then came the troubles of the revolution and the reign of William III., when the divisions of the Church at home, as well as the temper of those to whom the conduct of affairs was entrusted, prevented further steps being taken in the matter. Other difficulties also had now arisen. Though petitions were repeatedly sent, both from the clergy and laity of the American episcopal community, entreating this Church and nation to grant them the episcopate, yet amongst their fellow-countrymen were found some objecting to their reasonable prayer. Many of the colonies had, as we have seen, been founded by dissenters; and now they were multiplied in numbers, and grown into new sects of every name and form. The sending out of bishops would have been distasteful to them, and kindled the wrath of the upholders of dissent at home, whom William III. most sedulously courted. Our early neglect had made the line of present duty more difficult than ever; so that the scheme was was for the time wholly laid aside.

Queen Anne's accession promised better things; and in her reign the project of an American episcopate was heartily resumed.

The Society for the Propagation of the Gospel still led the way in the efforts which were made. As early as the year 1712, a committee was appointed " to consider of proper places for the residence, of the revenues, and me-

---

* The first letters of whose names formed the word *Cabal*. Lords Clifford and Arlington were papists, the Duke of Buckingham avowedly an atheist, Sir W. Ashley (two years afterwards Lord Shaftesbury) a deist, and Lord Lauderdale a presbyterian.

thods of procuring bishops and bishoprics in America." This committee sat from time to time; and agreeing that it was "a matter upon which the interests of religion, and the success of the designs of the society, do greatly depend,"* they moved both the body at large, and the archbishops and bishops especially, to proceed in it with vigor. Several times they laid before the crown their earnest representations of the great importance of the subject.

Nor were they without the promise of immediate fruit. Queen Anne was truly minded to be a nursing mother to the Church. Preparations were made for founding at once four bishoprics—two for the islands, and two for the continent of America. The society† prepared special subscription-rolls, towards raising a sum for the endowment of the sees; and from many quarters they received munificent bequests for this especial purpose. They applied to the Queen for the confiscated lands which had belonged to the popish clergy within the island of St. Kitt's, and received a most gracious answer in reply; and in 1712 they purchased Burlington House, within New Jersey, as the palace of one of the future bishops.

But just when all seemed most certainly to promise the success for which they had so long been waiting, the death of the queen again frustrated their hopes. With the accession of King George the First, and the change of the government, a blight fell upon the hopes of the friends of the colonial Church. Still the venerable society made its voice of remonstrance heard. They represented to the new monarch that, " since the time of their incorporation, in the late reign, they had used their best endeavors to answer the end of their institution, by sending over, at their very great expense, ministers for the more regular administration of God's holy word and sacraments, together with schoolmasters, pious and useful books, to the plantations and colonies in America." They recited their former arguments as to the great need of establishing colonial bishoprics, and with them the favorable answer they

---

* Manuscript papers of the Society for the Propagation of the Gospel.
† February 21, 1718. MS. proceedings.

had met with from the Queen. They entreated the King to carry out her unfulfilled intentions, and found four bishoprics, "that is to say, two for the care and superintendency of the islands, and as many for the continent."

These entreaties and remonstrances were not confined to this society. Some were always found who were ready to urge this duty on the nation. Foremost amongst these stands Bishop Berkeley, whose noble devotion to this great cause deserves more than a mere passing notice. Possessed of a most subtle understanding, he had already acquired fame and eminence, when the spiritual destitution of America attracted his attention. A finished and travelled scholar; the friend of Steele, and Swift, and Pope; and in possession of the deanery of Derry,—he was willing to renounce all, in order to redress this pressing evil. "There is a gentleman of this kingdom," writes Dr. Swift to the Lord-Lieutenant in 1724, "who is just gone to England; it is Dr. George Berkeley, dean of Derry, the best preferment amongst us. . . . . He is an absolute philosopher with regard to money, titles and power; and for three years past hath been struck with a notion of founding an university at Bermuda by a charter from the crown. He hath seduced several of the hopefullest young clergymen and others here, many of them well provided for, and all of them in the fairest way of preferment; but in England his conquests are greater, and I doubt will spread very far this winter. He shewed me a little tract which he designs to publish; and there your excelleney will see his whole scheme of a life academico-philosophical, of a college founded for Indian scholars and missionaries, where he most exorbitantly proposeth a whole hundred a year for himself, forty pounds for a fellow, and ten for a student. His heart will break if his deanery be not taken from him, and left to your excellency's disposal. I discourage him by the coldness of courts and ministers, who will interpret all this as impossible and a vision; but nothing will do. And therefore I humbly entreat your excellency either to use such persuasions as will keep one of the first men in this kingdom for learning and virtue quiet at home, or assist him by your credit to compass his romantic design, which, however, is very noble and generous, and directly proper for a great person of your excellent education to encourage." *

On this errand Berkeley went to London, and having found access by a private channel to George I., he so far interested him in the project, that the king granted a charter for the new foundation, and commanded Sir Robert Walpole to introduce and conduct through the House of Commons an address for the endowment of the college with £20,000. After six weeks' struggle against "an earnest opposition, from different interests and motives,"† the address was "carried by an extraordinary majority, none having the confidence to speak against it, and but two giving their negatives in a low voice, as if ashamed of it." But now, when it might have seemed that " all difficulties were over," they were little more than beginning, "much opposition being raised, and that by very great men, to the design." Sir Robert Walpole was averse to the whole measure; and a year and a half after the grant of the charter, it was "with much difficulty, and the peculiar blessing of God, that it was resolved to go on with the grant, in spite of the strong opposition in the cabinet council." But Berkeley's resolution was equal to every obstacle; though he complains of having "to do with very busy people at a very busy time," he was, by May 1727, " very near concluding the crown-grant to the college, having got over all difficulties and obstructions, which were not a few." At this moment, and before the broad seal was attached to the grant, the king died ;‡ and he had all to begin again.

With untired energy he resumed his labors, and "contrary to the expectations of his friends," so well succeeded, that by September, 1728, he was able to set sail with a new-married wife for the land of his choice. He went first to Rhode Island, where he intended to lay in some necessary stock for the improvement of his proposed college farms in the Bermudas. Here he awaited the payment of

---

* Life of Bishop Berkeley, pp. 17, 18.
† Letters of Bishop Berkeley.   ‡ June 1727.

the 20,000*l.* endowment of his college. But a secret influence at home was thwarting his efforts. His friends in vain importuned the minister on his behalf, and equally fruitless were his own earnest representations. The promised grant was diverted to other objects. With the vigor of a healthy mind, he was laboring in his sacred calling amongst the inhabitants of Rhode Island, making provision for his future college, and serving God with thankfulness for the blessings he possessed. "I live here," he says, "upon land that I have purchased, and in a farm-house that I have built in this island; it is fit for cows and sheep, and may be of good use in supplying our college at Bermuda. Amongst my delays and disappointments, I thank God I have two domestic comforts, my wife and my little son; he is a great joy to us: we are such fools as to think him the most perfect thing in its kind that we ever saw." For three years he patiently awaited the means of accomplishing his purpose; until Bishop Gibson extracted from Sir Robert Walpole a reply, which brought him home. "If," said he, "you put this question to me as a minister, I must assure you that the money shall most undoubtedly be paid as soon as suits the public convenience; but if you ask me as a friend, whether Dr. Berkeley should continue in America, expecting the payment of 20,000*l.*, I advise him by all means to return home to Europe, and to give up his present expectations."*

Thus was this noble project, and the labor of seven years of such a life, absolutely thwarted. One consequence alone remained. The library intended for his college was left by Berkeley at Rhode Island, and sowed in after-years the seed of truth amongst that people. He himself returned to England; and until his death, in 1753, repeatedly endeavored to arouse his country to the due discharge of its duty to the western colonies.

Other great men repeated his warnings. Bishops Butler,† Sherlock, and Gibson, enforced in turn our clear obligations in this matter. Thus we find, in 1738, the Bishop of London "laboring much, but in vain, with the

---

* Chandler's Life of Johnson, pp 53, 54.
† See Apthorpe's Review of Mayhew's Remarks, p. 55.

court and the ministry, and endeavoring to induce the archbishop, who had credit with both, to join him in trying what could be done to get a bishop sent into the plantations;"* and in the same year there was some hope that the bishop would be "appointed archbishop of the New World, the continent of America, and the adjacent islands, and invested with authority and a fullness of power to send bishops among them."

But the fears and the subtleties of worldly-wise politicians defeated all these promising appearances. Sir Robert Walpole's government was dead to all appeals founded upon moral and religious principles. The minister consented willingly to no proposal which could increase the strength of the Church at home; and whilst the sectarian opponents of the measure had put forward their objections in terms which could not be mistaken, there was no counter power to weigh against the irreligious bias of the administration. The nation knew too little of Church principles to feel much interest in the subject; while the Church herself languished beneath the benumbing influence of Hoadley, and others of his school. Still, the episcopalians in America continued their most reasonable prayer. From all parts of the continent memorials were still sent home, though the greatest earnestness upon the subject was manifested in the northern colonies, where, as we have seen, there was, from many causes, most of the life and vigor of religion.

One of these addresses touched on grounds which might have moved even Sir Robert Walpole. The bishops, who had been deprived of their temporalities for refusing to take the oath of allegiance to William III., did not thereby lose their spiritual character. They had still, therefore, as of old, the power of conferring holy orders, and of consecrating other bishops by the laying on of hands, although their doing so was plainly "irregular and schismatical."† This step unhappily they took, at the imminent risk of entailing a fearful schism on the English Church. Having founded a counter episcopate at home, they could feel little scruple

---

* Fulham MSS. † Perceval's Apology, p. 244.

in granting to America that boon which England had so long and so unwarrantably withheld from her. It was therefore natural that some of the American clergy should look to them for succor, and that they should lend a favorable ear to their requests. Accordingly, Dr. Welton, and Mr. Talbot, the oldest missionary of the Society for the Propagation of the Gospel, solicited and received consecration from the non-juring bishops: Dr. Welton was consecrated by Dr. Ralph Taylor in 1722, Mr. Talbot shortly afterwards by Drs. Taylor and Welton.* Political disqualifications made them unable to perform publicly any episcopal acts; but there is reason to believe that they privately administered the rite of confirmation, and, in some cases at least, ordained clergy. One such instance, traditionally recorded,† shows in an interesting manner what might have been done by resident bishops towards occupying the land with a native clergy, and so healing the divisions of the West.

A Congregationalist teacher in New-England, shortly before this time, began to doubt the lawfulness of his appointment to the ministry. His doubts and fears were often hinted, and became well known amongst his people. About the time of Dr. Welton's visit he left home for a few weeks, giving no intimation of the object or direction of his journey. On his return he resumed his pastoral charge, and now declared himself entirely contented with his ministerial commission. Whence this contentment sprang he never expressly stated; but there were reasons for the universal belief that he had received at Dr. Welton's hands the gift of ordination.

These Episcopal acts were performed with the utmost secrecy; but they were soon whispered abroad, and excited observation. Accounts of them were transmitted to headquarters; and good men, who distrusted non-juring loyalty, hoped to extort from the fears of the government what they could not obtain from higher motives. "We shall be very unhappy," they wrote home,‡ "if any measures are

---

* Perceval's Apology, p. 246. † Hawk's Maryland, p. 185.
‡ Fulham MSS.

taken to propagate disaffection among us. Now, though none of the clergy here have ever expressed the least disaffection to King George's person or government, but always the contrary, yet it is certain that the non-jurors have sent over two bishops into America, and one of them has travelled through the country upon a design to promote that cause. I had accidentally a little acquaintance with him; and though I had considered the matter too well to be wrought upon by them, yet many will be in great danger of being led aside; for their powers of insinuation are very considerable. Your lordship sees from hence how miserable the case of this country is, for want of bishops to preserve the flock of Christ from wandering out of one schism into another, and withal into disaffection to the king."

To the same effect speaks an address of the body of the clergy maintained by the Gospel-Propagation Society, setting forth "the many ill consequences that may follow from Dr. Welton's coming over, who is reported to have privately received the Episcopal character in England, by corrupting the affections of the people of that country to our most excellent constitution and the person of his most sacred majesty," and representing also "the great use and benefit of an orthodox and legal bishop residing among them."*

But not even political danger could extort this boon. These appeals only led to Dr. Welton's recall on his allegiance,† and to the dismissal of the venerable Talbot from his former office.

Still the question was not left to sleep; and even in the highest places of the Church at home a more lively zeal for its accomplishment was soon evinced. About the year 1764 a pamphlet was published on the subject in New-England, by the Rev. E. Apthorpe, a missionary at Cambridge, Massachusetts, which called forth an acrimonious rejoinder from a Congregational minister at Boston, of the name of Mayhew. In this, amongst other charges against the society in whose employment Apthorpe was,

---

* S. P. G. MSS.
† He returned to Europe, and died in 1726.

he specially attacked its aim and object in desiring American bishops.

This pamphlet was answered by no less a man than Archbishop Secker. His attention had long since been drawn to the question;* and, in a letter to Horace Walpole, written in January 1750, and published, by his order, after his decease, he had entered fully into the whole case. This letter was an answer to objections against the institution of an American Episcopate, urged, in a letter to Dr. Sherlock, bishop of London, by Robert Lord Walpole, brother of the late prime minister. Lord Walpole shared his brother's apprehension of increasing the power of the Church, and into this fear all his objections resolve themselves. These the archbishop fully met, and showed, as he does again in his reply to Dr. Mayhew's angry charges, how clearly due was such an institution to our Episcopalian brethren. "The Church of England," he maintained, " is in its constitution Episcopal. It is in some of the plantations confessedly the established Church; in the rest are many congregations adhering to it. . . . . All members of every Church are, according to the principles of liberty, entitled to every part of what they conceive to be the benefits of it entire and complete, so far as consists with the welfare of civil government. Yet the members of our Church in America do not thus enjoy its benefits, having no Protestant bishop within three thousand miles of them —a case which never had its parallel before in the Christian world. Therefore it is desired that two or more bishops may be appointed for them to have no concern in the least with any persons who do not profess themselves to be of the Church of England; but to ordain ministers for such as do, to confirm their children, when brought to them at a fit age for that purpose, and take oversight of the Episcopal clergy. . . . Neither is it, nor ever was, in-

* In 1745 he writes from London to Dr. Johnson: "Everything looks very discouraging here; ecclesiastical, civil, domestic, and foreign. God avert from us the judgments we have deserved. . . . . We have been greatly blameable, amongst many other things, towards you, particularly in giving you no bishops. *Life of Dr. Johnson*, p. 75.

tended to fix one in New-England; but Episcopal colonies have always been proposed."*

Such a plea seemed scarcely to admit of answer from the zealous advocates of religious toleration; but Dr. Mayhew still found grounds for opposition, and for the part he had taken in this matter the archbishop was maligned for years, as an overbearing violator of the rights of conscience.

Though no immediate steps were taken in the matter, the archbishop did not despair of its accomplishment. "Lord Halifax," he says (in 1671), "is very earnest for bishops in America. I hope we may have a chance to succeed in that great point, when it shall please God to bless us with a peace."† Nor was the cause let to drop amongst the northern colonists. Dr. Chandler of New Jersey, soon came forward as its advocate, and he expressed the views of all the northern clergy. Those of New-York, New Jeresy, and Connecticut, formed themselves into a union, under the title of "The Voluntary Convention," with a view to obtaining their desire. In May, 1771, the Connecticut clergy addressed another earnest appeal upon the subject to the Bishop of London. "Viewing," they began, "the distressed and truly pitiable state of the Church of England in America, being destitute of resident bishops, we beg leave to renew our addresses in behalf of it. We apprehend it a matter of great importance, considered in every view, that the Church should be supported in America. But this Church cannot be supported long in such a country as this, where it has so many and potent enemies thirsting after universal dominion, and so many difficulties to surmount, without an episcopate, which in any country is essential at least to the well-being of the Church. Must it not, then, be surprising and really unaccountable that this Church should be denied the episcopate she asks, which is so necessary to her well-being, and so harmless, that her bitterest enemies acknowledge it can injure none? While Roman Catholics in one

---

* Answer to Dr. Mayhew's Observations, &c.,—Archbishop Secker's Works, vol. ix. p. 324.

† Letter of Abp. Secker,—Dr Johnson's Life, p. 182.

of his Majesty's colonies are allowed a bishop, and the Moravians are indulged the same favor in another; nay, and every blazing enthusiast throughout the British empire is tolerated in the full enjoyment of every peculiarity of his sect; what have the sons of the Church in America done, that they are treated with such neglect, and are overlooked by government? Must not such a disregard of the Church here be a great discouragement to her sons? Will it not prevent the growth of the Church, and thereby operate to the disadvantage of religion and loyalty? . . . We believe episcopacy to be of divine origin; and judge an American episcopate to be essential to the well-being of religion here."*

The efforts of the clergy of Connecticut were not confined to sending such addresses to the powers at home. Their first endeavor was to secure the concurrent voice of episcopal America; and for this end they sent deputies† throughout the other states. Had such vigorous steps been taken earlier, there can be little doubt what would have been their issue. They would have called forth from all parts of that continent one general voice, which could not have been slighted here. But that season was gone by; there was now in many districts a clear indisposition to join in the attempt. Of this the convention of Connecticut avowed themselves " sadly sensible; some of the principal colonies are not desirous of bishops; and there are some persons of loose principles,—nay, some even of the clergy of those colonies where the Church is established,—who, insensible of their miserable condition, are rather averse to them. But this is so far from being a reason against it, that it is the strongest reason for sending them bishops; because they never having had any ecclesiastical government or order (which ought indeed to have obtained above seventy years ago), the cause of religion, for want of it, is sunk and sinking to the lowest ebb; while some of the clergy, as we

* Fulham MSS.
† The Rev. Dr. Cooper, president of King's College, New-York, and the Rev. Mr. M'Kean, missionary at Amboy, New Jersey, were sent to the southern part of the continent. Seabury MSS.,—apud Dr. Hawks' Virginia, p. 126.

are credibly informed (but are grieved to say it), do much neglect their duty; and some of them on the continent, and especially in the islands, are some of the worst of men: and we fear there are but too many that consider their sacred office in no other light than as a trade or means of getting a livelihood; and many of the laity, of course, consider it only as a mere craft; and deplorable ignorance, infidelity, and vice greatly obtain; so that unless ecclesiastical government can so far take place as that the clergy may be obliged to do their duty, the very appearance of the Church will in time be lost, and all kinds of sectaries will soon prevail, who are indefatigable in making their best advantage of such a sad condition of things. It is therefore, we humbly conceive, not only highly reasonable, but absolutely necessary, that bishops be sent, at least to some of these colonies (for we do not expect one here in New-England); and we are not willing to despair but that earnest and persevering endeavours may yet bring it to pass. We humbly beg your lordship's candor with regard to the warmth our consciences oblige us to express on this melancholy occasion."*

But these were not now the only hindrances. In many respects the time was wholly unpropitious for the effort. Discord had been long at work between the mother country and the colonies, and men's minds had become embittered against everything of English aspect. They associated the name of bishops with the institutions of the mother country, and were unwilling to receive them from her, even whilst they admitted and believed that their office was essential to the perfection of the Church. Other causes, too, were at work. There were some, no doubt, desirous of maintaining the union between England and America, who feared, at that moment of fierce and unnatural suspicion, to introduce any new cause of difference, or to alienate still further the sectarian population by the name of bishops. When, therefore, the Virginian clergy, who might be naturally thought most ready to unite in

---

* Letter from Convention of Connecticut to the Lord Bishop of London, Oct., 1766,—Fulham MSS.

this appeal, were called together by their commissary, in April 1771, for its consideration, so few appeared in council that the question was postponed. A second summons brought no more than twelve, a majority of whom, after one opposite decision, agreed to an appeal to the king in favor of an American episcopate. But against this vote, two at first, and ultimately four, out of the twelve, protested publicly; and such was the feeling of the laity, that these four received the unanimous thanks of the lower branch of the Virginian house of legislature, for "their wise and well-timed opposition to the pernicious project for introducing an American bishop." Yet of this very body the great majority would have termed themselves episcopalians; and the reasons given for the protest refer only to present expediency, whilst it professes to revere episcopacy. Three out of the four reasons on which it was grounded were, (1) the disturbances occasioned by the stamp-act; (2) a recent rebellion in North Carolina; and (3) the general clamor of the moment against introducing bishops; whilst the fourth, in fact, affected only the intended form of application, which, it was contended, should be first addressed to the Bishop of London for advice, before it besought the throne for the episcopate.

Under these reasons the true cause of this opposition may be read. There were already signs abroad of the approaching hurricane: the whole atmosphere, political and moral, was heated and disturbed. Old men looked around them with wonder and fear at the great change in opinions as to Church and State, which they saw passing upon all. They could "remember when, excepting a few inoffensive Quakers, there was not in the whole colony a single congregation of dissenters of any denomination,"* and when loyalty and love for their Church was the very characteristic of the "Virginian dominion:" but now all was changed. A popular candidate applied for votes upon the profession of "low churchmanship and whiggery."† It were as easy "to count the gnats that buzz about in a sum-

---

* Boucher's American Revolution: a sermon preached at St. Mary's, Caroline county, Virginia, in 1771, p. 97.
† Boucher's Sermon, p. 98.

mer's evening, as the numbers of sectarian and itinerant priests; and in particular of those swarms of separatists, who had sprung up under the name of Anabaptists and New Lights within the last seven years."*

With this increase of schismatics the Church was taunted as a proof of her remissness. It was in vain that she replied, that "itinerant preachers, with whom the colony was overrun, made their proselytes in parishes left vacant through the want of bishops to ordain successors:"† the temper of the time was against all authority in Church or State. The party papers of the day took np the contest. The discussion on the American Episcopate was conducted by the same organs and in the same temper as that on the recent stamp-act. Continued misrepresentation stirred up the feelings of the people into angry opposition to the plan. "It is our singular fate," boldly declared a preacher at the time, in the face of some of the warmest opposers of episcopacy, "to have lived to see a most extraordinary event in Church history: professed churchmen fighting the battles of dissenters, and our worst enemies now literally those of our own household." "Till now, the opposition to an American episcopate has been confined chiefly to the demagogues and Independents of the New-England provinces; but it is now espoused with warmth by the people of Virginia."‡

In such a state of things sober-minded men, who loved their country, looked onward with unfeigned alarm." "What evils,"§ declared one of them almost prophetically, in 1769, "this prevalence of sectarianism, so sudden, so extraordinary, and so general, may portend to the state, I care not to think. Enthusiasts conceive it to be the commencement of a millennium: but I recollect with horror that such were the 'signs of the times' previous to the great rebellion in the last century."

In this unhappy temper of the country, unanimity of effort to secure the episcopate was manifestly hopeless. Some of the southern clergy boldly rebuked their more

---

* Boucher's Sermon, p. 100.   † Ib.
‡ Ib. pp. 94, 103.   § Ib. p. 79.

time-serving brethren; and an "appeal" was published "from the clergy of New-York and New Jersey to the episcopalians in Virginia," full of arguments which, on their common principles, admitted of no answer. But events were hastening on to a far different end. The storm of revolution was already breaking on the land; and till its fury had swept past, the desire of every pious churchman must be unattainable.

CHAPTER V.

FROM 1775 TO 1783-4.

Revolutionary war—Loyalty of the Northern clergy—Persecution—Virginian clergy generally loyal—Treated with violence—Thomas Jefferson—Zeal of the Anabaptists—Their hatred to the Church—Repeal of all former acts in its favor—Incomes of the clergy stopped—They are stripped even of the glebes and churches—Conduct of the Methodists—John Wesley persuaded to consecrate Dr. Coke—Depressed state of the Church at the end of the war—Religion at a low ebb—The revolutionary war a consequence of the Church not having been planted in America.

THE first blood shed in the war of American independence was at Lexington, in the year 1775. The northern colonies, which had been all along the great fomenters of disturbance, now, true to the spirit of their ancestors, led the way in revolt. Amidst the general defection, one class of men alone continued loyal. Whilst hypocrisy found in Puritanism the forms it needed,* no one minister of the Episcopalian Church north of Pennsylvania joined the side of the insurgents; and, as if to make the lesson plainer to the mother country, the king's troops were fired upon for the first time from a meeting-house in Massachusetts Bay.† The great mass of the clergy here were missionaries of the venerable society, and depended for their incomes on the salaries they drew from it. But deeper motives lay at the root of their firm loyalty. They had learned to honor their king in the same holy oracles which bid them fear their God; and though there may be nothing in the constitution of the Church which makes it incompatible with republican institutions, yet those who had sworn allegiance to the crown of England knew not how to break those oaths without the crime of perjury.

* See p. 135. † Boucher's American Revolution.

PERSECUTION. 133

Their constancy was not a little tried; and it endured the trial. Mr. Beach, the venerable pastor of Newtown, answered an injunction to cease praying for the king, by the declaration, "that he would do his duty, preach and pray for the king, till they cut out his tongue."* One of the insurgent generals acquainted the Rev. Mr. Inglis that, " General Washington would be at church, and would be glad if the prayers for the king and royal family were omitted, or the word 'king' exchanged for 'commonwealth.'" Mr. Inglis paid no attention to the message, and declared soon after to Washington in person "that it was in his power to close their churches, but by no means in his power to make the clergy depart from their duty." To try his determination, one hundred and fifty armed men marched into the church in which he was officiating; but he fearlessly continued the appointed service. The officers sent to him for the keys of the church, that they might open it to the sectarian chaplains. He at once refused; took all the keys from the inferior servants of the church, and stood his ground so firmly, that the attempt was shortly after dropped.

But firmness would not always save the clergy from violence and wrong. Many received personal ill-treatment; and in 1777, Trinity Church, New-York was burned by incendiaries; and Mr. Avery barbarously murdered, becouse he refused to pray for congress. From the first outbreak of the revolution this spirit had been stirring; the builders of St. John's Church, Elizabeth Town, New Jersey, had, in 1774, to watch by night with swords in their hands over the rising walls of their new temple.† As the war proceeded, outrages became more general, until there was not in many of the northern provinces one church remaining open. In Pennsylvania one only was left, under the ministry of Mr. White, who, with Dr. Provoost, were the first Americans afterwards consecrated bishops by the Archbishop of Canterbury.

These passionate outbreaks were not confined to the

---

* Gadsden's Preliminary to the Life of Dehon, p. 37.
† Historical Notices of St. John's Church, p. 17, by John Rudd, D. D.

northern provinces, in which the clergy were, for the most part, missionaries of the Gospel-Propagation Society, and might for that reason be more closely identified with the English people. In Maryland and Virginia, where the clergy, supported by endowments, were entirely identified with colonial interests, they were similarly treated. The Church was an object of suspicion and dislike to the insurgents. They felt that her temper was against them, even when her sons, as in the case of General Washington, were found amongst their leaders. In these provinces, as well as in the north, the great bulk of the clergy remained loyal. Some of them continued to officiate and employ the English ritual, praying duly for the king, in spite of threats and violence, which were carried to the greatest lengths. Thus, for instance, one clergyman, who had offended the revolutionary party through his consistent loyalty, was enticed from home at night by a feigned message, which called for his attendance on a sick parishioner. He fell into the snare, was carried to the woods, and there tied up, and after being mercilessly flogged, left, till he was found and rescued in the morning.* Yet even here consistent firmness sometimes triumphed. One Virginian clergyman refused, when violence was at its greatest height, to close his church or change his service. He went weekly to his duty, after taking a last leave of all his family, and resolutely ministered as he had done of old. Such determination met with its reward: no one dared to interrupt him, and his house grew into a safe asylum for his persecuted brethren.

But, with some such instances of firmness, the clergy, on the whole, did not maintain the loyal tone which had so strongly marked the northern provinces. They were more under the control of local influence, and they were beset by many snares. No scruples withheld their opponents. If the rebellious spirit of the people flagged, the holiest things were craftily profaned in order to excite their passions. The deist Jefferson, looking back upon his life, records with self-complacent pleasure, that, thinking " the appointment of a day of general fasting and prayer would

---

* Ms. letter quoted by Dr. Hawks, Epis. Ch. of Virg.

be most likely to call up and alarm attention, he rummaged over the revolutionary precedents and forms of the Puritans, and cooked up a resolution for appointing a day of fasting, humiliation and prayer, to implore Heaven to avert from us the evils of a civil war."* Such hypocrisy was always at command. And in order to entrap the clergy, throughout the early stages of the war days of special fasting and prayer were publicly enjoined in terms of studied ambiguity, which did not express direct opprobation of the outbreak, but had a general reference to the disturbance of the times. Such orders could not reach the northern clergy; but here the Church was established, and the clergy were forced suddenly to choose whether they would check such wishes of apparent piety, or indirectly approve of the rebellion. As there was no bishop who could act as a common centre for the various members of the Church, each one took singly his own line; and the general tone being lower here than in the north, one-third of all the clergy joined the revolution, and more than one laid down his pastor's staff and censer to take up the musket and the sword. Two of the Virginian clergy had risen to the rank of brigadier-generals at the close of the war.

But compromise never saved the Church, and it did not shield it in Virginia. Its fiercest enemies, the Anabaptists saw at once the favorable moment, and resolved to seize it In their secret councils they had already doomed the provincial establishment,† and they set themselves at once to work out their design. Their first step was to address the convention with a declaration of their entire concurrence in the war, and to offer the assistance of their pastors in enlisting the youth of their own denomination. This done, they petitioned for freedom of worship, and for exemption from payments to any but their own religious teachers.‡ Their zeal was met by a permission to officiate in the army, in common with the established clergy, and by promises of future favor. Encouraged by these beginnings, they poured in on the legislature a multitude of similar petitions. In

---

* Jefferson's Memoirs, p. 6.
† Journals of Convention, August 1775, quoted by Dr. Hawks.
‡ Semple's History of Virginia Baptists, pp. 25-27.

their prayer, says the Anabaptist historian with wonderful simplicity, "the Presbyterians, Baptists, Quakers, Deists, and all the covetous," united. A long struggle followed in the legislative body, which gave rise to "the severest contests," says Mr. Jefferson, the chief opponent of the Church, "in which I have ever been engaged."* It resulted in an act repealing all former laws in favor of the Church; exempting dissenters from further contributions to its funds; only securing to the clergy existing arrears of salaries, with the glebes, churches, plate, and books, which they already possessed. In the present strife of parties, this act stopped at once the incomes of the great body of the clergy, and absolutely drove them from the country. Churches were now everywhere abandoned, flocks wholly broken up, and the sacraments administered only from time to time by a few zealous pastors, who travelled through the country for the purpose.

Yet even this did not satisfy the hatred of the Anabaptist faction. The title to the glebes was still in the Church; and till this was wrested from her, their spirit could not rest. Accordingly, as soon as the revolutionary war was over, they returned to the assault. The incorporation of religious bodies was rendered legal by the colonial legislature, and the Church availed itself of this permission. The first act of the dissenters was to repeal this measure, and dissolve the voluntary incorporation. This done, they rssted not until, in 1803, they procured the confiscation and sale of all the glebes and churches. Even the communion-plate was sold; and the offensive desecration of things long set apart to holy uses, which this violence occasioned, gratified their deep hatred to the Church.

Other evils pressed at the conclusion of the revolutionary war on her wounded and dismembered body. In Virginia, as at home, the Methodist connexion had been founded in communion with her. Some of the most pious of the clergy had lent their aid to nurture its beginnings. Its teachers at this time intruded themselves on no strictly ministerial office; they exhorted all their flocks to cleave to the Church;

* Jefferson's Memoirs, p. 33.

they with them received the holy eucharist from her appointed pastors; and only aimed at quickening and increasing the religious zeal of her members. Discipline was first openly neglected during the spiritual famine of the revolutionary war. Under its pressure some of the Methodist exhorters assumed a right to discharge the functions of ordained men. This, however, was completely checked by the authority of Mr. Asbury, a leader of their body, who with indefatigable labor succeeded in obtaining a public disavowal of the unwarrantable practice.

But after the revolution the blow fell from another quarter. John Wesley, then, as his brother Charles and his biographer suggest, enfeebled by the weight of fourscore years and two, was persuaded, by some of those into whose hands he was about to drop the reins which in his vigor none had ever shared with him, to attempt to give that which he had never received—the power of ordination. He found in Dr. Coke one who, with much zeal and piety, was predisposed by strong personal vanity to receive gladly the pretended consecration, and who even pressed strongly on Wesley his " earnest wish "* to obtain it. The unhappy step was therefore taken at Bristol in 1784; and " in spite of a million declarations to the contrary, the ordination of Methodist parsons on the Presbyterian plan"† commenced by Wesley. To the " uninfected itinerants," says Dr. Whitehead, himself one of the connection, it was " amazing and confounding." Even Charles Wesley, who was at Bristol with him, was not in his brother's secret; But in an evil hour John Wesley was "surprised into this rash action ;"‡ and with his commission, and the title of superintendent—soon changed by imperceptible degrees for that of bishop—Dr. Coke went out to America to involve the Methodist connection there in open schism.

Mr. Asbury was joined in this commission with the doctor. When it was first opened to him, he " expressed strong doubts about it ;"§ but the authority of Mr. Wes-

*Whitehead's Life of Wesley, vol. ii. p. 419.
† Ib. vol. ii. p. 416.
‡ Charles Wesley's Letter to Dr. Chandler.
§ Coke's Journal.

ley's name subdued him, and at length he joined the scheme; and the American Methodists were severed from the Church.

The reasons given by John Wesley for this step bear no marks of his vigorous understanding. At home he still declares, he would not suffer it; but where there were "no bishops with legal jurisdiction, his scruples were at an end." He seemed to himself to " violate no order, and invade no man's right, by appointing and sending laborers into the harvest." Every Churchman sees at once the vanity of such excuses. In admitting the power of bishops he sealed his own condemnation. For if such an order did indeed exist in the Church at all, possessed of powers and functions specially committed to it by the Lord, Wesley could not at his own desire arm himself with its peculiar gifts. Yet, whilst we see the weakness of his reasoning, it is most instructive to mark on what he grounded the lawfulness of this usurpation. Here as elsewhere, it is to the want of bishops that the injury may be distinctly traced.

The peace, which was proclaimed in April 1783, found the Church wasted and almost destroyed. The ministrations of the northern clergy had been suspended by their conscientious loyalty; and with the recognition of American independence the connection of the missionaries of the venerable society with the land in which they had labored hitherto was abruptly ended. In the south, its condition was not greatly better. Virginia had entered on the war with one hundred and sixty-four churches and chapels, and ninety-one clergymen spread through her sixty-one counties. At the close of the contest, a large number of her churches were destroyed; ninety-five parishes were extinct or forsaken; of the remaining seventy-two, thirty-four were without ministerial services; while of her ninety-one clergymen, only twenty-eight remained."[*] To this day, the mournful monuments of that destruction sadden the Churchman's heart throughout the " ancient dominion." As he " gazes upon the roofless walls, or leans upon the little

---

[*] Dr. Hawks' Virginia, p. 154. 154.

remnants of railing which once surrounded a now deserted chancel ; as he looks out through the openings of a broken wall, upon the hillocks under which the dead of former years are sleeping, with no sound to disturb his melancholy musings save the whispers of the wind through leaves of the forest around him, he may be pardoned should he drop a tear over the desolated house of God."* At the time, the prospect was indeed depressing. The flocks were scattered and divided ; the pastors few, poor, and suspected ; their enemies dominant and fierce. Nothing but that indestructible vitality with which God has endowed His Church could have kept it alive in that day of rebuke and blasphemy. Nor was it her communion only which had suffered ; a blighting influence pervaded all the moral atmosphere. Religion, in its most general form, was every where depressed. If the dissenters seemed to triumph, it was mainly because Jefferson—the friend of the infamous Tom Paine, and himself supposed to be a settled unbeliever—used them as his most convenient weapon of assault upon the Church. He and others like himself now held the reins of power, and in a great degree directed public opinion. They hated the Church alike for her loyalty and for her faith. Whilst she had learned to intercede for " kings and all that are in authority," they were teaching their young republicans to " besiege the throne of Heaven with eternal prayers to extirpate from creation this class of human lions, tigers, and mammoths, called kings."† And her faith was as hateful to them as her loyalty. They esteemed it a " form of tyranny over the mind of man, which had its birth and growth in the blood of hundreds and thousands of martyrs, against which they had sworn eternal hostility."‡ Her " clergy lived by the schisms they could create."|| Her saints were, like " Calvin or Athanasius, fanatics and impious dogmatists."§ The religious faith they would themselves inculcate may be learned from Jefferson's

---

* Hawks' Virginia. p. 155.
† Jefferson's Memoirs, vol ii. p. 224.
‡ Ibid. vol. iii. p. 499, and vol. iv. p. 368.
|| Ibid. vol. iii. p. 475.
§ Jefferson's Memoirs, vol. iv. p. 358

directions to a youth whose mind he wished to form. "Fix reason," are his words, " firmly in her seat, and call to her tribunal every fact, every opinion. Question even the being of a God. . . . Do not be frightened from this inquiry by any fear of its consequences. If it ends in a belief that there is no God, you will find incitements to virtue in the comfort and pleasantness you will feel in its exercise, and the love of others which it will procure you."* So large were his views, that he "threw the mantle of public protection alike over the Jew and Gentile, the Christian and Mahommedan, Hindoo and infidel of every denomination."† As was natural in such a state of things, infidelity was spreading all around, girdled every where by a fierce and unreasoning fanaticism. "From a pious Presbyterian," says a writer of the day,‡ " I learn that religion is at a low ebb among them. The Baptists, I suppose are equally declining ; I seldom hear anything about them. The Methodists are splitting and falling to pieces." " The war," says the Anabaptist chronicler of the state of his sect, " though very propitious to their liberty, had an opposite effect upon the life of religion among them. They suffered a very wintry season. . . . . . The declension was general. . . . . . Iniquity greatly abounded."∥

Such was the state of things at the end of the revolutionary war.

It is impossible to close the scene without reflecting how different it might have been, if the mother country had long before faithfully established the strong band of a true community of faith between herself and her colonies. Those whose minds the Church, weak as she was, had leavened, were by her healing influence kept loyal in the day of trial. What might not have been the consequence, if, instead of spreading division freely in that land, and keeping her maimed and impotent, we had, with a true faith in God, planted her amongst our western children in

---

* Jefferson's Memoirs, vol. ii. p. 217.
† Jefferson' Works, vol. i. p. 39.
‡ Life of Rev. Devereaux Jarratt, p. 180.
∥ Semple's Hist. Virginia Baptists, pp. 35, 36, quoted by Dr. Hawks.

her strength and beauty! The colonies might now, perhaps, have been as much an independent nation; but they might have reached that state by a gradual progress to natural maturity; their youthful affections might never have been torn from us; and England, America, and the world, might have been spared those bitter sufferings with which they have been visited in the war of independence, and its clear consequence, the French Revolution. But this the intrigues of party statesmen had prevented. In vain the Church at home protested; in vain America sent, year by year, her supplications for the boon; at one time their mutual suspicions; at another, fears of strengthening the Church at home; the hope, at another, of securing the support of schismatics in England or the colonies,—led these men to weave otherwise their fine-spun webs of cunning policy. Thus the cause of God was slighted; all seemed to prosper for a while; but the day of retribution came; and surely that hour of mortal struggle, closed by the sudden loss of those great settlements, was intended to teach England that her vast colonial empire was a trust from God; and that, if she would not use it for His glory, it should wither in her grasp.

CHAPTER VI.

'FROM 1783 TO 1787.

Depression of the Church—Parties—And Opinions—Attempted organisation in the south—Mr. White—Conventions in Virginia and Philadelphia—Agreement on common principles—First movements for general union—General voluntary meeting at New-York—Want of episcopate—Movement amongst the eastern clergy—They elect Dr. Seabury bishop—He sails for England—Disappointed of consecration there—Dr. Berkeley and the Scotch Bishops—Dr. Seabury applies to them—Opposition—his consecration—And return—First convention at Philadelphia—Difference of opinion—Dr. White—Proposed liturgy—Application to the English prelates for the apostolical succession—Their objections to some changes in the liturgy—These reconsidered—Drs. White and Provoost embark for England—Are consecrated at Lambeth—Return to America, April 1787.

It has been often seen, in the dealings of God with His people, that mortality becomes the seed of life. "Except a corn of wheat fall into the ground and die, it abideth alone; but if it die, it bringeth forth much fruit." "That which thou sowest is not quickened, except it die." And so it was now with the Church in America. Crushed it was, and almost brought to nothing; made the very prey of its enemies; abandoned, of necessity, by the fostering hand which from without had so long sheltered it; weak in the sunken spirits of its own children; yet even in that hour of darkness and depression, preparing to arise in a perfectness of discipline and strength which it never had known, and never could know, whilst, instead of being planted as a substantive communion, it was treated as a distant, incomplete, and feeble branch of one settled in another land. It had within itself the principle of life; and now that it was cast out into the field of the world, although suddenly and rudely, it began to strike its roots, and put forth its tender buds.

Yet dangers of the most various character threatened its existence. A twofold object was before those who watched over it; to provide, through the possession of the Episcopal succession, for the independent existence of the Church, and to gather up into a national communion the scattered congregations of the old "Church of England in America." It was no easy matter to secure either of these objects, and peculiar difficulties opposed their combination. There always have been, and, from the constitution of the human mind, there always must be, in the Church two extremes of opinion, towards which, on the one side or the other, its members will incline. On the one side are ranged those who are disposed to set a high value on external observances and forms; on the other, those to whom the inner spirit seems so exclusively important that they are inclined to undervalue and despise all outward organs through which only it can act. Between those who belong to these extremes, mutual suspicions must from time to time spring up, which too often harden into obstinate separation. Of this there was now the greatest danger in America. In the eastern states the distinctive features of Church discipline and order were passionately valued; whilst in the south the great majority were not unwilling to give them up entirely; separation between the two parties seemed inevitable, and the very existence of episcopacy was in peril with the last.

But at this dangerous time God had richly endued one of His servants with those gifts of judgment and temper which were needful for the crisis; and hence the name of William White will ever be recorded by the grateful remembrance of the Western Church. The revolutionary war found him assistant minister of Christ Church and St. Peter's, Philadelphia. Mild in manners, meek in spirit, and large in toleration of the views of others, he was yet firm and decided in his own. Early in the war, he joined, from conviction, the side of the colonists, and, at its darkest moment, publicly committed himself to it, by undertaking the chaplainship of congress. The progress of the war left him the sole minister of Christ Church and St. Peter's, and the election of the vestry made him their rector. When the cause of colonial independence triumphed, his presence in a great measure turned aside the angry jealousies with which the young republic looked on the connexion to which he belonged. His consistent conduct was well known; and Washington was one of those who worshipped at his church. Men would hear from him what they would not from another. Nor was he slow to employ this advantage the general good. His views were early turned to gathering the various flocks which were scattered through the states into one visible communion. Early in August 1782, despairing of the speedy recognition of American independence, and " perceiving their ministry gradually approaching to annihilation,"* while England was as unwilling to give, as America to receive the episcopate from her, he proposed a scheme for uniting the different parishes in convention, and on behalf of their whole body, committing to its president and others the powers of ordination and discipline. This proposal sprung from no conscious undervaluing of episcopacy, but from a belief " that in an exigency in which a duly authorised ministry could not be obtained, the paramount duty of preaching the Gospel, and the worshipping of God on the terms of the Christian covenant, should go on in the best manner which circumstances permit."† Should more favorable prospects dawn upon them, and the succession be obtained, he proposed, by a provisional ordination, to supply any deficiencies of ministerial character in those who had been thus ordained. Happily no such scheme took effect, since it would, in all probability, have laid the foundation of widespread and endless separation. In the very month in which Mr. White's pamphlet was published, the hearts of all were gladdened by clear symptoms of approaching peace between the mother country and her now independent colonies. This was no sooner established than Mr. White abandoned his scheme, and, daring to look on to greater things, set himself to gather into one the various limbs of

* Letter to Bp. Hobart, quoted in Life of Bp. White, p. 80.
† Note of Bp. White's to his Letter to Bp. Hobart, Dec. 1830.

the episcopal communion, that they might apply in concert to the mother country for the consecration of their bishops. He began with his own state of Pennsylvania, calling together first his own vestries, and then (on the 31st of March, 1784) the other clergy of the state who happened to be present in the town, to deliberate upon the measures rendered necessary by the present posture of the episcopal communion. They agreed to send a circular to all the episcopalian congregations in Pennsylvania, inviting them to delegate one or more of their vestry to meet the clergy of the state in a general consultation on the 24th of May. On the day appointed they assembled, and agreed to certain fundamental principles as a basis for after action as a body. These were :—

1. That the episcopal Church is, and ought to be, independent of all foreign authority, ecclesiastical or civil.

2. That it hath, and ought to have, in common with other religious societies, full and exclusive powers to regulate the concerns of its own communion.

3. That the doctrines of the Gospel be maintained, as now professed by the Church of England, and uniformity of worship continued, as near as may be, to the liturgy of the same Church.

4. That the succession of the ministry be agreeable to the usage which requireth the three orders of bishops, priests, and deacons; that the rights and powers of the same respectively be ascertained, and that they be exercised according to reasonable laws to be duly made.

5. That to make canons or laws, there be no other authority than that of a representative body of the clergy and laity conjointly.

6. That no powers be delegated to a general ecclesiastical government, except such as cannot conveniently be exercised by the clergy and laity in their respective congregations.

Resolutions to a somewhat similar effect were passed in Maryland, in June 1784, and at Boston, in Massachusetts, in September of the same year. By agreement upon these common principles, a basis for internal unity of action was formed within the separate provinces; but there was still wanting some common bond which should hold together the episcopal communion in the several independent governments which together form the confederation of the United States. This was Mr. White's great object, and his character and conduct were most effectual in securing it. His early efforts were especially addressed to the members of the southern states, and amongst them his reputation for moderate views gave great weight to his advice. He had at first to deal with most discordant materials. One state (South Carolina) clogged a tardy consent to apply for the episcopate with the condition that no bishop should be planted in her borders; and something of this jealousy was widely spread. But there was in him nothing to inflame it, and he was thus able to win over to better views those who were ready to oppose themselves. In the month of May 1784, a few clergymen of New-York, New Jersey, and Pennsylvania, met at Brunswick in New Jersey, to renew a charitable society which had been chartered, before the revolution, for the relief of the widows and orphans of the clergy. At this meeting the present state and prospects of their Church, and the best means of uniting its scattered parts, came naturally under their discussion. To obtain this end, it was determined to procure another and more numerous gathering at New-York, by which some common principles might be defined. In October 1784, the projected council met, eight of the different states furnishing some voluntary delegates. These agreed on seven leading principles of union, which they recommended to the several states, and which, with little alteration, have formed ever since the basis of their combination. Of these the chief resolutions were the following:—

1. That there should be a general convention of the Episcopal Church in the United States of America.

2. That the Episcopal Church in each state should send deputies to the convention, consisting of clergy and laity.

3. That the said Church shall maintain the doctrines of the Gospel as now held by the Church of England, and adhere to the liturgy of the said Church as far as shall be consistent with the American revolution and the constitutions of the several states.

4. That in every state where there shall be a bishop duly consecrated and settled, he shall be considered as a member of the convention *ex officio.*

5. That the clergy and laity assembled in convention shall deliberate in one body, but shall vote separately; and the concurrence of both shall be necessary to give validity to every measure.

6. That the first meeting of the convention shall be at Philadelphia, the Tuesday before the feast of St. Michael next.

Such were the first efforts made within this Church for visible and outward unity. That they should be made at all bespoke the living energy which was dormant even in their most imperfect body: that they should have been required is a heavy charge against the mother Church. Never had so strange a sight been seen before in Christendom, as this necessity of various members knitting themselves together into one, by such a conscious and voluntary act. In all other cases the unity of the common Episcopate had held such limbs together; every member, that is, of the Church, had visibly belonged to the community of which the presiding bishop was the head. That bishop was himself one member of an equal and common brotherhood, all of whom, with the same creed and in the same succession, were partners in one common power which each one separately administered; and so each member of the Church under them belonged already to one great corporation, needing to make no voluntary alliance between its several parts, because it was already one; and they that were grafted into it were thereby grafted into unity with their fellows. But this common bond we had left wanting in our colonies; and it was the want of this which had thus dismembered their communion. As soon, therefore, as the political connexion of the state with England was dissolved, some measures, for which no precedent existed, were forced upon them; nor would it have been easy to devise a wiser course than that which they adopted, in their present want of bishops, who have ever been the organs of communication between different portions of the Church.

A delegate from Connecticut had attended the convention which framed these recommendations, but he took no part in the deliberations; for Connecticut had early moved in a somewhat different manner. Amongst the eastern clergy, as we have seen, was the most earnest piety, wedded to the strongest and most clearly ascertained Church principles. In their new circumstances, they esteemed it their first duty to perfect their system by securing the presence and rule of a bishop. In this they were confirmed by the avowed temper of the south, from which they greatly feared the adoption of a spurious and nominal Episcopacy. They began, therefore, at once to act for themselves, and refused to take any share in organizing their scattered communion until they had a bishop at their head. As soon as the peace made it possible,* the clergy met in voluntary convention; and before the British troops had evacuated New-York, Dr. Samuel Seabury, formerly a missionary of the Gospel-Propagation Society in Staten Island, and now elected bishop by the clergy of Connecticut, had sailed for England to obtain consecration there. Besides the certificate of his election, Dr. Seabury bore with him testimonial, from the leading clergy of New-York,† and letters earnestly requesting of the English bishops the boon which America had so long sought in vain.

Dr. Seabury reached England at a time when the mutual relations between this country and her late colonies were new and uncertain, and when the government at home were full of care lest any apparent interference on their part should stir up the jealousy of new-born independence. Hence, when Dr. Seabury made his application to the Archbishop of York, (the see of Canterbury being vacant,) he found at once great difficulties in his way. Without a special act of parliament, the archbishop could not consecrate a citizen of America; for no subject

---

* March 1783.

† He had been treated with great severity by the insurgents during the revolutionary war; and though hunted from place to place, and more than once imprisoned, had maintained his ministry till the last moment.

of a foreign state could take the oath of allegiance, to dispense with which the archbishop had no power; and for such an act ministers would not apply, until they were assured that the step would not offend America. Delay and uncertainty became thus unavoidable; whilst the motives which had led to the attempt pressed strongly on Dr. Seabury. Under these circumstances, he looked anxiously around, to see if he could properly obtain from any other quarter the Episcopal succession. The Church in Scotland at once attracted his attention. There the true succession, derived of old time from ours, was carefully preserved; whilst the bishops, unlike those in England, were fettered by no connexion with the state. The Presbyterian kirk had been long established in Scotland, and the Episcopalians were barely tolerated there. They consequently would be able, without any application to the state, so to vary, if need were, the form of consecration, as to make it suit a citizen of the American republic.

Other circumstances had been preparing the way for this application. In the autumn of 1782, before the recognition of the independence of the North American colonies, the attention of the Scottish bishops had been specially called to the state of the Church there. In October of that year, Dr. George Berkeley, eldest son of the great Bishop Berkeley, the heir of his father's virtues, and of his interest in the welfare of America, writing to the Rev. Mr. (afterwards Bishop) Skinner, expressed his hope, " that a most important good might ere long be derived to the suffering and nearly neglected sons of Protestant Episcopacy on the other side of the Atlantic, from the suffering Church of Scotland." "American rebellion," he continues, " has widened her religious, or rather irreligious, bottom so extensively, as to require, from those who bear office under her baleful shade, a simple declaration 'that they believe in the existence of the Supreme Being.' I would humbly submit it to the bishops of the Church *in* Scotland (as we style her in Oxford), whether this be not a time peculiarly favorable to the introduction of the Protestant Episcopate on the footing of universal toleration, and before any anti-Episcopal establishment shall have taken place. God direct the hearts of your prelates in this matter."*

Such a suggestion as this, from such a quarter, attracted immediate attention. Dr. George Berkeley was a man of the highest station in the English Church. He had been the intimate friend of the late Archbishop Seeker, was himself a prebendary of Canterbury, and had two years before refused the bishopric of Killala. The episcopalians of Scotland had been little accustomed to any great respect in England, and were therefore the more attracted by such an overture. Many difficulties, however, met them on the threshold, but none to which Dr. Berkeley would yield. "As to American *Protestant* episcopacy (for *popish* prelacy hath found its way into the transatlantic world), one sees not any thing complicated or difficult in the *mere planting* it. A bishop consecrated by the English or Irish Church would find considerably stronger prejudices against him in the revolted colonies, than would one who had been called to the highest order by a bishop or bishops of the Scotch Church; our bishops, and those of Ireland, having been nominated by a sovereign against whom the colonists have rebelled, and whom you have never recognised. The Americans would, even many of the episcopalians among them, entertain political jealousies concerning a bishop by any means connected with *us;* they would be apt to think of him as of a foe to their wild projects of independency, &c.

"I am as far removed from Erastianism and from democracy as any man ever was; I do heartily abominate both of those anti-scriptural systems. Had my honored father's scheme for planting an episcopal college, whereof he was to have been president, in the Summer Islands, not been sacrificed by the worst minister that Britain ever saw, probably under a mild monarch, (who loves the Church of England as much as I believe his grandfather hated it), episcopacy would have been established in America by succession from the English Church, unattended by any invidious temporal rank or power. But the dis-

---

* MS. Seabury papers. The italics are those of the original letter.

senting miscellaneous interest in England has watched, with too successful a jealousy, over the honest intentions of our best bishops. . . .

" From the Churches of England and Ireland America will not now receive the episcopate ; if she might, I am persuaded that many of her sons would joyfully receive bishops from Scotland. The question, then, shortly is, Can any proper persons be found who, with the spirit of confessors, would convey the great blessing of the Protestant episcopate from the persecuted Church of Scotland to the struggling persecuted Protestant episcopalian worshippers in America ? If so, is it not the duty of all and every bishop of the Church in Scotland to contribute towards the sending into the new world Protestant bishops, before general assemblies can be held and covenants taken, for their perpetual exclusion ? *Liberavi animam meam.*

" Deeply convinced as I am of the necessity of episcopacy towards the constitution of a Christian Church, I hope that no consideration would (I know that no consideration ought to) restrain me in this matter, if I was a bishop. A Scotch bishop consecrating one or more good men, of sound ecclesiastical principles, might now sow a seed which, in smallness resembling that of mustard, might also resemble it in subsequent magnificence and amplitude of production. I humbly conceive that a bishop at Philadelphia, who had never sworn to king George, would be very well placed. The Quakers are a tolerating people. I have written to you *currente calamo.*

" If, as I suspect, persecution shall have tended to damp the spirits of our right reverend fathers in Scotland, *I*, (who never knew experimentally what persecution meant,) must not presume to censure. Zeal without knowledge—(without knowledge of one's own heart)—is a dreadful enemy of true religion."*

In answer to these earnest representations, Bishop Skinner (for he had just been raised to the episcopate) laid before his friend the great difficulties which opposed themselves to such a course.

* MS. Seabury papers.

"Nothing," he suggests, "can be done in the affair with safety on our side, till the independence of America be fully and irrevocably recognised by the government of Britain; and even then the enemies of our Church might make a handle of our correspondence with the colonies, as a proof that we always wished to fish in troubled waters—and we have little need to give any ground for an imputation of that kind." He urges, further, the difficulty of finding a proper person, and the uncertainty of his reception in America. To all this Dr. Berkeley answers, on the 24th of March:—

"I beg leave to observe, with all becoming deference, that I cannot consider the immediate and unsolicited introduction of episcopacy into America in the same light wherein it is viewed by yourself and your venerable brethren, the bishops of the Scotch Church.

"From the papists one learns that no time is to be lost, and that substances are to be preferred to shadows—*things** essential, to the *paraphernalia* of a Church. If I ever wrote a sentence under the influence of an humble spirit, I write so at this moment, when I do yet adventure to differ from *my fathers in Christ*. A *consecration* in Scotland might be very secret; it could not be so elsewhere. A *consecration* from a persecuted, depressed Church, which is barely tolerated, would not alarm the prejudices of opponents. I need not say to Bishop Skinner or his brethren, that an episcopal Church may exist without any *legal* encouragement or establishment, and without the definition of country into *regular* and *bounded* dioceses. *Provincial assemblies* will never invite a prelate; provincial assemblies, if they establish anything, will establish some *human device;* but *provincial assemblies* will not, now or soon, think of excluding a Protestant bishop, who sues only for toleration. Popish prelates are now in North America exercising their functions over a willing people, without any aid or enconragement from provincial assemblies. In a *short time*, we must expect all Protestant episcopalian principles to be totally lost in America. They

---

* The italics throughout are preserved from the original letter.

are not so now; and yet episcopacy must be sent before it be asked: these are lukewarm days. Christianity waited not at the first, the Church of Rome waits not *now*, for any invitation or encouragement. Bishop Geddes told me that the pope allows him 25*l.* per annum, and that he has no other settled support; the other popish bishops in Scotland have 5*l.* each per annum from the Bishop of Rome. *Out* of Scotland there is but little known concerning the episcopal Church there; and, generally it is conceived to be a society *purely political*. I believe a secret subscription could be raised, adequate to the purposes of supporting one pious, sensible, discreet bishop, at least for a season after his arrival in Virginia; and I think I know *one* person competent and willing for the great work."*

Thus matters stood when Dr. Seabury reached England; and finding the difficulties which beset his application to the English bishops for the present insurmountable, began to turn his eyes to Scotland. In Nov. 1783, a letter was despatched by Mr. Elphinston, a man of literary reputation, the son of a Scotch clergyman, in which the following question was put to the primus or presiding bishop of the Church in Scotland: "Can consecration be obtained in Scotland for an already dignified and well-vouched American clergyman, now at London, for the purpose of perpetuating the episcopal reformed Church in America, particularly in Connecticut?"†

At the same time, Dr. Berkeley thus re-opened his correspondence with Bishop Skinner:—" I have this day heard, I need not add with the sincerest pleasure, that a respectable presbyter, well recommended from America, has arrived in London, seeking what, it seems, in the present state of affairs, he cannot expect to receive in our Church.

" Surely, dear sir, the Scotch prelates, who are not shackled by any *Erastian connexion*, will not send this suppliant empty away.

" I scruple not to give it as my decided opinion, that the king, *some* of his cabinet counsellors, all our bishops (except, peradventure, the Bishop of St. Asaph), and all

---

MS. Seabury papers.   † Ib.

the learned and respectable clergy in our Church, will at least secretly rejoice, if a Protestant bishop be sent from Scotland to America; but more especially if Connecticut be the scene of his ministry. It would be waste of words to say anything by the way of stirring up Bishop Skinner's zeal."*

The Scotch bishops, in reply, required information as to the personal merits of the candidate for the episcopate, as well as on the hindrances with which he had met in England. On both points Dr. Berkeley answered them, urging strongly that they need anticipate no opposition from the English government to their granting "a consecration, which can contradict no law, for a foreign and an independent state. My reading," he continues, "does not enable me to comprehend how, without an episcopacy, the gospel, together with all its divine institutions, can possibly be propagated. In the present state of matters, I do not see how the English primate can, without royal license at least, if not parliamentary likewise, proceed to consecrate any bishop, except for those districts which erst were allowed to give titles to assistant bishops. In this state of things, I think the glory of communicating a Protestant episcopacy to the united independent states of America seems reserved for the Scotch bishops. Whatever is done herein ought assuredly to be done very quickly, else the never-ceasing endeavors of the English dissenters, whose intolerance has kept back the blessing of prelacy from the Protestant prelatists of America, will stir up too probably a violent spirit in Connecticut against the bishop *in fieri*. If the Church of England was to send a bishop into any one of the United States of America, the congress might, and probably would, exclaim, that England had violated the peace, and still claimed a degree of supremacy over the subjects of that independent state. The episcopal Church of Scotland cannot be suspected of aiming at supremacy of any kind, or over any people. I do therefore earnestly hope, that, very shortly, she may send a prelate to the aid of transatlantic aspirants for the primitive ordinance of confirmation."†

* MS. Seabury papers. † Ibid.

The Scotch bishops now expressed, in answer, "their warmest approbation of the new proposal." Their primus (Bishop Kilgour) expressed his "hearty concurrence in the proposal for introducing Protestant episcopacy into America. All things," he continues, "bid fair for the candidate. I hope, indeed, that the motion is from, and the plan laid under, the direction of the Holy Spirit. But as it is a matter of the greatest importance, it is necessary we go about our part in it with the utmost circumspection." "The very prospect," writes another bishop, "rejoices me greatly; and considering the great depositum committed to us, I do not see how we can account to our great Lord and Master, if we neglect such an opportunity of promoting His truth, and enlarging the borders of His Church."*

At length, upon the 31st of August, 1784, Dr. Seabury made a distinct application to the Scottish bishops. "I thought it my duty," he says, referring to his application for English consecration, "to pursue the plan marked out for me by the clergy of Connecticut, as long as there was a probable chance of succeeding. That probability is now at an end; and I think myself at liberty to pursue such other schemes as shall ensure to them a valid episcopacy. Such I take the Scotch episcopacy to be, in every sense of the word; and such, I know, the clergy of Connecticut consider it, and always have done so. But the connexion that has always subsisted between them and the Church of England, and the generous support they have hitherto received from that Church, naturally led them, though now no longer a part of the British dominions, to apply to that Church in the first instance for relief in their spiritual necessity. Unhappily the ministry have refused to permit a bishop to be consecrated without the formal request, or at least consent, of congress, which there is no chance of obtaining, and which the clergy of Connecticut would not apply for, were the chance ever so good. They are content with having the episcopal Church in Connecticut put upon the same footing with every other religious denomination. A

* MS. Seabury papers.

copy of a law of the state of Connecticut, which enables the episcopal congregations to transact their ecclesiastical affairs upon their own principles, to tax their members for the maintenance of their clergy, for the support of their worship, for the building and repairing of churches, and which exempts them from all penalties and from all other taxes on a religious account, I have in my possession. The legislature of Connecticut know that a bishop is applied for; they know the person in whose favor the application is made; and they give no opposition to either. Indeed, were they disposed to object, they have more prudence than to attempt to obstruct it. They know that there are in that state more than seventy episcopal congregations; many of them large; some of them making a majority of the inhabitants of large towns, and, with those that are scattered through the state, composing a body of near or quite 40,000—a body too large to be needlessly affronted in an elective government.

" On this ground it is that I apply to the good bishops in Scotland; and I hope I shall not apply in vain. If they consent to impart the episcopal succession to the Church of Connecticut, they will, I think, do a good work, and the blessing of thousands will attend them. And perhaps for this cause, among others, God's providence has supported them, and contiued their succession, under various and great difficulties, that a free, valid, and purely ecclesiastical episcopacy may, from them, pass into the western world. As to any thing which I receive here, it has no influence on me, and never has had any. I indeed think it my duty to conduct the matter in such a manner as shall risk the salaries which the missionaries in Connecticut receive from the society here as little as possible; and I persuade myself it may be done, so as to make that risk next to nothing. With respect to my own salary, if the society choose to withdraw it, I am ready to part with it.

" It is a matter of some consequence to me that this affair be determined as soon as possible. I am anxious to return to America this autumn; and the winter is fast approaching, when the voyage will be attended with double inconvenience and danger, and the expense of continuing here another winter is greater than will suit my purse. I know you will give me the earliest intelligence in your power; and I shall patiently wait till I hear from you. My most respectful regards attend the right reverend gentlemen under whose consideration this business will come; and as there are none but the most open and candid intentions on my part, so I doubt not of the most candid and fair construction of my conduct on their part."*

One more hindrance was interposed to the fulfilment of these wishes. When the Scotch bishops had resolved to consecrate, an earnest appeal was sent to them from an American clergyman, whose own views, as it afterwards appeared, would be in some measure thwarted by the consecration of Dr. Seabury; but who now assured them that he desired " to divert a heavy stroke from episcopacy, which was likely to suffer through this consecration," which, he asserted, was " against the earnest and sound advice of the Archbishops of Canterbury and York, to whom Dr. Seabury's design was communicated, they not thinking him a fit person, especially as he was actively and deeply engaged against congress; that he would by this forward step render episcopacy suspected there, the people not having had time, after a total derangement of their civil affairs, to consider as yet of ecclesiastical; and if it were unexpectedly and rashly introduced among them at the instigation of a few clergy only that remain, without their being consulted, would occasion it to be entirely slighted, unless with the approbation of the state they belong to; which is what they are laboring after just now, having called several provincial meetings together this autumn, to settle some preliminary articles of a Protestant episcopal Church, as near as may be to that of England or Scotland. . . . . See," he concludes, " if you value your own peace and advantage as a Christian society, that your bishops meddle not in this consecration," &c.†

When this letter reached Scotland, Dr. Seabury was there. His sincerity and zeal convinced Bishop Skinner of his great fitness for the post to which he was designed.

---

* MS. Seabury papers. † Ibid.

The concurrence of the clergy of Connecticut was easily established; and Dr. Berkeley having ascertained that the English primate, though he could not give to it a formal sanction, was yet by no means hostile to the step,* all difficulties were removed, and he was solemnly admitted into the episcopate at Aberdeen on the 14th day of November, 1784, by three bishops of the Scottish Church (the whole college then consisting but of four)—namely, Bishops Kilgour, Petre, and Skinner, of Aberdeen, Ross, and Moray. After his consecration, which was in the Scottish form, the new bishop signed, on behalf of his brethren in America, certain articles which might serve as a basis for permanent and friendly intercourse between the sister Churches. Shortly after, he returned to London, whence on the first of March he was about to sail for America in the ship Triumph, " the master of which was his partienlar acquaintance ; a friendly obliging man and a good Churchman, and very anxious to have the honor of carrying over the Bishop of all America."

By the "latter end of June" Bishop Seabury was again in Connecticut. His "reception from the inhabitants" was "friendly," and he "met with no disrespect."† The Presbyterian ministers appeared to be rather alarmed ; and, in consequence of his arrival, assumed and gave to one another the style and title of bishops, which formerly they reprobated as a remnant of popery. On the 3rd of August he met his clergy, and "joyful indeed was the meeting." The letter from the good bishops and the concordat were laid before them, " and cordially received." Only as to one article, which engaged them to receive the Scotch form for the admistration of the Holy Eucharist, it was thought best to wait for a season until by preaching

* Dr. Berkeley wrote to the Archbishop of Canterbury, that application had been made by Dr. Seabury to the Scottish bishops for consecration, and begged that, if his Grace thought the bishops here ran any risk in complying with Seabury's request, he would be so good as to give Dr. Berkeley notice immediately; but if his Grace was satisfied that there was no danger, there was no occasion to give any answer. No answer came." A MS. note of Bp. Skinner's on Dr. Seabury's letter of application.

† MS Letter of Bp. Seabury to Bp. Skinner.

and conversation the minds of the communicants were prepared for receiving the Scots office. They feared, too, to encourage by their example a disposition to effect changes in the Liturgy, which had showed itself in the south. Such was Bishop Seabury's entrance upon the duties of his office.

He arrived at a critical time for the American Church. The first general convention was soon to meet at Philadelphia; and the knowledge that a bishop already presided over one of their Churches, greatly strengthened the hands of those who desired at once to apply for the episcopate.

The first American convention met according to appointment, in October 1785, at Philadelphia; seven out of the thirteen states sent to it deputies both clerical and lay, and they entered at once on their important duties. Three leading subjects claimed their chief attention. The first of these was the general ecclesiastical constitution of the meditated union; the second, the formation of a common liturgy; the third, the steps to be taken for obtaining an American episcopate.

Upon the two first questions warm discussion arose. The various tempers of the eastern and the southern states were soon displayed. Thus, on the general terms of union, the two parties disagreed; one proposing to declare the bishop *ex-officio* president of the convention; the others fearful of the bishop's power, and so denying him this right. The grounds too of this difference lay deep. The southern states would have restrained the bishop from all rule; made him subject to his own convention; and distinguished him from other presbyters only by his possession of the powers of ordaining and confirming. The eastern states, with a more instructed faith, truly acknowledged the bishop as possessing, by the appointment of Christ, the charge of spiritual government. Their tendency, indeed, lay strongly to the opposite extreme. They would not only have given to the bishop spiritual rule, but would have deprived the laity of that power of co-ordinate deliberation and assent, which appear to have been in the earliest times their Christian birthright. The plans of the eastern Churchmen would have excluded from conventions all lay deputies, and confined deliberation on things ecclesiastical to those in holy orders.

The like difference was shown in the revision of the Book of Common Prayer. While one of the Virginian deputies proposed to omit the four first petitions of the Litany, in order to get rid of the direct acknowledgment of the Trinity in the adorable Godhead; and whilst in Virginia generally the rule most objected to in all the Prayer-book was that which allowed the minister to repel from the Eucharist notorious evil-livers: the wishes of the eastern states would have restored to the Communion-service some of those early devotions which the peculiar aspect of their times had led the Anglican reformers most wisely to omit.

Such differences boded ill for the result of the convention; but the meek wisdom of its president brought it to a safe and harmonious conclusion. Doubtful things were left for discussion when their body should be fully organised. Whether the bishop should preside or not, remained for the present undetermined; but the point was at once conceded in practice, and afterwards adopted willingly as law. A proposed Book of Common Prayer, varying as little from the English ritual as the temper of the council would allow, was suggested to the various state conventions; and the time thus gained saved the Church from the direct proposal of many alterations, which, if they had been all at once resisted stiffly, would have been as hotly urged upon the other side.

On the measures to be taken for obtaining the episcopate the convention happily agreed. Bishop Seabury had declined, with his clergy, attending its session, from a fear that it would carry measures to which his principles would not allow him to assent. The southern states were known to hold loose opinions upon church matters, and expected evils were greatly exaggerated. "I have thought it my duty," writes a clerical correspondent of Bishop Skinner, in 1786, "to advise you and the college of bishops of the ancient Church of Scotland, of the tendency of the bill just brought into the House of Lords by the Archbishop of Canterbury, to enable the English bishops to consecrate for foreign countries, viz. the overthrow of Bishop Seabury of Connectient. Dr. Smith, Dr. White, and Dr. Provoost, three Socinians, have been recommended to the Archbishop of Canterbury, for consecration; the first to be Bishop of Maryland, the second of Pennsylvania, the third of New-York, who are to be answerable to a consistory, composed of presbyters and lay delegates," All this was gross exaggeration; but Bishop Seabury had ground for apprehension. The doctrinal tenets of one of the two first elected bishops were probably not wholly orthodox; and Dr. Smith, who was generally named for the episcopate, was an ambitious and dangerous man, with low views of the Church, and great self-confidence. Accordingly the bishop thought it safer to remain away from the convention, writing an apology* for not appearing, and explaining plainly and fully his sentiments concerning their general mode of procedure, and especially their degradation of the episcopal dignity. But though he was not present, his experience helped to guide their decision. It was at once resolved, that the succession should be obtained, if possible, at the hands of the English rather than the Scottish bishops.† To this end an address of convention to the English bench was drawn up and signed, and a sub-committee named to communicate with the archbishop; while, to remove all political objections, the deputies applied to the executive within the various states for a certified assent to the request now urged.

These points being settled, and a general ecclesiastical

* MS. Letter of Bp. Seabury to Bp. Skinner.

† My attention has been called, by a paper in the *Christian Observer*, August 1845, to a letter from Granville Sharpe, Esq., in 1786, in which he states that this decision was the result of his advice to the convention. That great and good man had long been zealous in the great cause of American episcopacy, and had labored diligently with the archbishop on the one side, and his American friends on the other, to obtain the succession for the West. His biographer, however (Prince Hoare, Esq.), overstates, I think, his actual services in saying of them, " Few, if any, examples can be found of more momentous or more successful exertions in the service of the Church. By the active intelligence of a single person, the mutual prejudices and doubts of the two countries were removed, and the functions of the episcopal order duly established in America." *Life of Granville Sharpe*, part ii. c. vii. p. 231.

constitution ratified, which provided for a triennial convention, to consist, besides the bishops, of deputies, not more than four, clerical and lay, from the Church in every state, who should vote state by state, each order possessing a negative upon the other, the clergy of each state being subject only to its own ecclesiastical authorities,—the council adjourned until the following June, when it hoped to receive the answer of the English bishops.

The address of the convention, with certificates from the executives of Maryland, Virginia, Pennsylvania, and New-York, was forwarded to the Archbishop of Canterbury, through the American minister. The part taken by Mr. Adams is highly to his credit. Not himself an episcopalian, and so well aware of all the prejudices which his conduct might excite, that he deemed it "bold, daring, and hazardous to himself and his,"* he made, without hesitation, the required address to the archbishop. Here, again, the consecration of Dr. Seabury had greatly prepared the way. He had been well received in America, and it was plain that if the mother Church continued to refuse the boon, she would effectually alienate her western daughter. The archbishop's answer was received by the committee in the following spring. It expressed, on his part and on that of all the English bishops, an anxious readiness to grant the episcopal succession to America, but delayed giving a specific pledge until they had seen the intended alterations in the liturgy and the proposed ecclesiastical constitution. "While we are anxious," they concluded, "to give every proof not only of our brotherly affection, but of our facility in forwarding your wishes, we cannot but be extremely cautious lest we should be the instruments of establishing an ecclesiastical system which will be called a branch of the Church of England, but afterwards may possibly appear to have departed from it essentially either in doctrine or in discipline."

Another letter soon followed, written after the receipt of the amended liturgy, and pointing out some changes in it with which the English bishops were dissatisfied.

* Letter to Bp. White, Oct. 27, 1814.

Amongst these were some unnecessary verbal alterations, and the disuse of the Athanasian Creed. But that to which they mainly objected was the omission of the Nicene Creed, and one clause in the Apostles' ("He descended into hell"). With one provision also of the constitution they found fault, from its seeming to subject bishops to trial by the laity and the inferior clergy; and they suggested hints as to the care that should be taken in the choice of those who were to be elected bishops, reminding the convention that the credit of the English Church would be at stake in the prosperity of this her daughter branch. On these points, therefore, they expressed their earnest hope that the ensuing convention would give them satisfaction, in which expectation they would at once prepare a bill, by which the necessary powers would be imparted to them. Before this letter reached America, the convention had assembled and revised the constitution in the very point to which the bishops had objected, but the alterations in the liturgy remained untouched. Great fault had been found with them by all the more consistent Churchmen of America. "I learn from others," writes Bishop Seabury to his friends the Scottish bishops, "that at this convention they have discarded the use, at least left it discretional, of the Athanasian and Nicene Creeds, and the observation of saints'-days; omitted the article of the descent into hell, in the Apostles' Creed; reduced the Thirty-nine articles to twenty; made such alterations in the liturgy and offices as makes a new Prayer-book necessary."

On receiving the remonstrance from the English bishops, it was resolved, by the committee charged with the negotiation, that these points should again be taken into full consideration; and for this purpose the convention was called together in October. There was a general wish to satisfy the English prelates, of which the friends of peace made careful use. They might, indeed, receive the true succession from the Scottish bishops, and by the Danes it had been already offered; but the whole body earnestly desired to receive it from the Church which had originally sent them forth. In this spirit they entered on the question, and, after full debate, resolved to restore to its place the clause they had omitted in the Apostles' Creed, and to replace in their liturgy that of Nicæa. On some minor points, and as to the liturgical employment of the Athanasian Creed, they still affirmed their former sentence.

With these concessions they doubted not the English prelates would be satisfied, and they proceeded therefore to sign the testimonials of three presbyters, the Rev. William White, the Rev. Samuel Provoost, and the Rev. David Griffith, who had been elected to the office of a bishop by the conventions of Pennsylvania, New-York, and Virginia. Early in the following month, Dr. White and Dr. Provoost sailed for England. A painful cause is given for Dr. Griffith's absence from their company. He was too poor to bear the necessary cost of such a journey, and the Virginian Church had not raised funds to forward him upon his way. On Wednesday the 29th of November, the bishops elect arrived in London, and on the following Monday they were presented by Mr. Adams, the American ambassador, to the Archbishop at Lambeth. Several interviews succeeded. The conclusions of the convention, and the testimonials of the bishops, satisfied the English prelates; and after a gratifying audience of the king, on Sunday, the 4th of February, 1787, in the Archiepiscopal Chapel of Lambeth, these two presbyters of the Church of America were consecrated bishops by the two archbishops and the bishops of Bath and Wells and Peterborough. Thus, at last, did England grant to the daughter Church this great and necessary boon.

For almost two whole centuries had she, by evil counsels, been persuaded to withhold it, until, as it would seem, the fierce struggle of the war of independence, and the loss of these great colonies, chastised her long neglect, and by a new and utterly unlooked-for issue, led her to discharge this claim of right. Awful, doubtless, was the hour to these two when the holy office was conferred upon them; when, at the hands of him, whom Bishop White, full of affectionate respect for his mother Church, calls this "great and good archbishop," they were set apart to bear into the western wilderness the likeness and the office of the first apostles. Solemn must have been their landing on the 7th of April, the afternoon of Easter Sunday (1787), upon the shores of their own land, as the especial witnesses of that resurrection of which "the holy Church throughout all the world" was on that day keeping glad remembrance,—the especial stewards of those mysteries which she was on that day dispensing unto all her faithful children.

CHAPTER VII.

Convention assembles—Case of Dr. Bass—Bishop Seabury joins the Convention—The Liturgy—First and succeeding consecrations—Period of depression—Its causes—Ecclesiastical constitution—Parish—Diocese—Convention—Laity in convention—Anglo-Saxon usage—Difficulties of true organization in America—Neglect of the mother country.

THE Church assembled in convention after the arrival of the bishops at Philadelphia, July 28, 1787. For the first time it was gathered together in the full likeness of that council to which "the apostles and elders came together at Jerusalem."* For now, as then, it met with bishops at its head, with presbyters and deacons, each in their own order, ministering under them, and with the laity, "the multitude of the faithful," taking solemn counsel for the welfare of their Zion.

There was great need in that synod of meekness and heavenly wisdom. The minds of men were still angry and unsettled. They knew little of the principles on which they were to act; and points of the utmost delicacy and moment were sure to come under consideration. On the third day of their meeting, after some preliminary business, an application from the clergy of Massachusetts and New Hampshire gave rise to much discussion. The "act" of these states, after setting forth their "gratitude to God for having lately blessed the Protestant Episcopal Church in the United States of America with a complete and entire ministry," proceeded to declare that to secure for their people "the benefit and advantage of those offices, the administration of which belongs to the highest order of the ministry, and to encourage and promote a union of the whole Episcopal Church in their states, and to perfect and

* Acts iv. 6.

compact this mystical body of Christ, we do hereby nominate, elect, and appoint the Rev. Edward Bass, a presbyter of the Church, to be our bishop : and we do promise and engage to receive him as such, and to render to him all canonical obedience and submission, when canonically consecrated and invested with the apostolic office and powers. And we now address the right reverend the bishops in the states of Connecticut, New-York, and Pennsylvania, praying their united assistance in consecrating our said brother, and canonically investing him with the apostolic office and powers."

This address brought at once before the convention the relation of Bishop Seabury to its own body, and to the two bishops of the English line. Happily Bishop Provoost was not at Philadelphia, and it was therefore left to the moderate and healing spirit of his brother bishop to frame an answer to the clergy of the east. The convention first solemnly recorded its conviction of the rightful consecration of the Bishop of Connecticut; and afterwards resolved that a "complete order of bishops, derived as well under the English as the Scottish line of Episcopacy, now subsisted within the United States; and that they were fully competent to every proper act and duty of a bishop's office." It further proceeded to express its wish that these three bishops (the number always held canonically necessary for a rightful consecration) should proceed to consecrate the elected bishop of the eastern clergy, so soon as the New-England Churches should have agreed in convention to articles of disciple and union with the general body.

To allow time for this union, the convention, after a session of ten days, agreed to a two-months' adjournment, having first determined that as soon as the united Church possessed three bishops, the members of that order should constitute a separate house from that of the clerical and lay deputies.

On the 29th of September 1787, the adjourned session opened; and, to the joy of all, the attendance of Bishop Seabury and two of his New-England clergy was announced. Their presence was indeed important; for it not only secured the union of the Church throughout the several states, but it brought to those counsels by which their infant institutions must be formed, the aid of principles which were most wanting in the southern states. Amongst them the prevailing tone, both as to discipline and doctrine, was low and uncertain. Hence had arisen the desire of removing from the opening of the litany the addresses to the blessed Trinity. Hence their jealousy of even the lightest discipline. Hence, too, it happened that the lay deputy sent by Virginia to convention was an ordained presbyter, who, in the time of the Church's sufferings, had renounced his orders. And thus, all through this convention, he who, in purer times, would have been marked out for spiritual censure, took, without doubt or remonstrance, a leading part in fashioning the discipline and order of their infant communion. To a temper thus bordering on latitudinarian views, Bishop White, if he had stood alone, would, from natural kindness, and perhaps from personal inclination, have been too much disposed to yield, and some fatal bias might have been given to their earliest institutions; but in the presence of Bishop Seabury and those about him, a check was provided on such innovations. With the strongest attachment to the distinctive articles of the Christian faith, the New-England clergy held, as we have seen, most firmly to the model of apostolical order; and in these counteracting tendencies was the best hope of the convention coming to a safe and sound conclusion.

This difference of views between the east and south was seen at once. Before the eastern clergy gave in their adhesion to the articles of union, they required that, by the alteration of the third, there should be given to the board of bishops the power of originating acts for the concurrence of the lower house, with a negative on their conclusions. The first point was easily conceded. The second, for the present, was made the subject of a compromise. It was agreed that the non-assent of the bishops should negative all acts to which four-fifths of the lower house did not still adhere. The absolute negative was referred to the collective judgment of the several diocesan conventions. Upon this agreement Bishop Seabury, and the three New-

England presbyters, gave in their adhesion to the general constitution, and took their seats in the convention.

Important matters came at once into discussion. The proposed Prayer-book, drawn up in 1785, had kindled a flame of opposition. Some were offended at the alterations of the English ritual, and more at the want of alteration. Its compilers had unwisely printed a large edition, and from this were understood to regard it rather as a settled than a projected form. The lower house accordingly entered with some warmth on this discussion. Instead of proposing, as before, to take the existing liturgy, and merely alter in it what required adjustment, they, the more completely to dismiss the obnoxious book, appointed committees " to prepare a litany," " to prepare a communion-service," " a morning and evening prayer," and other " offices."

In this they ran no slight peril. Scarcely with any thing beside is the well-being of the Church bound up so closely as with the full orthodoxy of its liturgies. On this depends, not only the unity of all her children, but also, in great measure, their whole religious character. Hence from the earliest time these have been a matter of especial care. By one Council* it was ordered, " that the prayers, prefaces, impositions of hands, which are confirmed by the synod, be observed and used by all men ;" and another† gives the reason for this order, " lest through ignorance or carelessness, any thing contrary to the faith should be vented or uttered before God, or offered up to him in the church."

In this wholesome dread, during times of purity, change had always been brought cautiously and with a sparing hand into the older offices. Nor was there a more certain sign and instrument of increasing corruption than when the public liturgies, which had been first veiled from common sight by the mystery of a learned language, began to embody largely the errors of a later time. These, however, were rather additions than substitutions. So that even in the worst times the golden thread of primitive truth might be traced by the spiritual eye through all the subtle entan-

---

* Con. Carth. can. 106. † Council of Milan, can. 12.

glement of more modern error. The endeavor of our own reformers was, to keep this precious thread unbroken, whilst they freed it from the false inventions by which it was well-nigh concealed. The old books of common English use had been taken by the bishops and doctors to whom this work was entrusted; and from them the new insertions which had crept gradually in with the spread of Romish errors were cast out, that the oldest offices might still remain amongst us, and set the tone of such additions as the change of customs and of times required. On this point there had been a long and anxious struggle between English Churchmen and the Puritans; for these wished for new prayers, whilst the true sons of the old English Church strove to retain this sure mark and instrument of their oneness with the body of Christ from the beginning, that they spoke in praise and prayer, and in intercession and confession, as far as might be, in the same accents in which their forefathers had worshipped God from the time when the little flock were gathered in " an upper chamber," where " the doors were shut for fear of the Jews."

The existence of such a liturgy was put at hazard in America; but, by God's blessing, the danger was averted. The house of bishops was now duly constituted; and in the continued absence of the Bishop of New York, it was composed of Bishops Seabury and White. Their first entrance on their duties afforded a hopeful promise for the issue; for as meekness ever waits upon true wisdom, there was a token of wise counsel in Bishop White's instant cession of precedence to his eastern brother on the ground of his seniority of consecration. Their harmonious action turned aside the danger; they took as their guide the old offices of their communion; and making only needful changes, by degrees won over the general voice on nearly every point.

Bishop White has recorded the remark of a by-stander, which strikingly illustrates the working of more thoughtful minds at that important crisis :—" When I hear these things I look back to the origin of the Prayer-book, and represent to my mind the spirits of its venerable compilers ascending to heaven in the flames of martyrdom that consumed their bodies. I then look at the improvers of this book in . . . .

. and . . . . . and . . . . . The consequence is, that I am not sanguine in my expectations of the meditated changes in the liturgy."

The character of the chief changes which were made is curious and instructive. They show the great peril of attempting to improve such fixed and ascertained forms; for they are marked by a tendency to opposite extremes. Thus, on the one side, there were struck out from the Prayer-book the Athanasian Creed and the absolution in the Visitation of the Sick; whilst the use of the sign of the cross in baptism; and "Receive ye the Holy Ghost" in the ordinal, are left to the choice of the minister. Thus, also, whilst to the question, "What is the inward part or thing signified in the Lord's supper?" the answer of the English Catechism, "The body and blood of Christ, which are *verily* and *indeed* taken and received by the faithful in the Lord's supper," is changed into "The body and blood of Christ, which are *spiritually* taken and received by the faithful in the Lord's Supper;" at the same time, upon the other side, in the Office for the Holy Communion there were inserted the prayers of invocation and oblation which are contained in the earliest liturgies. These had been retained in the first English Book of Common Prayer put forth in the reign of Edward VI. by "the archbishop and other learned and discreet divines;"* but upon its subsequent revision they were both omitted; their essential parts, as our reformers thought, being found in other parts of the service, whilst their use must prove dangerous at a time when popish superstition had obscured that holy mystery, and lowered its spiritual reality to a gross and carnal conceit. In the ancient Scottish Prayer-book, which was compiled at a later period, these forms had been restored; and in it their use was familiar to Bishop Seabury. He was disposed to overvalue their presence; hardly, as he owned to Bishop White, considering the service from which they were absent as "amounting strictly to a consecration." He therefore pressed earnestly their restoration. From his brother bishop he met with no opposition;

---

* A.D. 1548. Statutes at large, vol. ii. p. 393.

Bishop White having always admired "the beauty of those ancient forms, and seeing no superstition in them."* No remark of any sort was made on their insertion in the lower house; and they accordingly form part of the American Prayer-book.†

One other important change came into debate. From the services of "the proposed Prayer-book" had been struck out the whole Nicene Creed, and that clause of the Apostles' which declares of our Lord that "He descended into hell." The Nicene Creed was now reinserted; and after

---

* Appendix to Bishop White's Memorial.

† The Communion-office, therefore, is thus altered from our own. After what is with us the conclusion of the prayer of consecration, the prayer of oblation follows, in these words: "Wherefore, O Lord and heavenly Father, according to the institution of Thy dearly beloved Son our Saviour Jesus Christ, we Thy humble servants do celebrate and make here before Thy divine Majesty, with these Thy holy gifts which we now offer unto Thee, the memorial Thy Son hath commanded us to make; having in remembrance His blessed passion and precious death, His mighty resurrection and glorious ascension: rendering unto Thee most hearty thanks for the innumerable benefits procured unto us by the same." Then succeeds the Invocation, in these words: "And we most humbly beseech Thee, O merciful Father, to hear us; and, of Thy almighty goodness, vouchsafe to bless and sanctify with Thy word and Holy Spirit these Thy gifts and creatures of bread and wine, that we, receiving them according to Thy Son our Saviour Jesus Christ's holy institution in remembrance of His death and passion, may be partakers of His most blessed body and blood. And we earnestly desire Thy fatherly goodness mercifully to accept this our sacrifice of praise and thanksgiving; most humbly beseeching Thee to grant, that by the merits and death of Thy Son Jesus Christ, and through faith in His blood, we, and all Thy whole Church, may obtain remission of our sins, and all other benefits of His passion. And here we offer and present unto Thee, O Lord, ourselves, our souls and bodies, to be a reasonable, holy, and living sacrifice unto Thee; humbly beseeching Thee, that we, and all others who shall be partakers of this holy communion, may worthily receive the most precious body and blood of thy Son Jesus Christ, be filled with Thy grace and heavenly benediction, and be made one body with Him, that He may dwell in them and they in Him. And although we are unworthy, through our manifold sins, to offer unto Thee any sacrifice, yet we beseech Thee to accept this our bounden duty and service, not weighing our merits, but pardoning our offences; through Jesus Christ our Lord; by whom and through whom, in the unity of the Holy Ghost, all honor and glory be unto Thee, O Father Almighty, world without end. Amen."

much discussion, the use of the disputed clause allowed; the lower house not consenting to its absolute adoption. In the first printed Prayer-books it was inserted between brackets; but this seeming to stamp it as apocryphal, the next convention placed, instead of them, this discretionary rubric: "And any Churches may omit the words, 'He descended into hell;' or may, instead of them, use the words, 'He went into the place of departed spirits,' which are considered as words of the same meaning in the creed."

A selection of Psalms, fixed portions of which might be used instead of those which came in daily order in the Psalter, was inserted in the Prayer-book. This was the work of the lower house, and is another instance of the risk attending all such changes. The first principle of any such selection is manifestly false. It is a denial of the great truth, that in those words of inspiration we find the spirit-struggles of the King of Israel answer to our own as face to face. And this first error led to many others. One aim of the compilers was to shorten the service; their success may be gathered from the words of Bishop White, who considers "the omissions as very capricious, and the selections in general as having added to the length of the morning and evening prayer." Some of his expressions show, that even he was unawares drawn, by the fault of his position, into an unconscious disrespect to Holy Scripture, or he would not have ventured, as if dealing with some human composition, to commend "the excellency of psalms overlooked by gentlemen of judgment and taste." These were the chief changes in the Common Prayer; the others aiming chiefly, and with small success, at introducing greater verbal correctness into our old Saxon dialect.

Such is the Book of Common Prayer, "declared by the bishops, the clergy, and the laity of the Protestant Episcopal Church in America in convention to be the liturgy of" their "Church:" and upon the whole, in spite of some alterations which we must deem unhappy, and more which we esteem needless, it remains as a living proof of that gratitude which its preface expresses to the Church of England, "to which, under God, she is indebted for her first foundation and a long continuance of nursing care and protection," since, upon the whole, it fulfils the profession, that "she is far from intending to depart from the Church of England in any essential point of doctrine, discipline, or worship, or farther than local circumstances require."*

The convention broke up without the consecration of the elected bishop of Massachusetts; a direct vote, as we have seen, acknowledged Bishop Seabury's consecration; and with his co-operation, Dr. Bass might have been admitted to the highest order of the priesthood. But Bishop White conceived that he was pledged to the archbishop to hand on the English line unmixed. The consecration, therefore, was postponed until this engagement should have been relaxed. In the event, this proved needless, since, in the following year (Sept. 1790) Dr. Madison, elected as Bishop of Virginia, crossed to England, and was duly consecrated bishop; and thus, 184 years after her planting, the Church in Virginia first saw a bishop of her own within her borders.

The ensuing convention witnessed the first American consecration. At its session the upper house consisted of Bishops Seabury, White, Provoost, and Madison. This first meeting of Bishops Seabury and Provoost was full of interest, although the unhappy temper of the latter made it a time of much anxiety. Narrow to a high degree in mind, and full of prejudice against his eastern brother, the Bishop of New-York resisted bitterly the title to presidency, which by the canon of the last convention would be his in right of seniority; and was even ready to deny, at all hazards, the regularity of his consecration. The first point was, with Christian meekness, ceded by the elder bishop; and through the influence of Dr. White, all further open opposition was dropped by Bishop Provoost.

On the 17th of September, 1792, Dr. Claggett, bishop elect, was consecrated by the laying on of hands of Bishops Provoost, Seabury, White, and Madison. Thus was the Church at last complete in all its functions, and able to expand itself as God might give it grace and opportunity, to meet the many wants of that vast continent in which it

---

* Preface to American Common Prayer.

was now fully planted. Other consecrations soon succeeded. In 1795, Dr. Smith was consecrated bishop of South Carolina; and in 1797, Dr. Bass of Massachusetts; whilst in the same year Dr. Jarvis was called to succeed the first bishop of Connecticut. The system of the Church was every day becoming more perfectly consolidated. In the conventions of 1792, 1799, and 1801, the question of articles was frequently discussed. Various opinions from time to time seemed to predominate. Some in leading station, and of great laxity as to the first truths of the faith, were, like Bishop Provoost, desirous to avoid entirely what they unhappily conceived to be a needless restriction on the right of private judgment. Wiser councils defeated this proposal; but what should be the articles adopted still remained an anxious question. The English articles had been at first assumed to be the nucleus of the new collection; and into them such changes as appeared expedient were to be inserted. The result may easily be guessed; one party objected to one set of propositions, the retrenchment of a second was required by others, until absolute division seemed rapidly approaching. In this dilemma it was resolved, as a means of securing peace, that the English articles should be received, with such changes only as would make them suit republican America, and consist with the alterations in the creeds detailed on a former page.*

At this time the Church may be considered as rooted in that land. Native Bishops witnessed for the resurrection of the Lord; from one, obtained almost by stealth from Scotland, they had already multiplied to seven, and promised to hand on unbroken the appointed orders of the ministry. Already (1795) the first bishop (Seabury) had entered on his rest, and his successor been admitted in his room into the apostolic college. There was now, in truth, an American Church. Of old the proper title of the body so described would have been the English Church in America, if indeed that sickly and almost severed branch could claim true union with the parent stock. But it was now

---

* The use of the Book of Homilies is suspended until they have been cleared from "obsolete phrases and local references."

planted in the wide western continent; and many and earnest were the prayers of faithful men, that its branches might spread unto the sea and its boughs unto the river. It had taken root, as in every other soil; and good hope there was that it would cover the land. The Church might now be read there by her distinctive characters. This was a great matter gained. For this, through long years of weakness and destitution, the most zealous and devoted hearts in America had longed and prayed. By a most unexpected turn had the answer of those prayers been sent as one healing fruit of the American rebellion. Surely it was thus given as a reproof to the mother country for her long denial to her offspring of the most valuable part of their inheritance.

But though the Church was now thus complete in its organisation, it did not as we might fondly hope, shoot forth at once into full strength and vigor. Almost every where there was much of feebleness about its growth, and there were districts in which it seemed to languish and decay. "The period through which for some years our narrative has been taking us," says Dr. Hawks,* referring to this time, "is one, for the most part, of such gloomy darkness, that the smallest ray of light is felt to be a blessing." Even when "the dawning light of a brighter day" was rising on Virginia, "the journals of the convention by which Bishop Moore was elected show the presence of but *seven* clergymen and seventeen laymen. We look back upon the past, and are struck with the contrast. Seven clergymen were all that could be convened to transact the most important measure which our conventions are ever called on to perform, and this in a territory where once more than ten times seven regularly served at the altar. We look back farther still, and find the Church, after the lapse of 200 years, numbering about as many ministers as she possessed at the close of the first eight years of her existence."

But little better is the account of things in Maryland. "In 1803 there was a spirit of indifferenc to religion and the Church too extensively prevalent in the parishes;

---

* Contributions to Eccl. Hist. of Virginia, p. 295.

nearly one half of them were vacant ; in some, all ministerial support had ceased. Some few of the clergy had deserted their stations ; and of the residue, several, disheartened and embarrassed by inadequate means of living, had sought subsistence in other states. Infidelity and fanaticism were increasing ; and, on the whole, there never was a time when ministers were more needed, or when it was more difficult to obtain them."* In Pennsylvania it was much the same. The number of the clergy here continued still so small, " that even the old parishes, existing before the revolution, could not be supplied, much less could the formation of new congregations be attempted."† Such was the general state of things during the first years of this century

Many causes tended to produce this deep depression · some of these were inherent in the general temper of American society and manners, but many more may undoubtedly be traced to the peculiar condition under which the Church was now established. To gain a clear view of the history of those times, we must shortly glance at each of these, and endeavor to trace in action the working of the ecclesiastical constitution as it had been recently remodelled. The first great hindrance to its strength was the low tone of feeling and of doctrine which in the former days of our neglect had crept over its members. There was little attachment to the Church, little veneration for her character, little knowledge or value of her distinctive claims ; there were many recollections of careless shepherds, of clergy who had disgraced their calling. Thus there was widely spread abroad a want of reverence for holy things and holy persons ; there was among the laity a feverish readiness to constitute themselves watchmen over their appointed watchmen, which was most injurious in its effect both to the clergy and to themselves.

These evils were further aggravated by the peculiar position of the newly-constituted body with respect to the communions round it, which claimed equally the Christian

---

* Dr. Hawks' Memorials of Virginia, pp. 350, 351.
† Life of Bishop White, p. 154.

name, but were strangers to the apostolic form and discipline; for it was thus subjected, at the same time, to the weakness both of infancy and of decrepitude. In all those associations and prescriptive rights whereby an hereditary Church maintains her hold upon the love and reverence of men, she was necessarily wanting. She had no territorial existence; men belonged to her not because they were born within her pale, because in the old time holy pastors of her communion had stood up there amongst their pagan forefathers, and bowed their rugged hearts by the message of the everlasting Gospel, and then gathered them into a visible fellowship, into which they too, in their turn, had been baptised, and to which they owed from infancy an hereditary reverence; nor even because they now joined a company of others who had been trained amidst such associations;—but they belonged to her because they chose to join her—because she was more reasonable or more comely in their eyes than others---because they willed it: and to this action of their will, and that of others round them, it seemed as if she owed her being: like the constitution of their nation, she seemed self-formed through their agency. They were not grafted into a pre-existing body—they were the framers of a new society; and they felt towards it, therefore, ever afterwards, as towards that which they might support, remodel, or forsake at will—as their cause so long as they maintained it—as that which they had a title to conduct as they would. And hence they were almost strangers to the reverence and affection of children to a spiritual mother: this, under their circumstances, could only grow up with time and slowly formed associations; and so for the present, the weakness of infancy was on her.

On the other hand, there was amongst them little of the strength of the Church's youth; for this is founded on the ardent affection of fresh converts to the great heart-truths of Christ's blessed Gospel. The small company of gathered believers in any land where, for the first time, the cross of Christ is planted, are a body every one of whom is personally convinced of the reality of that common spiritual life into which he is now admitted. They are all well nigh overpowered by the first discovery of their true greatness and blessedness in Christ, and their utter misery without Him The Church has brought them the glorious message of their new creation, and for it they are ready, if need be, to go through fire and water ; and so, though they may be few in number, they are great in strength, for every one of them is a host: each may go forth in God's strength and chase a thousand. But this could not be the case with this infant communion. She was young indeed, but she was shorn of the strength of her youth. The message she bore was familiar to the ears of those to whom she spoke; she had to deal with a population calling itself Christian, or, at least, well acquainted with all the offers of Christianity ; she stood but as a new sect amongst sects ;* she seemed to them to be contending for nice distinctions, subtle refinements, perhaps doubtful claims. This weakened everywhere the effect of her testimony with others, and it tended to lower her own tone,—to lead her to stand upon the defensive,—to act and speak, and often, we may fear, think of herself, as nothing more than one amongst the many round her, and of her errand, as rather to make proselytes to the dogma of Episcopacy, than to win living souls to Christ.

In these circumstances may doubtless be found reasons for the comparatively small effect which, at first, followed her implanting in America as the true Church of that great people. But beyond this cause, weakness existed in her peculiar organization. To enter fully into these, we must review shortly the system of ecclesiastical polity which was at that time established. This, in outline, was as follows:—The union of the whole Church was maintained by a "general convention" or assembly "of clerical and lay deputies" elected by each diocese, not to exceed four of each order, which met once in three years

---

* The language of the preface to her Prayer-book unhappily, favored this view, in declaring that the result of the war of independence was to "leave the different denominations of Christians at full and equal liberty to model and organize their respective churches and forms of worship and discipline, in such manner as they might judge most convenient for their future prosperity."

to pass general canons, and determine any question which concerned the common interest of the whole Church; each diocese to have one vote; all questions to be settled by a majority of voices, each order having a negative upon the other whenever they should be required to vote by orders. Further, a like body of lay deputies and clergy met every year in "diocesan convention," to order, in subjection to the general canons, all which specially concerned that diocese. One function of the diocesan convention was to nominate a "standing committee," which, during the intervals between its session, carried its decisions into execution in the diocese, and, with its fellow-committees, formed, in some respects, a standing council of the whole Church. Within the diocese, again, each separate parish had its own vestry, which, besides possessing many administrative powers, elected its delegates for the "diocesan convention."

A very little inspection will show the deficiencies of all this scheme of polity, which was, in fact, copied, in the main, from the political institutions of the newly-founded republic, and rested, therefore, far too much upon the choice and self-government of all its members. It is of great moment that we trace this out, because it will show us the root of many of the infirmities and difficulties by which the Church has been beset. We can, indeed, only trace the outward side of such evils; we can inquire into defects of organization and errors in systems of polity and discipline, and we can do no more; but in doing this we must never overlook the master-truth, that in the presence of the blessed Spirit of the Lord is the only life and strength of the whole Church. His gracious breath revives its love and purity; His withdrawal leaves it dry and withered. The secret history of a multitude of hearts may therefore account, in any land, for its welfare or decline, but that history is secret as the pathway of the Lord amongst the mighty waters. On this, therefore, we cannot enter; not from undervaluing its first importance, but because it is a hidden thing, to which we cannot reach. We must be contented if we can discover the external causes with which these mighty influences are by God's will connected; and this is our intention here.

To begin, then, with the lowest subdivision. The title "parish" in America has a widely different meaning from that which it bears with us. It is not a certain district of a diocese committed by its bishop to the spiritual care of a presbyter, who is to regard all within it as his charge, for whom he is to care now, and to give account hereafter, "whether they will hear or whether they will forbear;" it was merely a set of persons who associated themselves together and agreed to act and worship together in a certain place, and under certain rules, because they preferred the episcopal form to any other. Their very corporate existence was the consequence of their own choice and will, not the result of care taken for them; and this principle was present every where. After a time these men determined upon building a church; they built it, and divided its area into pews, which they took to themselves; so that the poor were from the first excluded, because they could not pay their share towards the expenses of the building, which now belonged to the body corporate in whose decision it originated. Here was the first grievous fault: "to the poor the gospel was" not "preached." The next was of a different kind, but no less real. The body thus formed applied to the convention of the diocese in which it was situated for admission as a part of that diocese; it obtained from the legislature the privileges of a body corporate, and it began to exercise its rights. Accordingly, in Easter week of every year, all the holders of the pews met together to elect by ballot a vestry, which might consist of any number not exceeding ten. From this number two wardens were appointed, one by the clergyman[*] and one by the vestry. The vestry being thus organised, elected out of their own body a treasurer, secretary, and delegates to the diocesan convention.

To this vestry the management of all the affairs of the parish was committed, and this lay body not only conducted its pecuniary concerns, but settled the payment of the minister, "engaged the services of a clergyman in cases of a

---

[*] In the greater number of cases the wardens are both appointed by the vestry.

vacancy;"* and if it deemed it right, provided also an assistant minister. Thus, by this system, not only was the pastor dependent on the offerings of his flock, but he derived his authority from them, and to them he was responsible. They at first nominated him to his post, and afterwards, through the vestry, in a great measure controlled his conduct. The practical evils which flowed from this unsound principle need scarcely be pointed out. The course of this history will require us to notice hereafter some striking instances in which the Episcopal clergy, as a body, have not dared to raise an open testimony against national corruption. Such must be too often the result of arrangements such as these. The very notion of the Christian ministry presupposes in the witness for his Lord entire independence of those to whom he is sent. He must be ready to withstand and to rebuke evil principles and evil practices wherever they are found; and if he be not, it is soon discovered that the salt of the world hath lost its savor. For this end it was, that since the power of working miracles has been withdrawn, the whole system of the Church has sought to provide for the independence of those who were to be, by the necessity of their office, bold rebukers of sin, and, if need be, patient sufferers for the truth. The wisdom with which it had secured this end, by making the clergy dependent only on itself, was one great secret of the power and prevalence of papal Rome. Amongst ourselves the same end has been greatly promoted by the existence of an endowed national establishment. For, though the spirit which fills the heart of confessors and martyrs is of far too high and noble a character to be directly affected by such an influence, yet in the long run the temper of any large body of men will be surely, though unconsciously, depressed or raised by the dependence or independence of the position which they occupy.

In America, all things tend to make the clergy keenly feel their want of independence. So far does this extend, that it can hardly fail to act injuriously upon their own estimate of their spiritual position. It is hardly to be ex-

* The American expression. Caswall's American Church, p. 66.

pected that men who are thus taught from the first to view themselves merely as the selected and paid agents of a lay board can, as a body, fully realize their high character as the fearless witnesses for Christ's truth in the face of an evil generation. Noble exceptions, indeed, there have been among the western clergy—Christian heroes, who have risen above the weakening influence of the system under which they live; but of that system the tendency is no less certain. It is to make the pastor wholly dependent upon those to whom he ministers.

Next to the parish comes the diocese, which consists of all the parishes within any one state, which, having organised themselves according to the rules of the general convention, have been admitted into union with it. Here, again, the same faulty principle was present. A "diocese," in the language of the Church, has ever meant a certain portion of Christ's flock committed to the special charge of one chief pastor, who fills for it the office which our Lord entrusted to His first apostles. But in America a diocese meant nothing more than a federal commonwealth of "parishes," associated on certain prescribed conditions with each other and the general convention. So far from dependence on one bishop defining its character and marking its limits, it might, and often must,* for years, by the general canons of the Church, have no bishop at all. For, while any number of parishes in any state were invited by the constitution to form themselves into a "diocese," it was specially enjoined† that they should not have the right of electing a bishop until six presbyters had been duly settled within that state, in charge of six duly organised parishes, for the space of one year. The reason of this rule is plain. Without it, any ambitious presbyter who could gather one or two supporters, might have "organised a diocese" in some new state, and presented himself for consecration as its elected bishop. But the necessity of such a rule is a striking instance of the evil which resulted from this new principle of self-creation; by which,

* This necessity has since been happily removed, as will appear hereafter.
† By the second canon of the Church.

like some mere commercial association aiming at pecuniary profits, the members of the Church formed themselves at will into a body corporate, to act together by mutual agreement, without their appointed head.

The practice of earlier times, indeed, and the necessities of this, would have allowed, if need be, any scattered presbyters to act, singly or together, on their own commission, waiting for and expecting the time, when the rulers of the Church should crown their labors, by sending forth one chief witness more, to gather them together into a visible unity. But this would have been wholly a different arrangement from that, which directed the laity or clergy to constitute themselves an organised diocese, though they remained for years without a bishop.

The evils of this state of things are well expressed by a living bishop of America :*—" If due perpetuation of the Church, and chief authority, and the protection of God's promise, appertain to bishops as successors of the apostles of the Lord, how can we encourage, so far as we have rightful influence, the extension, or even the existence of the Church without a bishop? If it be 'evident,' as we declare,† 'to all men diligently reading holy scripture and ancient authors, that from the apostles' time there have been these orders of ministers in Christ's Church, bishops, priests, and deacons,' by what warrant can we withhold from any portion of the Saviour's family the chiefest of the three? If it be sound and true in practice, as it is certainly of primitive authority, 'not to do any thing without the bishop,'‡ upon what principle is it that we permit the organisation of dioceses, yet, until they have a certain number of duly organised parishes and duly settled presbyters, compel them to remain without a bishop ?"

One evident effect of this rule was, to afford temptations to all sorts of subterfuges through which a state could be made to seem possessed of the number of parishes and

---

* George Washington Doane, D. D., bishop of the diocese of New Jersey, in a sermon preached at Philadelphia, September 25, 1833

† Preface to the Ordinal.

‡ See the Epistles of Ignatius, the disciple of St. John.

pastors to which was annexed the exercise of this right. Another and a greater evil belonging to this rule was the weakness with which it infected all the aggressive acts of the Church upon those whom she should conquer to save. In the outskirts and border-land of Christendom the spiritual struggle is always most severe. There, where the old standard can be carried forward only by hard fighting, is the greatest need of those true champions who are ready to spend their breath and shed their blood in the holy cause. There is ever the greatest need of disciplined ranks, of completeness of authority, of ready obedience, of concentred command, of our Master's promised presence; there, more than any where beside, must the successors of the twelve be found ready to do constantly apostle's works. Nothing, therefore, could be more disheartening than the lacking this secret of strength exactly where that strength was most required.

Again, another evil resulted from this rule. It fostered the very spirit of self-will and independence from which it sprang; for, by allowing the organisation of a diocese without a bishop, it led practically to the undervaluing of the office of a bishop, to its being esteemed an ornamental part of the Church machinery, and not as the power of government and the instrument of a visible unity. The "convention," and not the episcopate became really the ruling power. That is, while called Episcopal, the Church was, in fact, in great measure Presbyterian.

There was much in the constitution of the diocesan "convention" to increase this evil. It was a synod, of which laymen, many of whom were not even communicants, formed the greater part.† Each parish sent one, two, or three delegates to this convention; and they passed canons, administered the discipline of the diocese, decided on the alteration of creeds, liturgies, and articles, elected a bishop, and even held that when appointed he would be "amenable to" them.† Of a

---

* There is nothing to prevent even an unbaptised man representing the Church in general convention; and it is too certain that such men have actually been found amongst the delegates.

† Canons of the Church in Virginia.

like character was the constitution of the standing committee, which commonly consisted of laymen and clergy, in equal numbers.* This, which was elected by a diocesan convention, was, till the next assembled, the governing body of the diocese.

A few extracts from the minutes of one of the Virginian conventions will show the working of this system in detail. They are taken from the journal of May, 1790,† four months before the consecration of the first bishop of that diocese.

On Wednesday, May 5th, a sufficient number of clergymen and lay deputies to form a convention having met according to appointment, the Rev. T. Madison, D. D., was unanimously elected president. After this they elected a secretary and a committee to examine into the certificates of the appointments of sitting members, and adjourned till two P. M., to receive the report of this committee. This having been received, and the list of actual members of convention ascertained, they then adjourned until the morrow.

On Thursday, May 6th, the proceedings opened with prayers and a sermon; after which, amongst other things, it was "resolved, that this convention will to-morrow resolve itself into a committee of the whole convention, on the state of the Protestant Episcopal Church; that this convention will, to-morrow, proceed to the nomination of a bishop of the Episcopal Church in Virginia; that a committee be appointed to amend the canons which respect the trial of offending clergymen." This committee was composed of five laymen and five clergymen.

On the following day the convention proceeded by ballot to the nomination of a bishop, when it was found that the numbers given were—for the Rev. James Madison, 46; for the Rev. Samuel Shield, 9—a majority, therefore, of the whole convention was in favor of Dr. Madison, and

---

* "In Pennsylvania it consists of five clergymen and as many laymen. In Ohio three of each order are elected; in Tenessee two of each." Caswall's *American Church,* p. 74

† Journals of Virginian Conventions. Appendix to Dr. Hawks's Memorials, p. 31, &c.

it was accordingly resolved that he should be nominated for consecration as their bishop.

The convention then appointed five clergymen to "visit" the different districts of the province; and agreed to recommend any bishop to whom Mr. Stephen Johnson might apply for ordination, to dispense in his case with the knowledge of the Greek and Latin languages, required by the seventh general canon of the Protestant Episcopal Church in America. After transacting some of the temporal business of the diocese, the convention adjourned. At their meeting on the following day, which ended the synod, besides other business, they received from the committee some new canons respecting the trial of offending clergymen, which were read and finally adopted, and agreed to a general "ordinance for regulating the appointment of vestries and trustees, and for other purposes." Some extracts from these "canons" and this "ordinance" will show the nature of the questions decided by this convention, in which there were twenty-seven clergymen to thirty-three lay deputies. "Be it ordained," says the ordinance, "that future conventions shall consist of two deputies from each parish, of whom the minister shall be one, *if there be a minister*, the other a layman, to be annually chosen by the vestry, who shall also choose another, where there is no minister in the parish,"—a minister being no more essential to a parish than a bishop to a diocese.

"Convention shall regulate all the religious concerns of the Church, its DOCTRINES, DISCIPLINE, and WORSHIP, and institute such rules and regulations as they may judge necessary for the good government thereof, and the same revoke and alter at their pleasure."

To the same purport speak the canons. "All questions, whether they relate to the order, government, discipline, DOCTRINE, or worship of this Church, shall be determined by a majority of votes." "The clergy of several neighboring parishes shall assemble in presbytery annually, at some convenient place in the district. One in each district shall be appointed by the convention to preside at their meetings, with the title of visitor; who shall annually visit each parish in his district—shall attend to and inspect the morals and conduct of the clergy—shall admonish and reprove privately those clergymen who are negligent or act in an unbecoming manner—and shall report yearly to the bishop, if there be one, or if there be no bishop, to the next convention, the state of each parish in his district." Other canons carried these principles still further. "Bishops," says canon 25, "shall be amenable to the convention, who shall be a court to try them, from which there shall be no appeal;" and (canon 27) " on a bishop's being convicted of offences, he shall be reproved, suspended, or dismissed, at the discretion of the court."

Of the same character are some of the rules for the lower orders in the ministry. "No minister," says the 13th, "shall hereafter be received into any parish within this commonwealth till he shall have entered into a contract in writing . . . by which it shall be stipulated . . . that he holds the appointment subject to removal upon the determination of the convention of this state." And the 28th canon, one of those adopted at this time, constitutes the chairman and three-fourths of the standing committee (a lay body) a court to try all clergymen accused of offences, giving them the power of "passing such a sentence as the majority shall think deserved, which shall be either reproof, dismission, or degradation." The tendency of such a set of rules is plain. They do not merely secure to the laity that share of power which, in the best times, belonged to them, but they give to the convention the whole government; and confer upon a synod of deputies, clerical and lay, the office of degrading presbyters and bishops—of taking, that is, from them, what it had no authority to give or to remove.

In the organization of the general convention the same evils may be found. Some, indeed, there were, and amongst them Bishop Seabury, who contended that laymen should not sit at all in synods of the Church. But for this there seems to be undoubted warrant. From the intimations of the Acts of the Apostles, we can hardly doubt that, in some way or other, the laity took part in the disscussions of the primitive Church. It is as plain that they made up the body in which dwelt the Holy

Ghost, as that the power of discipline and rule was vested in the hands of the apostles. The general history of the Church in the succeeding age suggests, that then also the believing people ratified with their expressed consent the decisions of the earliest synods. That such was the custom in our own land is clear from plain historical records. It is proved by the earliest remains of our annals, that the bishops presided over ecclesiastical councils in England, and, with a vast attendance of the people, settled all matters of religion against heresies,

After the subjugation of this island by the Saxons, their kings, with the chiefs and bishops, held councils, in which they decided all which concerned the safety of the Church and kingdom; and to maintain their peace and discipline, enacted laws, with the sanction both of the laity and prelates. Further, if at any time canons were passed in a merely ecclesiastical synod, they were not binding on the body of the clergy until they had received the sanction of the monarch, as the representative of the laity; for no decrees of ecclesiastical councils possessed the character of public enactments until thus sanctioned by the king's authority.*

Both in Scotland and England, in the ninth, tenth, and eleventh centuries, councils were held for settling both civil and ecclesiastical affairs, in which it is plain, from their signatures, that kings and great men of the laity sat with and even outweighed the bishops.†

On this point our ancient records cannot be mistaken. "Let the bishop and the senator," say the laws of Edgar (about A.D. 950,) "be present at the provincial synod, and afterwards let them teach divine and human laws."‡

"King Eadmund," says the code of Anglo-Saxon laws, "assembled a great synod at London-byrig, as well of ecclesiastical as secular degree, during the holy Eastertide. There was Odda, archbishop, and Wolfstan, archbishop, and many other bishops, deeply thinking of their souls' condition and of those who were subject to them."§

---

* Wilkins, Concilia, vol. vi. p. viii.   † Ibid. p. xxvii.
‡ Wilkins, Leges Anglo-Saxonicæ, pp. 78, 79.
§ Anglo-Saxon Laws, p. 92.

"In the reign of the most bountiful Wihtred, king of the Kentish men, there was assembled a convention of the great men in council: there was Birhtwald, Archbishop of Britain, and the forenamed king; and the ecclesiastics of the province of every degree spoke in union with the subject people."*

So speak the laws of King Alfred. "After this it happened that many nations received the faith of Christ,† and that many synods were assembled throughout all the earth; and also among the English race after they had received the faith of Christ, of holy bishops, and also of other exalted witan." And even in later times, when the clergy and laity no longer sat together, the decisions of the synod were ratified by the assent of the assembled laity.

It is not, therefore, to the presence or votes of the laity in the American convention that objection can be made. In this respect the constitution of the synod did but follow primitive examples. But there were other points for which no such warrant can be found. The Episcopal character was not distinctly marked in its organization. The veto of the bishops is as essential to the completeness of the system as the possession of their due share of power by the believing laity: and this was withheld from the bishops in America; the agreement of four-fifths of the lower house forced upon them any measures approved by the majority.

If Episcopacy be indeed of Christ's appointment, such infractions on its principles must have weakened this infant Church; and that it did so, there is ample proof. To these various errors admitted into its constitution we may doubtless trace much of the slow and feeble progress of the body. Conventions never, even in America, have commanded the respect which has always waited on the personal rule of a holy and devoted bishop. Hence sprung "angry contentions" in diocesan meetings, in which "both sides charged their adversaries with unholy motives, and

---

* Anglo-Saxon Laws, p. 14: A.D. 695.
† About 880: p. 23.

disingenuous, unchristian conduct."* To such a pitch did these conflicts sometimes rise, that we find them preventing the possibility of the election of a bishop from the fierce opposition of contending factions. From this course, also, there was diffused on all sides amongst Churchmen a low estimate of God's gifts, and of the powers of His spiritual kingdom. Hence sprung such propositions as, "that the canons should be so modified as to give rectors and vestries the power of admitting to the pulpits of the churches clergymen of other denominations;"† hence wanton alterations in the creeds and liturgy; hence a feeble and faltering tone, which soon infected thought and action, first amongst the clergy, and then amongst the laity, and helped on the impression, at one time " common in the south, that the Church was cold and lifeless, and indifferent to the religion of the heart."‡

But even as we remark these errors in the early organization of this now independent body, we must bear in mind to whom belongs the real fault implied in their adoption. It was the Church and nation of England which had accustomed these our western sons to reverse the ancient rule, and " do every thing in the Church without the bishop." It was our past neglect which left them now to seek their principles, and at the same time to set up the very framework of their body spiritual.

Nor should their peculiar difficulties be overlooked. The American revolution not only shook the Church to its base, but left the minds of the people disinclined to episcopacy, merely because it was the form of English religion. Even Churchmen were infected with this feeling. They had known nothing of bishops except the name; and they had always associated their office with the customs and usages of the mother country. Episcopacy was commonly supposed to be of necessity allied to monarchy; and hence in republican America the whole tide of men's strongest passions set full against it. Here, then, was a great temptation to the framers of the new ecclesiestical constitution,

---

* Dr. Hawks's Maryland, p. 389.   † Ibid. p. 391.
‡ Ibid. p. 376.

to mingle, as far as possible, the ruling principle of self-government with the fabric of the episcopal communion. They needed, undoubtedly, to be reminded, that "the rights of the Christian Church arise, not from nature or compact, but from the institution of Christ ; and that we ought not to alter them, but to receive and maintain them as the holy apostles left them. The government, sacraments, faith, and doctrine of the Church are fixed and settled. We have a right to examine what they are, but we must take them as they are."* They were besides almost forced to give their laymen too large a share of spiritual government, for they had no bishops to rule over them.

While, therefore, we regret the compromise, and see too clearly the evils to which it has given birth, we must rejoice that still more of ancient truth was not lost in those perilous times ; and we hail with peculiar pleasure many after-modifications of injurious practices, and many gradual returns to higher and more primitive principles. The Churchmen of America had amongst them the true principle of life, and the true law for its development ; and year by year they have cast off some cause of weakness, and, through God's good guidance, carried on the mighty work to which His grace has called them.

* Letter of Bishop Seabury to Dr. White.

CHAPTER VIII.

FROM 1801, TO 1811-12.

Death and character of Bishop Seabury—Bishop White—Bishop Provoost—His character—Resigns the episcopal jurisdiction—Nomination and consecration of Bishop Moore—His character—Improvement of the state of the Church—Maryland—Bishop Claggett—Party spirit—Bishop Claggett applies for a Suffragan—Division of convention in 1812—Method of electing a bishop—The laity negative the nomination of the clergy—Convention of 1813—No attempt at an election made—Dr. Kemp elected suffragan in 1814—Consequent party feuds—Bishop Claggett's death Dr. Kemp succeeds—His death—Renewed contests as to the Episcopate—Bishop Stone elected—Troubles on his death—The see vacant—State of Delaware—No bishop—Application to Maryland—Refused—Decay of the Church there—And in Virginia—Issue of the long struggle with the Anabaptists and others—The glebes confiscated—Prostration of the Church.

AT the opening of the new century seven bishops presided in America over their several sees. Of these, three were of European and four of American consecration. The first of the four fathers of the western episcopate had been already, as we have seen, gathered to his rest. Bishop Seabury died in 1796. His death was a heavy loss to his infant communion; yet he had lived long enough to leave a marked impress of his character upon its institutions. His influence was most important whilst the foundations of the ecclesiastical fabric were being laid. For he was a clear-sighted man, of a bold spirit, and better acquainted than any of his coadjutors with those guiding principles which were then especially required. His own bias, indeed, was to extremes in the very opposite direction from that to which their inclination led them. Trained amidst the New-England sects, he had early learned to value the distinctive features of his own communion : and receiving consecration from the Scotch bishops, the affections of his heart opened freely towards them, and drew the whole bent of his mind towards their forms and practices. Had it been left to him alone to form the temper and mould the institutions of the western Church, there would have been little hope of its ever embracing the whole of the jealous population of that wide republic. But his views were a wholesome check upon those with whom he had to act. Of these, Bishop Madison had been bred a lawyer in the worst days of Virginian laxity. He was an elegant scholar, a good president of a college, and a mild and courteous gentleman; but he had none of the Christian learning and little of the untiring energy in action which his difficult position rendered needful. Bishop White, mild, meek, and conciliatory, inclined always to those councils which bore most faintly the stamp of his own communion, and fulfilling, through these qualities, a most important part in the common work, was indisposed by character and temper from taking resolutely the position which the times required. From that which he was sure was right, nothing indeed could move him; but he was naturally over-tolerant of all opinions.

These very qualities made him a most useful coadjutor to the Bishop of Connecticut. For, as it was his great endeavor to secure unanimity of action, he was ready to take part in many things to which he was himself indifferent, when he saw his brother's earnestness concerning them. The same easy temper as to things he judged indifferent, which would have led him, for the sake of peace, to concede to the most opposite objections what ought not to be yielded, now made him take the stricter side in matters which he saw would not be given up by Bishop Seabury. On this principle he voted for reinserting in the liturgy the Athanasian Creed, whilst he scrupled not to say that he would never use it; and agreed to place in the Communion-office the prayers of invocation and oblation, though he himself had never regretted their omission. His temper in these things was of the more importance from the peculiar character of Bishop Provoost. He was not a man to whom the destinies of an infant Church could with safety be committed. The whole tone of his theological views was cold and harsh; and in Church principles he was remarkably deficient. Before the revolutionary war he was assistant-minister of Trinity Church, New-York, but had retired in 1770 from the work, and lived for fourteen years on a small farm in Dutchess county.* To this step he was led in part by his violent political feelings, which made him unwilling to hold any preferment under British influence, and in part by the extreme unpopularity of his ministry. It was urged commonly against him that he brought forward with but little prominence those peculiar features of the Christian dispensation which are usually distinguished as the doctrines of grace. There seems to have been too much foundation for the charge. The language of his own defence is by no means satisfactory. He was accused, he says, of endeavoring to sap the foundations of Christianity, because he made a point of preaching the doctrines of morality, guarding his flock at the same time against " placing such an unbounded reliance on the merits of Christ as to think their own endeavors quite unnecessary, and not in the least available to salvation." This language savors of a most dangerous school, and implies no small indistinctness as to Christian truth. Morality, indeed, in its highest sense, the Christian teacher must always enforce, and he must lead men to be most strenuous in " their own endeavors" after salvation, " working" it " out with fear and trembling ;" but not as if (which this mode of speech implies) there were some opposition between the fullest statement of Christian doctrines and the enforcement of morality ; or between laboring heartily themselves, and " placing an unbounded reliance on the merits of Christ."

He was elected for consecration as the first Bishop of New-York, chiefly, as it seems, because his known democratic opinions were likely to make it an unsuspected and even popular choice. But zealous Christian men in different parts viewed the appointment with unfeigned sorrow, fearing that he was inclined to opinions of little less

* Life of Bishop Hobart by M'Vickar, p. 296.

than a Socinian character. His conduct during his episcopate did not materially lessen these impressions to his disadvantage. It could not be denied that he was to a great extent, cold and indistinct in doctrine, distant and reserved in personal bearing, and indolent and inactive in his work. Against Bishop Seabury, whose opinions and character were ine very respect most unlike his own, he was strongly prejudiced, and long denied the validity of his consecration, even though in this he stood almost alone amongst his own clergy, and when the neighboring states had received as pastors those whom his eastern brother had ordained. Most happily for the infant Church, the mild urbanity of Bishop White checked this discord and prevented the threatened separation; and from this time, though there was little sympathy of feeling, yet they acted in concert till the death of Bishop Seabury in 1786. Bishop Provoost's own public life lasted little longer. In September 1800 he resigned the incumbency of Trinity church; and in the following year he called together the diocesan convention, and resigned to it his episcopal jurisdiction. Different causes led him to this step. He had little sense of the spiritual greatness of his charge, no burning ardor in fulfilling it; its duties pressed heavily upon an inactive temperament; he had long withdrawn himself from all but those which he could not escape; and the loss of his wife in 1799, and his son in 1800, induced him at once to retire from the discharge of an office which he felt to be an irksome burden rather than a blessing.

His resignation led to anxious debates in the general convention, and the house of bishops refused to allow what they thought might be an unseemly and inconvenient precedent. They acted, however, so far upon it, that they agreed to consecrate Dr. Benjamin Moore as his assistant now, and his successor at his death. Much good resulted from this choice. Bishop Moore was a man of tender gentleness of character; and the vigor and determination of his successor would probably have suited the temper of events less than his winning mildness. Under the rule of his predecessor all had been dormant, if not apathetic. Of this lethargic character had been his temper who should have been the spring of life and energy in others. Bare toleration seemed to Bishop Provoost all that could be hoped for by a body branded with the stigma of British descent. They who invite suspicion and contempt are seldom slow in meeting with them. So it was now: common opinion looked suspiciously upon the Church, and the sense of this oppressed its members. Neither the clergy nor the laity ever rose under him to any sense of the importance of their position. The apostolic gentleness of Bishop Moore brooded with a loving energy over the scattered and disheartened flock, and prepared the way for a better state of things. During the ten years of his episcopate, though there was little evident increase, there was a gradual upgrowth of sounder principles within his diocese.

On no other side was there the same amount of promise. Maryland* was at this time, and until 1816, under the charge of Bishop Claggett, a mild and courteous ruler, and a zealous Christian minister; but wanting somewhat of that habitual firmness which was needful to give tone to his episcopate. His flock, as we have seen,† was in a languishing condition; it was, moreover, sorely harrassed by internal disputes; parties ran high within it, and it seemed as if the unity of the spirit had departed from the land. Bishop Claggett could scarcely repress the feuds which were rife among his clergy; and as soon as opportunity allowed, they broke out into visible dissensions.

The opportunity too soon occurred. For twenty years Bishop Claggett had been overburthened by the united weight of those cares which belong to a laborious parish priest and those which press upon a faithful bishop. Such an incongruous union, which breaks down prematurely the best men, is almost universal in America. While the fear of exalting the class of prelates has led some conventions (that, for instance, of Virginia) to make the retention of a parish-cure imperative upon a bishop, the need of securing a certain income to support the episcopate has made this the general custom. " Episcopal funds," to

---

* From Dr. Hawks's Memorials, Maryland, Preface.
† P. 176.

meet this want, have, indeed, often been proposed; but, except in the diocese of New York, they have never met with full success; and thus they on whom is laid the charge of government and the daily "care of all the churches," are obliged, at the same time, to serve the most laborious cures in order to secure themselves a necessary income.

Worn out by such labors, yet unwilling wholly to desert his post, Bishop Claggett, after twenty years of service, applied, in 1812, for a suffragan to share his toils. The right of electing a bishop is lodged by the constitution of the American Church in the diocesan convention; their choice is submitted to the general convention, if it be the year of its session, and if approved by it, is acted on by the bishops. In the recesses of the general convention, a majority of the "standing committees" of all the dioceses in union must approve of the choice before the bishops consecrate. By the rule of election in the state of Maryland, a vote by ballot of two-thirds of the clergy in session nominates the clergyman to fill the vacant see: this nomination then becomes the subjcet of a ballot among the lay deputies; and if two-thirds of them approve of it, the bishop elect is nominated to the president of the house of bishops, who collects the opinions either of that body or of the standing committees of the union.

When Bishop Claggett's message reached the diocesan convention, they proceeded to a ballot, and Dr. Kemp was nominated for the office. He was a native of Scotland, born of pious parents attached to the Presbyterian kirk. What first changed his religious views is now entirely unknown. In his youth the Episcopal oommunion was oppressed in Scotland by the severest penal laws; and when he was first permitted to attend its services, he was wont to be led blindfold to the house of prayer, lest he should afterwards prove a traitor, and expose his fellow-worshippers to the severe enactments of a persecuting code. Probably this attachment to the Church led to his emigration to America. Here he lived for some years as private tutor in a respectable family of Maryland; in 1789 he was ordained by Bishop White both deacon and priest; and having been the year before chosen to the associate rectorship of St. Paul's, Baltimore, was now, by a majority of clerical suffrages, nominated as assistant bishop to Dr. Claggett. This nomination, however, was negatived by the lay delegates, and the convention adjourned before any choice was made. At the convention of the following year the equal strength of the two parties prevented all attempts to make a nomination; and when, in 1814, Dr. Kemp's election was carried by a constitutional majority, the defeated party charged his friends with the grossest fraud, and stirred up a bitter and lasting opposition to the elected suffragan. He, however, made good his ground. The house of bishops rejected a protest laid before them by his enemies; and in the eastern coast of the diocese of Maryland, which was specially committed to him, his temper and his zeal soon gained him the esteem of all good men.

Yet the embers of ill-will which had been stirred up in this contest broke out afresh into a flame at every opportunity. A party in the Church besought Dr. Provoost, the retired bishop of New-York, to consecrate one of their number in opposition to Bishop Kemp; and the strife was not allayed till it had led to the suspension of the chief opponent of the choice; and even then it only slept. Bishop Kemp, indeed, succeeded without question to the see on Dr. Claggett's death; but when he in turn was, in 1827,* gathered to his fathers, the strife was renewed. In the convention of the following year three fruitless attempts to nominate a bishop prolonged the strife; five such followed in the convention of 1829. In 1830, a compromise between the hostile parties seated Dr. Stone upon the bishop's seat, which for full seven years he occupied with a meek quietness which might have stilled the spirit of division; but the meeting of convention shortly after his death, soon showed that it was unallayed. The synod was opened with a most touching address, prepared for delivery by Bishop Stone; but now, in consequence of his decease, read by another. From its words of peace the convention

* Bishop Kemp's death was sudden and violent, owing to the overturning of the carriage in which he was returning from the general convention.

passed to bitterness and strife. Each party put its candidate in nomination; and though the two principals agreed in recommending a third party for the office, their adherents would permit no compromise. After twenty fruitless ballotings, a bishop was still unappointed. The see was declined by one presbyter of New-York (Dr. Eastburn), and one missionary bishop (Dr. Kemper), and in 1838 was still untenanted.

In all this narrative we seem scarcely to be reading the annals of that Church which glories in possessing the apostles' "doctrine and fellowship." Rather do we seem engaged with the perverse wranglings of the adherents of some worldly sect. But it is, in fact, a striking comment on that intertwining of lower principles with the single thread of apostolic order which weakened at so many points the Western Church. It was the result of allowing men to organise themselves, and so become and remain a headless diocese; instead of sending the Church to them as the constituted ordinance of God.

While there was this distempered life in Maryland, in the neighboring state of Delaware there was almost the apathy of death. This was one of those American anomalies—a diocese without a bishop. It seems to have been constituted a diocese in 1785; but the episcopal chair had never yet been filled. The cause of this does not appear; but it was probably the want of funds to support the office. In 1803, Delaware proposed to the Maryland convention, that the eastern shore of that state should with itself constitute a new diocese. The application was declined; and with it seem to have ended all their efforts for this object. Religion was at the lowest ebb. Before the Revolution, matters had been widely different. Numerous congregations had been wont, throughout that district, to worship in goodly churches their fathers' God. Of these buildings many have perished utterly; many are still in ruins. "The traveller," says Dr. Hawks,* "in going down the line that separates Delaware from Maryland, might at a recent period have seen within a few miles of

---

* Memorials of Maryland, p. 354.

that line the tottering remains of five churches, and the spots on which had stood three or four others. There are few things more calculated to touch the soul of a pious Churchman than to journey over those southern states, and to mark the crumbling remains of ruined temples that attest the piety of our forefathers. More than once have we paused in our travel to step aside, and stand alone within the roofless and, perchance, shattered walls of some house of God that caught our eye and lured us from the road. There is a sermon in the very stillness of the quiet air around the hallowed spot, as one sits down on some half-sunken tombstone, and, in the calm loveliness of one of those bright and beautiful days that belong to a southern clime, calls up the scene of former times, and fills that forsaken church with the worshippers of a buried generation."

The state of things in Delaware was desolate indeed. The whole peninsula on which it stands,—which includes the state of Delaware, the east shore of Maryland, and two counties of Virginia,—contained, at the time of making this request, but nineteen clergymen. In 1827 they had dwindled to fifteen; and there was still almost forty churches in a fit state for worship, surviving the wreck of time to testify against a love which had grown cold, and a candlestick already well removed from its place, It is surely worth notice, that the districts in which Church principles had long been lowest were those in which piety the soonest flagged. So it was in Maryland, and so it was in the neighboring diocese of Virginia. From this state had come the strongest opposition to the distinctive features of the Church. It was a Virginian deputy who proposed to omit the first four petitions of the Litany; it was Virginia which resisted the rubric allowing the clergy to expel unfit communicants; it was Virginia which sent as lay deputy to the general convention a priest who had abandoned his orders; Virginia headed the opposition to the Athanasian Creed; directed her representative, by an unanimous vote, to express "the highest disapprobation" of the proposed allowance of a negative to the house of bishops; and declared her bishops "amenable to their conventions;" it was in Virginia that clergymen were found who began to substitute extemporaneous prayer for the appointed Litany;* it was in Virginia, also, that deadness to all spiritual things was the most perceptible. One name amongst her clergy is still fresh in the grateful remembrance of the few surviving members of his flock. Devereux Jarratt, ordained in London in 1762, returned the same year to Virginia; and till his death, in 1801, never ceased doing faithfully the work of an evangelist. Earnest, simple, and eminently heavenly-minded, his ministry was greatly blessed by God; "his converts were exceedingly numerous; and a few aged disciples still living in Virginia acknowledge him as their spiritual father."† But, alas, he seems long to have stood literally alone; "at his first answer no man stood with him:" and the final loss of the glebes almost made the Church low.

This disastrous conclusion of the long struggle between their united enemies and Churchmen took place in the year 1804. Its last stages were remarkable. In 1799 an act had passed the assembly of Virginia, professedly intended "to declare the construction of the bill of rights and constitution concerning religion;" but really meant to repeal every act favorable to the Church which had passed since the Revolution. This was followed by another in January 1802, by which it was declared that the title to the property the Church had held before the Revolution was vested in the state at large; and that, whenever they were vacant, the glebes should be sold for the benefit of the poor of the parish. Under this law those acts which always mark confiscation followed. The glebes were sold at prices merely nominal; and the small sums which did accrue from them flowed into various channels of private profit. The churchyards, and the churches with their furniture, were exempted from the operations of this law; yet they, and even the communion-plate, were seized and sold. The fruits of this confiscation are still to be found. "Within our own time," says Dr. Hawks, "a reckless sensualist has administered

---

* Dr. Hawks's Memorials, Virginia, pp. 269, 270.
† Henshaw's Life of Bp. Moore, p. 15.

the morning dram to his guests from the silver cup which has often contained the consecrated symbol of his Saviour's blood. In another instance the entire set of communion-plate of one of the old churches is in the hands of one who belongs to the society of Baptists." The Bishop of Virginia, when on his visitation, has witnessed the conversion of a marble baptismal font into a trough for horses.*

The act under which these offences were committed did not pass without a struggle. When adopted, its constitutional legality was questioned, and its enforcement resisted by processes of law. The decision of the lower courts was on the side of confiscation. This judgment was carried by appeal before the highest tribunal of Virginia. This court consisted of five judges, of whom four only (one as a Churchman, deeming himself an interested party) sat upon this trial. Of these Judge Pendleton was by seniority the president. His judgment, and that of two of his assessors, was against the courts below; and he was about to reverse the previous sentence, and so, in fact, repeal this most injurious law. The morning came on which the final sentence was to be pronounced, when Judge Pendleton, who was already past fourscore, was found dead in his bed from a stroke of apoplexy. In his pocket was discovered the decision which another day would have made law, securing to the Church the full possession of her glebes; but it had not been pronounced, and so was void of all authority. The case was heard again before Judge Pendleton's successor. His judgment was the other way; and thus (Judge Fleming still refusing to take part) the court was equally divided. The decree from below was therefore officially confirmed, and its property taken for ever from the Church.

Some good and wise end was doubtless answered by this reverse; but its present effect was most disastrous. It extinguished wholly the spirit of Churchmen, and was followed by a complete prostration of hope and exertion. How entire this was has been already seen. One more instance may be mentioned.† In the year 1722, within

---

* Hawk's Virginia, p. 236.
† Ibid. p. 267.

six counties of what is termed the northern neck of Virginia, there were more than twelve churches, all supplied with the ministrations of the Gospel. Almost a hundred years had passed, and instead of any growth throughout an extent of country one hundred miles long and fifteen broad, every church and chapel had been forsaken. The road to the Chesapeake was studded with mouldering ruins of what had once been houses of the Lord; and if here and there one or two seemed at first sight to maintain their fair proportions, a closer examination showed that it was only that the piety of earlier days had built them of a massive strength,* which had enabled them thus long to resist the injuries of time.

Such was the deadly trance which had fallen on the Church. From such a state Bishop Madison was not the man to rouse it. He was an elegant scholar, with no great warmth of Christian character, and a low estimate of the spiritual power inherent in the office which he held. How far he was fit to discharge its arduous duties in that day of reproach, may be gathered from the fact that he obtained the eulogies of Thomas Jefferson, the deist in religion, and in politics the man who purchased the votes of the opponents of the Church† by so framing the constitution of Virginia as to refuse corporate powers to all religious societies, and thus prevent their holding property at all. Bishop Madison seems to have felt his own unfitness for the post he filled. At first, indeed, he manifested some activity; but his early efforts were not crowned with success, and he had not energy enough to persevere without such direct and sensible encouragement. In 1805 he applied to his diocese for an assistant bishop; the subject was deferred until the convention reassembled in the following year. It was never resumed;—for the convention never sat again within his lifetime. During fifteen years of his Episcopate the state of things grew more and more disastrous: " he seemed to be like a pilot with his ship amongst

---

* These churches are built of bricks which were brought from the mother country. Many such still remain, needing little more than a roof to render them fit for immediate use.

† Voice from America, p. 30.

the breakers, who in despair resigns the helm, in expectation that his noble barque will soon be stranded as a shattered wreck upon the shore."*

"It was the dark day of the Church, when all slumbered and slept."† They owed their awakening from this slumber to that office which Virginia had so greatly undervalued; for it may be clearly traced, under the blessing of Almighty God, to the appointment and devoted labors of another bishop.

* Dr. Henshaw's Life of Bishop Moore, p. 112.
† Dr. Hawks.

CHAPTER IX.

1811, 12.

Death of Bp. Madison—Renewal of diocesan convention—Election of Dr. Bracken to the episcopate—He refuses it—Dr. Moore elected—His early life—Ministerial success—He visits the diocese—Stirs up the spirit of Churchmen—Revival of the Church—Growth of Church principles—Improved canons—Theological seminary founded—And poor scholars' fund—Dr. Meade elected Suffragan, with a restriction—Conduct of the house of bishops—Removal of restrictions—Bishop B. Moore of New-York applies for an assistant bishop—Dr. J. H. Hobart elected—His origin and youth—First ministerial charge in Pennsylvania—Removes to New-York—His studies—Publications—Services in state and general convention—Controversy with Dr. Mason—Elected bishop—Opposition—Bishop Provoost's claim to the bishopric of New York—Disallowed by the convention—Bishop White's treatment of Bishop Hobart—And high esteem for him.

THE dark day through which our recent history has taken us began at last to break away, and, at the period we have reached, the sky already glowed in many different directions. The old generation was passing away. The deists who, with Thomas Jefferson to head them, had long held undisputed sway, no longer carried every thing before them. There had been a secret upgrowth of a better race, and in the Church, as well as elsewhere, men of another temper took their places on the stage. Both among the laity and clergy, the cold and timid councils of the former generation were beginning to give way to energy and zeal. In Virginia, Bishop Madison expired in March 1812; and the first sign of vitality within the diocese was the meeting of the convention to elect his successor. It was now seven years since it had assembled; and in a state which of old could number its hundred clergy, and which required the attendance of fifteen to make a quorum, and the presence of twenty-five to pass any canon, thirteen clergymen and twelve laymen were all who could be brought together,* Having voted nine a quorum, they proceeded to elect a bishop, and chose Dr. Bracken. When the convention met the following year (1813), it was to hear that Dr. Bracken had declined their offer. This was a disheartening answer. The few who had assembled did not proceed to make another choice ; but feeling strongly their well-nigh hopeless destitution, they drew up an address urging on their brethren the duty of making fresh exertions in their common cause. This " most earnestly entreated them to consider the necessity of adopting zealous measures for the restoration of religion," especially as, " from the destitute state of the churches, many piously disposed persons who were attached to the doctrine, worship, and discipline of the Protestant Episcopal Church, were deprived of the means of worshipping God according to her venerable forms, to the great unhappiness of themselves, as well as to the great detriment of the Church at large ;" it besought them " to raise a fund for the purpose of aiding in the support of such clergymen of piety and talents as may be obtained to perform divine service in such districts in the state as may be assigned to them by the convention."

In May 1814 the annual convention re-assembled ; seven clergymen and seventeen laymen met in council,† and proceeded to elect a bishop. They felt the great importance of the crisis, and looked far around them for the qualities they needed. They plainly saw that it was not a time when a merely blameless life or classical attainments would be enough for him who, amidst their busy and disordered population, was to sit on the apostles' seat. After full deliberation, they elected Dr. Richard Moore, rector of St. Stephen's church, in the city of New-York. They had been guided to a happy choice. Dr. Moore had received a classical education, but at the close of the war of independence he entered on the medical profession, and followed it for nearly nine years. His childhood had been

---

* Journals of Virginian Convention, p. 181.
† Vide supra, p. 239.

marked by sincere and decided piety; and though this had seemed for a while "choked" by the cares of other things, and he entered upon life too much like other men, yet he was not long suffered to wander, but in early manhood was recalled to the service of the Cross. For a while he continued in the practice of medicine, but his soul now thirsted for the labors and rewards of the Christian ministry; and at the time of the Church's most entire prostration, when there was least, in possession or in prospect, to gratify ambition, he yielded to those guiding impulses, quitted his more lucrative profession, and determined to prepare for holy orders. In 1787 he was admitted deacon by Bishop Provoost, being the first ordained by him,—the first therefore ever set apart for this high calling in New-York,—and making then the sixth clergyman in that large diocese, which has now for several years numbered more than its 200. The blessing of a religious youth rested on the new-made deacon; within this same Church he had been baptised into the name of Jesus Christ, confirmed, in due season, in the faith, and first admitted to the holy eucharist. From it he went forth to his work in the fulness of the blessing of the gospel of peace. His first field of labor was on Staten Island, where for one-and-twenty years he was rector of St. Andrew's. An unusual increase crowned his ministerial labors; although he raised before his flock a high standard of pastoral piety, yet no fewer than 100 new communicants were gathered in one year around the altar of his church. In 1809 he moved to St. Stephen's, on the outskirts of his native city of New-York. Here all was yet in its infancy. About thirty families attended, and the communicants numbered not more than twenty. For five years he labored among them; and when called to the Virginian episcopate, he left behind him a body of 400 communicants.

When the see was first offered to him, he shrunk from the charge, and refused to leave New-York. Many circumstances added weight to that Christian diffidence which might well lead any man to shun, as far as lawfully he may, the perilous height of the episcopate. Moore, though devoted with all the ardor of feelings more than usually warm to the distinctive doctrines of the gospel of God's grace, and even laboring from this cause under some reproach from men of a colder and more unimpassioned temper, was yet conscientiously attached to the distinctive principles of his own communion. Previous to his settling there, the chief families of Richmond had formed " a kind of joint spiritual charge, watched over with alternate services by an Episcopalian and a Presbyterian."* The invitations which he now received hinted at the probable expediency of some concessions to sectarian feelings, and took for granted from his well-known character, that he would be a likely man to further their adoption. It was notorious that there were points on which his judgment had differed widely from that of Bishop Hobart; that he had encouraged, under due restrictions, social meetings for prayer; that he favored meetings of the clergy for the purpose of devotion; and that he maintained such doctrine as found utterance in the following letter to his future coadjutor :—" That we are too cold is a solemn truth. To remedy this evil is in our power, provided we will seek the aid of God's Holy Spirit in sincere and fervent prayer; and I am persuaded that if we HONESTLY call upon God to assist us with His grace, and honestly preach His OWN word, He will make that word quick and powerful to the conversion of those who hear it."† But these principles implied no bias to sectarian views : and so his correspondents soon discovered.

" The state," they tell him, " of the Church in Virginia is indeed most deplorable. The desolations of many generations are to be repaired—now is the trying and critical moment—now is to be decided whether God means to keep a remnant of our Church alive among us, or to destroy it entirely. The town of Richmond contains by far the largest body of Episcopalians in the southern country. If some one of suitable talents and real piety does not go there, it will either fall into the hands of some miserable creature (many of whom have already been fawning for it), or, if a

* Life of Bishop Moore.
† Letter to Mr., afterwards Bishop Meade,—Life of Bishop Moore, p. 98. The capitals are the bishop's.

clever Presbyterian should offer, they will throw away Episcopacy, and fall under his banners. And if Episcopacy dies there at the heart, of course it dies elsewhere. . . Certain I am, that unless we have a bishop of real piety, zeal, and talents in Richmond, Episcopacy is gone for ever."

The apprehension of these dangers so fully occupied the minds of these good men as to incline them to attempt to tread the fatal path of compromise and false conciliation. "The Church," they say, "in Virginia," (for it is always under this delusion that this temptation is disguised), "is in a peculiar situation. Its having been once the established Church, the prevalence and virulence of other denominations, the sequestration of its glebes, the irregularity of the lives of its ministers, and various political causes, have combined to swell high the tide of public opinion, and indeed of odium, against her public form of service, her surplices, and all the paraphernalia of clerical costume. . . . . Under these circumstances, to hearts thus constructed, it appears to me that no man can carry out our forms in all their rubrical vigor with any prospect of success. . . . . We want a bishop who will watch over his clergy with tears and tenderness; who will be an example as well as teacher to his flock; ·who will know nothing amongst us save Jesus Christ and Him crucified; and who, whilst he inculcates a due reverence for our venerable forms of doctrine, discipline, and worship, as being of apostolic authority, will at the same time direct his best endeavors towards the end of all religious institutions, namely, the deliverance of immortal souls from hell. Such a bishop will have our co-operation, our love, and our prayers."

The temptation was here masked in much to which the warm heart of Moore was sure readily to answer; but it was put aside without hesitation.

"The prejudices," he tells his correspondent, "which are entertained by many of the Virginians against the services of the Church and the appropriate costume of the clergy, afford matter of considerable surprise to a person bred in this part of the union. . . . Educated in the bosom of the Episcopal Church, I have always been taught to entertain the most profound respect for all her services.

.... Let the ministers of the Church tread in the steps of their divine Master; let them visit the sick and bind up the broken-hearted; let the poor of Christ's flock be the objects of their care; and I will venture to predict that the mountains of opposition will, in a little time, become plain; the Prayer-book will be venerated, our ceremonies approved, the cause of the Church will be promoted, and penitent sinners will seek for an asylum in our bosom."

To these principles he adhered throughout the correspondence, steadily maintaining, at the same time, his first position, that he would not come "on trial;" but if elected rector of Richmond, he would then, with the approbation of the Bishop of New-York, accept the offered charge.

An application to Bishop Hobart as to the character of Moore drew forth the assurance, that from "the confidence felt in his fidelity to his principles, and in his prudent and zealous efforts to advance the interests of the Church, he would remove to Virginia with the regret of him whose diocese he quitted, and with the good wishes and prayers of his brethren generally."

The Virginians at length assented to his terms; and his bishop judging that he ought not to refuse what was pressed on him with such urgency, he was chosen rector of the Monumental Church in Richmond; and (which had never befallen a clergyman residing in another diocese) was, directly after, elected by convention, to the vacant see.

On the 18th of May, 1814, he was consecrated to the office of a bishop in St. James's Church, Philadelphia. Bishop Hobart, in the consecration-sermon, ventured to predict that "the night of adversity had passed, and that a long and splendid day was now dawning on the Church in Virginia." And a little further on he adds, addressing publicly the newly elected bishop, "How fervent will be our thanks to God, who hath made you the instrument of this great good!"

Much was expected from his labors; and the expectation was not disappointed. The bishop set to work at once in the visitation of his diocese; and wherever he went, his fervent spirit awoke the slumbering energies of those to whom he came. He returned to report to the convention of 1815 the rising promise of the Church. Some of its first-fruits might be seen in the increased attendance at this synod of the diocese, at which the number present exactly doubled that of the preceding year. He encouraged them to seek and look for great results: he told them of the earnest desire which he had found in many districts to repair the waste places of their fathers' Church: of parishes which had seemed wholly extinct suddenly aroused to life and vigor; of others where the whole congregation had burst into tears as he spoke to them of the ancient glory and present desolation of their Church.

The bishop did not raise his voice in vain. The laity were manifestly roused. From parish after parish he received earnest applications for a resident minister. In the succeeding year ten new churches were reported as in progress of erection, and eight formerly dismantled as now under repair. His own labors were unabated. He traversed the whole diocese repeatedly; crossing the mountains of the Blue Ridge, and even advancing to aid the destitute state of North Carolina. His tone of preaching was earnest, affectionate, and simple. It raised the Cross of Christ and His salvation before the eyes of all; and God gave him the hearts of men. His zeal was contagious; and zealous pastors of the flock quickly gathered round him.

The younger clergy undertook the work of missionaries in the widely scattered field, and collected new congregations throughout all the province, whilst he had the joy of sending many fresh laborers into his Master's vineyard. Many were the dry and withered hearts which were thus awoke to Christian life and gladness. This was the especial work of Bishop Moore; and a blessed work it was. But there still was little done to impress on their disjointed body the sense of its unity, to gather up its scattered parts into a living and self-conscious whole. Here and there, indeed, there were signs of returning life. There were faint reachings forth after discipline and order; some irregularities were laid aside. A few of the clergy, in the vain expectation of removing prejudice, had begun to substitute in part, unauthorised devotions for the service of the liturgy.

Against this the bishop raised his voice in timely warning, and led his convention strongly to condemn the practice.* Other tokens of improvement may be found. In the year 1815, the offensive canon which declared a bishop amenable to his convention had been rescinded : while new rules committed the trial of a bishop to his brethren in the sacred college, and specially provided, that " none but a bishop shall pronounce sentence of deposition or degradation from the ministry on any bishop, presbyter, or deacon."†

The time had been when, from a misplaced jealousy, Virginia had declared that every bishop should continue to discharge the duties of a parish priest ; but now, not only was this rule withdrawn, but it was proposed to found a fund for the episcopate, that no bishop might be kept by ministerial duties from his higher charge.

Another mark of life may be discovered in the new provision made for the education of the clergy. Two plans promoted this important end ; one, the foundation of a theological seminary, which has proved of the greatest value both in supplying candidates for the ministry, and also in raising the tone of clerical character; the other, the formation of a fund (in 1818) for the education of young men of piety, who were desirous of entering into holy orders. Such an institution was greatly needed in America, where there are few endowments left by the piety of earlier days. No discredit is attached to the student who is thus supported ; though he who is maintained by living benefactors cannot know the independence of the scholar of an English University. Yet this institution has proved most important ; it has opened a way to the ministry to those whose hearts longed for its sacred work, but whose narrow means would have made due preparation for its duties unattainable by them.‡ Nearly one-tenth of the clergy had, in 1836, in whole or in part, been assisted by this society ; one-sixth of the present clergy of Ohio, one-eighth of those of Pennsylvania, one-fifth of those of Maryland, and a large proportion of those in Virginia, had de-

* Journals of Virginia Convention.
† Acts of Convention in Virginia, 1815.
‡ Dr. Hawks (1836), note to Memorials, Virginia, p. 261.

rived aid from its funds, while it was still affording assistance to about one-seventh of all the students in the several theological schools of the Church in the United States. Many of the leading clergy in the west have owed their early training to this source.

All these were movements in the right direction. But much yet remained to be corrected. There still appear on the journals of convention notices which startle an English eye. Such are, the "grateful acceptance of Presbyterian and Baptist Churches for divine service during the session;"* the record of "churches nearly completed, but not exclusively episcopal;"† and the return of "forty communicants, only fifteen of whom may be considered members of the episcopal Church," whilst the attendance of members of "other denominations" is spoken of as "gladly witnessed and affectionately encouraged."‡

But perhaps the least favorable feature of the whole is the result of various contributions attempted at this time for the promotion of the common purposes of Churchmen. It is not that they were poor; for never was the Church of Christ so full of strength as when its poverty was deepest; never was it so truly rich as before it had gathered in the treasures of the earth. Such entries, therefore, as an extra vote of a few dollars for the unusual charge of the carriage-hire for a part of their bishop's visitation might bespeak times of primitive simplicity.§ But it is painful to know, that these things marked the Church's poverty when Churchmen were rich. This clearly bespoke some great want in their system.

It is painful to find the aged Bishop Moore "thanking his laity for the patronage extended by them to his clergy and himself;"‖ and the more so when we see the utter failure of all efforts to raise funds for the support of the episcopate. Year by year the subject was renewed, and always with the same result. In vain did conventions

---

* Journal of 1821.   † Ib., 1826.   ‡ Ib., 1827.

§ Of a like character is the notice of a horse, worth a hundred dollars, being left on hand by a missionary, who, after it had been purchased for him, declined that sphere of labor.

‖ Journal of 1832.

dwell upon the need of the bishop's "visiting every part of the diocese, encouraging the desponding, rousing the thoughtless, giving direction to the zeal and energy of the pious, and impressing upon the whole a salutary impulse;" in vain they urged that "words alone were cheap, and insufficient to make their cause flourish;" in vain did the aged bishop himself press on them, time after time, that he thought this "a matter of leading importance;" that the "wants of his own parish made his visitations in a diocese of 70,000 square miles in extent, hurried and ineffectual;" in vain did he, when his age made it impossible that he should reap any personal advantage from it, supplicate them earnestly to make provision for his successor,—still the proposed fund made no perceptible advance and scarcely could a few dollars be annually raised to supply him with assistance when he was well nigh worn out in their service.

The same evil may be traced as pressing with its heavy weight on the inferior clergy. The bishop traces* to their "inadequate support, their frequent removal from one parish to another; removals often attended with results injurious to the clergy, and always to the congregations left in a destitute state." He speaks "of the want of support producing uneasiness in their minds and paralysing their efforts," and of "extreme penury borne with silent suffering by the pious, excellent, and well educated clergyman."

These are painful features. Some of them are evils inherent in the voluntary system; some of them were the remains of the torpid numbness which had long entranced religion. But from these we turn gladly to the brighter prospect. There was a great rekindling of personal devotion. An ardent zeal largely pervaded the younger clergy; poor as was their earthly recompense, their ranks were now recruited from the best blood of Virginia, the most aristocratic district of the Union. Though still far too few for the population, their number was greatly on the increase. The seven who met in convention at the election of Bishop Moore had multiplied to thirty-five.

* Journal of 1835.

This was, in a great measure, his work. For fourteen years Bishop Moore continued, without interruption, his successful labors; and then feeling the infirmities of age beginning to abate his vigor, he applied in 1828, to his convention, begging them to nominate a clergyman for consecration as his suffragan. In the convention of the following year his wish was gratified by the election of the Rev. Wm. Meade to fill the office. It was, however, cogged with one unwise condition. Dr. Meade was elected suffragan only for the life of Bishop Moore; and on his death a new election was to nominate his absolute successor. Against this the house of bishops instantly protested; and as Virginia jealously maintained her own arrangement, a dispute, and probably a breach, appeared to be at hand; but it was happily avoided by the consecration of the suffragan elect, while the danger of the precedent was turned aside by the enactment of a general canon, which defined the office, and secured in every instance the succession of assistant-bishops. Virginia showed her sense of the judicious kindness of this treatment, by removing, in 1829, of her own act, the restriction she had placed on Dr. Meade's succession. In him Bishop Moore found a meet assistant and a worthy successor.

The two worked happily together; and, till the aged principal was gathered to his rest, he watched with full rejoicing over the prosperous labors of his younger coadjutor. "To the neighborhoods and distant congregations I once visited with great delight," he says, a little while before his end, "I have bidden, through the effects of infirmity, a final adieu; and it is only on the return of our conventional meetings that I am blessed with the sight of my old friends, and am permitted to shake by the hands a family of clergymen who have been set apart to the ministry of the Gospel by myself. From the record of the clergy of the diocese, I find that, out of sixty-six, forty-four have received the imposition of my own hands, and been clothed with ministerial authority by myself. Be determined," continues the aged bishop, "I beseech you, to make full proof of your ministry. Preach Jesus Christ and Him crucified. · In all your trials, my beloved sons, may the

Almighty be your place of refuge; and underneath you may He place the everlasting arms of his love."* With his " latest voice," it was, he declared, his own hope that he should " proclaim the riches of redeeming grace," and assert, in his " last moments," that " God is love."†

To keep unbroken the thread of Virginian history, we have followed out the life of Bishop Moore, and advanced far beyond the dates to which we must now return.

The blessing which Virginia thus received in 1814, had been given some years sooner, not only to New-York, but to the whole Church of North America, in the Episcopate of Dr. John Henry Hobart. For ten years after Bishop Provoost's resignation, New-York remained in the care of the gentle-hearted Bishop B. Moore. But, in March, 1811, an attack of paralysis brought his active labors to a sudden close. Feeling keenly his unfitness for the charge which rested on him, he called at once a special convention, and urged them to appoint an assistant-bishop, who should share or undertake the anxieties and labors of his post. The convention followed his advice; and proceeding at once to the election, nominated John Henry Hobart, one of the assistant-ministers of Trinity, New-York.

This was a turning-point in the history of the Western Church. Hobart was a man who at any time would have left on his communion an impress of his own character; in the unformed state of institutions and opinions in that land, it could not fail of being deeply and broadly marked. Identified as is his personal history with the great movement we have now to trace, we shall better understand his principles and influence, if we first mark the formation of his character, and the course of his life.‡

Hobart was sprung from the best of the old Puritan stock. His ancestor, the Rev. Peter Hobart, the son of

---

* Journals of Virginian Conventions.

† Life of Bishop Moore, p 210.

‡ The events of Bishop Hobart's life are drawn freely from Dr. M'Vickar's Memoir, except where a special reference indicates another source.

"parents eminient for piety,"* and himself "a painful servant of the Lord," settled at Massachusetts in 1635. He was "a person that met with many temptations and afflictions,"† and who, amongst the New-England worthies, bore away the palm for "well-studied sermons." Though so devoted to his views of truth that he quitted a beloved home to avoid what he esteemed the "blackening cloud of prelatical impositions," he was a man of a Catholic spirit; with a "heart knit in a most sincere and hearty love towards pious men, though they were not in all things of his own persuasion. He would admire the grace of God in good men, though they were of sentiments contrary unto his, and would say, I can carry them in my bosom." There were none, indeed, from whom he so much turned away, as those amongst his own people, "who, under a pretence of zeal for Church-discipline, were very pragmatical in controversies; but at the same time most unjust creatures, destitute of the life and power of godliness." These he would bridle with the saying: "Some men are all Church and no Christ."

Of his race proceeded a goodly company of preachers; amongst whom the Apostolic Brainerd must be mentioned as his daughter's son. From this Peter Hobart, sprung in the fourth generation the future bishop of New-York: and in many traits of character the stamp of the old pilgrim-father was repeated in him. His immediate parents had migrated to Philadelphia, and rejoined the ancient Church of their old English forefathers. There his early youth was spent beneath the pastoral charge of the venerable Bishop White. It was a youth of the fairest promise; the joy and hope of his early-widowed mother. At the close of his education he was almost drawn into a life of business. But better things were in store for him; and the guiding Hand led him, instead, to devote his energy and powers to the ministry of Christ's Church. His preparation for its duties was patient and severe. The head of his college wished him to begin by studying a system of

---

* Cotton Mather's Magnalia, b. iii. p. 153.
† Ibid. p. 155.

divinity; but from this easier mode of obtaining a general dogmatic accuracy, the healthy instincts of his soul revolted; and complaining of the plan of "studying Scripture to support preconceived opinions," he wisely resolved " to take up systems when he had gone through the study of the Bible." After due preparation he presented himself for ordination before the good old man by whom he had already been first received at the font, and then confirmed by the laying on of hands; and from him received his orders and mission as a minister of Christ. Truly humble was his estimate of himself: " I am far from thinking that I am qualified for the ministry either in mental or spiritual acquirements. . . I am afraid that my views are not sufficiently pure. . . Sacred and awful will be my duties; the grace of God can alone enable me to execute them. . . . Oh, pray with me, that I may have a single eye to His glory and the salvation of immortal souls; that He would subdue within me every desire of honor, emolument, or human praise; and that I may serve Him with sincerity and truth."* With such self-suspicion did he turn away from those paths which would have led him straight to earthly fame, and addict himself to the humble walk of the American ministry.

He was ordained, in 1798, to the charge of two small parishes within the diocese of Pennsylvania; one of them amongst the earliest gathered in that district by the missionary labors of George Keith; and still, to the grief of its young pastor, a " dispersed flock, with little zeal, and much intermixed with other denominations."† Here he stayed a year; and having thence removed, first to New Brunswick, and then to Hampstead in Long Island, he settled, in the autumn of 1800, as assistant-minister of Trinity Church, New-York. This was a prominent situation, and one to which, under common circumstances, no deacon of two years could have aspired; since New-York might be considered the metropolis of North America, and Trinity stood at the head of all its churches.‡ Unlike the

---

* M'Vickar's Life, p. 152.
† Letter to the Rev. E Grant,—M'Vickar's Life, p. 170.
‡ Before the Revolution it stood 146 feet in length, 72 in width,

rest, its revenues were ample, having been endowed by Lord Cornbury, the royal governor, with a farm, which is now covered by the increasing town. Its ministers had always been the leading men of their body.* Here, then, Hobart took his station, and was soon conspicuous for the zealous assiduity with which he discharged its duties. Though when he first settled in New-York he " panted for the country," and thought that he " could never like a city," yet he was soon fixed in it for life ; declining a call to his native town because he possessed where he was " every opportunity for the exercise of whatever means of usefulness" he could command.

These opportunities were manifold. As a preacher he rose quickly to the highest rank ; in pastoral visits, and the distracting detail of ministerial life, he was active and unwearied : and yet for the labors of his study he saved many hours by late watching and early application, and snatched others by ready diligence from the intervals of busy days.

"His earliest residence was a very small two-story house, the rear of which was rendered airy by the proximity of the river. The attic chamber here formed his study, as being the most retired and quiet spot in the house, with windows looking out over the noble expanse of the Hudson to the opposite shores of Jersey, and having for the back-ground of the view the distant hills of Springfield.

" In this little sanctum, surrounded, or, to speak more justly, walled in, by piles of folios and heaps of pamphlets, through the zig-zag mazes of which it was no easy matter

---

and with a spire of 180 feet in height. In 1776, in common with the city round it, it was consumed by fire, and lay in ruins through the war of the Revolution. A new church was built in 1788, which though 42 feet shorter, was of a higher character than its predecessor. This, in its turn, has given place to the present imposing structure.

* Rev. Charles Inglis, D. D. (afterwards first Bishop of Nova Scotia) . . . . . . was rector from 1777 to 1783.
    Right Rev. S. Provoost . . .   1783 to 1800.
    Right Rev. B. Moore . . . . . . 1800 to 1816.
    Right Rev. J. H. Hobart . . .   1811 to 1830.

for a stranger to make his way, you might find the young theologian entrenched, and passing every minute both of the day and night that could be snatched from sleep and hasty meals, or spared from the higher claims of parochial duty. These latter interruptions were so numerous, that by one less vigorously resolute in gathering up the scattered crumbs of time, they would have been pleaded as a sufficient apology for the remission of all study beyond necessary preparation for the pulpit."*

But this was far from Mr. Hobart's habit. From this study proceeded many devotional and other works, some original, and some remodelled by his pen; and here he devised, and, till his accession to the episcopate, conducted, "The Churchman's Magazine," a monthly publication which contributed in no slight measure to raise the principles and hopes of those to whom it was addressed. To these more private occupations he added the discharge of public duties. He was early† elected secretary to the diocesan convention of New-York; and chosen one of the deputies to represent the diocese in the general convention which met the same year. In each department he was at once distinguished as a man of business. From 1801 till 1811 he discharged the duties of the first, and was always re-elected to the second. He was also annually chosen on the standing committee of the diocese.

But it was not in this course of labor, useful as it was, that his chief services were rendered. To understand these we must look more closely into his character and principles, and see their peculiar action on the state of things around him. He came, then, to New-York when the universal tone of thought and feeling in the body which he joined was low and torpid. The impression of their first bishop's character was plainly legible upon the Churchmen of New-York: with indistinct views of Christian doctrine; moralists for the most part, rather than believers; conscious of being objects of suspicion, and almost thinking that suspicion just,—they never ventured in defending their position beyond the cautious tone of timid apology.

* M'Vickar's Life. † In 1801.

In this state Hobart found matters; but their continuance in this state he would not endure. Trained in a Presbyterian college, he was a Churchman on the fullest conviction of his reason. He early declared* his own principles to run up in brief into these two: "That we are saved from the guilt and dominion of sin by the divine merits and grace of a crucified Redeemer; and that the merits and grace of this Redeemer are applied to the soul of the believer by devout and humble participation in the ordinances of the Church, administered by a priesthood who derive their authority by regular transmission from Christ, the divine Head of the Church, and the source of all the power in it."

Many a sleeper must have been startled by such a voice as this, whether true or false in its announcement, from one resolute, and thoroughly in earnest; and Hobart was both. He was convinced that this was the truth, and he was ready to live or to die for it. All his ministry spoke this conviction. In the pulpit " he warned, counselled, entreated, and comforted, with intense power and energy. His manner and voice struck you with the deep interest which pervaded his soul for their salvation. He appeared . . . as a herald from the other world, standing between the dead and the living . . entreating perishing sinners not to reject the message of reconciliation which the Son of the living God so graciously offered for their acceptance."† "He never ceased to preach 'Christ crucified,' the only Saviour of sinners; and to exhort them, 'even with tears,' to lay hold upon that salvation, by entering into covenant with Him in that Church which He had purchased with His blood."‡ And what he was in the pulpit he was everywhere; by the sick-bed or in society, abroad or at home, this was still his watch-word—"The Gospel in the Church," "Evangelical truth and apostolical order:" these he pressed on all as the subjects closest to his own heart, and the most concerning theirs. The awakening sleepers of his own communion

---

* Preface to a Companion to the Altar, by J. H. Hobart. 1804.
† Letter to the Rev. T. Chalmers, D. D., on the Life and Character of the Right Rev. Dr. Hobart, by Archdeacon Strachan.
‡ Dr. M'Vickar, p. 187.

could not understand him; and feeling only his warmth reprove their coldness, they knew not whether to reproach him as a " High Churchman or Methodist." Still he rose daily in general esteem. His sincerity could not be questioned, and none could doubt his kindness; whilst his talents for business were seen and felt by all. Hence his constant re-election as secretary to his own, and delegate to the general, convention.

Other effects also were soon visible. The cold timidity which had benumbed all men began to pass away. He was gathering round him a band of younger men, laity as well as clergy, of a new temper—men who believed that Christ had indeed founded a spiritual kingdom, and that they had functions in it to discharge, and powers with which to fulfil them. The fruit of this was soon seen on all sides; in the increased attendance on conventions; the growing snpport of Church societies; and, which was far better, in the new religious earnestness of all. It is clear that he was raised up to do a special work; to consolidate and bind together the loose and crumbling mass; to raise the general tone; to animate their zeal; to save them from the fatal apathy into which they were subsiding.

But this change could not pass on his own communion and not be felt abroad. The Church of that day was utterly depressed. The time, indeed, was in some degree gone by, when the " prejudices against the name and office of a bishop were such as to make it doubtful whether any person in that character would be tolerated in the community."* But it was " a time of loose principles and morals;"† and suspicion had given place only to contempt. " He had been invested," was the language used concerning Bishop Seabury's consecration, " or imagined himself invested, with certain extraordinary powers by the manual imposition of a few obscure and ignorant priests in Scotland."‡ Under such a stigma Churchman had been hitherto contented to remain; unresisting, if not half persuaded of its justice. But this was now passed; and the

---

* Bishop White's Dedication of Mem. of Epis. Chur.
† Letter of Bishop J. H. Hobart,—M‘Vickar's Life, p. 235.
‡ American Unitarianism, p. 15: quoted by Dr. M‘Vickar.

altered temper of the Church was felt. It was not that Hobart assailed those without; he addressed his own people; but so his voice passed of necessity abroad, and stirred up attacks to which he rejoined. He was called out by the times, and he was needful for them. Dr. Mason, the leading Presbyterian of the day, in a review which he conducted, aimed a blow intended to "give a quietus to the aspiring ambition of the young Churchman." With this formidable opponent Mr. Hobart calmly and gravely joined issue, in "An Apology for Apostolic Order and its Advocates," published in 1807, which is said to have drawn from his keen antagonist himself the remarkable admission: "Were I compelled to entrust the safety of my country to any one man, that man should be John Henry Hobart."

Nor was it only by the pen that he had to defend this cause. His chief power lay in action. It would be hard to find in his writings any of the stamp of genius. They are plain, energetic, forcible, and marked throughout by the strong common sense of a man of business. In his practical power was his strength; action was natural to him. This strength was first tested as trustee of Columbia College. Open to all denominations, this had received its endowments from the gift of the Episcopalians of Trinity Church, New-York. Its board-meetings were a field of battle on which each persuasion sought to obtain the mastery, and in this strife the true interests of the college were neglected. After many struggles, the Presbyterian Dr. Mason had attained to almost undisputed sway. Of commanding size and features, bold, eloquent, and bitter, few men dared to face his withering and scornful sarcasm. But he now met one who feared him not. Wanting in the gifts of person, Hobart had all the mental and moral qualities which make men leaders of their fellows. Undaunted, ready, and sagacious, he never abandoned a principle, deserted a friend, or quailed before an enemy. "The Church needs no abler representative," was the judgment of a bystander, a sectarian and a lawyer, who witnessed these contentions; "he has all the talents of a leader; he is the most parliamentary speaker I ever met with; he is equally prompt, logical, and practical. I never saw that man thrown off his centre." In these struggles Hobart gained the day. His position was, that there must be one distinct line in the management of such a trust; that for this there must be an ascertained majority in favor of one party; and that here, the body which supplied the funds was justly entitled to the supremacy. His success was complete; and the undivided energy with which the interests of the college were promoted when this majority was ascertained, justified the conflicts by which it was secured.

One other quality which fitted him to lead was shown in these contentions. During these ten years of public strife, it may be doubted if he made one private enemy. He had inherited his pilgrim-father's largeness of affection; and whilst identified with that which he esteemed the cause of truth, he lived on terms of unrestrained friendship with those of other views.

It was in the midst of this active course that Hobart was elected bishop. Difficulties beset his consecration; for the American episcopate was already so reduced in number, that it was no easy matter to obtain the presence of three bishops. Bishops Seabury, R. Smith, and Bass had entered on their rest; Bishop Moore was incapacitated by paralysis; Bishop Claggett was turned back by dangerous sickness; and Bishop Madison was bound by oath to residence within his college in Virginia. There remained only Bishops White, Jarvis, and Provoost—himself in great infirmity, and having, for the last ten years, performed no act belonging to his office. By these three, however, after some embarrassment, Dr. A. V. Griswold, elected bishop of the eastern diocese (now formed by the addition of Vermont and Rhode Island to Massachusetts and New-Hampshire), and Dr. J. H. Hobart, were admitted to the highest order of the priesthood. To the presiding bishop it was an affecting service. Dr Hobart, though not an untried, was yet a young man,* and to the spiritual father who had formerly baptised and confirmed him seemed to belong

---

* Aged 35.

naturally the words of "Paul the aged,"* "Thou therefore, my son, be strong in the grace that is in Christ Jesus."† "I shall have peculiar satisfaction," he declared, "in the consecration of a brother, known in his infancy, in his boyhood, in his youth, and in his past labors in the ministry, and look with the most sanguine prospects to the issue." The old man dwelt with pleasure on the recollection of counsels he had given formerly to one who, for the future, was to be a colleague, and "who may," he added, "in the common course of affairs, be expected to survive .... when he who gave those counsels shall be no more." In this only was his augury untrue. The younger ministry was first accomplished; the younger man was gathered soonest to his rest; and the aged saint survived to weep nineteen years later over his grave.

No second candidate divided with Hobart the votes of the convention, and he opened his episcopate with general acclammations. But amidst these one voice of unworthy jealousy was loudly uttered. Another presbyter, a fellow-assistant at Trinity Church, New-York, published his "solemn remonstrance" against this election. The ineffectual weapon recoiled at last, and with destructive force, against himself. But for the present the remonstrance awoke a a tumult of bitterness and strife. One of its effects was to bring Bishop Provoost in a most unseemly manner again before the Church. No doubt he recognised in Hobart some of those features which had formerly been so distasteful to him in the first bishop of Connecticut; and under these impressions he became, in the weakness of old age, the tool of others to wound the assistant-bishop on whose head his own hand had just been laid. His first step was to claim a right to that jurisdiction which he had of old resigned. This was met at once by the diocesan convention. Distinguishing with careful accuracy between the indelible office of a bishop, which it had not given and could not remove, and that local jurisdiction to which he had been elected by itself, it resolved that "the Right Rev. Samuel Provoost, immediately after the acceptance of his resigna-

---

* Philemon 9. † 2 Tim. ii. 1.

tion by the convention of the Church in this state, ceased to be the diocesan bishop thereof, and could no longer rightfully exercise the functions or jurisdiction appertaining to that office; that having ceased to be the diocesan bishop as aforesaid, he could neither resume nor be restored to that character by any act of his own, or of the general convention, or either of its houses, without the consent and participation of the said state convention, which consent and participation the said Bishop Provoost has not obtained; and that his claim to such a character is therefore unfounded."

Upon the passing of this resolution, Bishop Provoost no longer urged his ill-advised claim. It was clear that he was altogether wrong. His spiritual order the convention could not touch; but the jurisdiction which he exercised in virtue of their choice, which he had resigned, and which had passed to Bishop Moore on his election by convention, it was as impossible for Dr. Provoost to resume at will.

It is pleasant to contrast with this unhappy conduct the course of the aged Bishop White. Of a wholly different school, he did full justice to the solid excellence of Hobart; no creeping jealousy alloyed his praises. "Never," he afterwards declared, had he "known any one on whose integrity and conscientiousness of conduct he had more full reliance;" and in the prospect of his own approaching end, he had thought, he said, with "gratification, that he should leave behind him one whose past zeal and labors were a pledge that he would not cease to be efficient in extending the Church and preserving her integrity."

CHAPTER X.

FROM 1810 TO 1820.

Episcopate of Bishop Hobart—Two first years of opposition—Rise of Church societies—Effect upon the laity—New tone of feeling and action—Bishop Hobart with his clergy—His language as to the Church of Rome—His visitations—General spread of the Church—Increase of bishoprics—State of " the West"—Need of missionary pastors—Pioneers of the Church—Lay readers—Samuel Gunn—His early years—Labors—Removal to Ohio—Consecration of Bishop Chase—His life—Founds Kenyon college—Its building—Students—Their missionary excursions—How received —Funds for domestic purposes—Jackson Kemper—Bishop Hobart's canon—His labors amongst the Indians—Oneida reserves —Eleazar Williams—His history—The bishop's visit.

The episcopate of Dr. Hobart fulfilled the promise of his earlier years. It was that of one who had " purchased to himself a good degree" in the lower functions of the ministry, and now entered with " boldness" and faith on the discharge of the highest.

Yet his two first years were years of trial and discouragement. The opposition which had followed his election had raised the troubled waters of angry contention, and they did not suddenly subside. It may be that his ardent spirit rendered such a check needful for one who was thus early raised to the seat of government and power. Assuredly it was borne meekly, and yielded for himself and many more the good fruits of a disciplined patience. At the close of these two years he had lived down this opposition, and was able to carry out his plans for the improvement of his diocese. These were all aimed in one direction. He desired to " stir up the gift of God" which he firmly believed was " in him ;" and to awaken all around to greater zeal and earnestness within the Church. Surrounded as it was with sects, with none of those civil distinctions or hereditary prepossessions which, in the mother country, tend to define its separate form, all depended in America on the vigor of its inner life sufficing for its own development. This induced him, from the first, to direct the zeal of its members to the formation, within their own body, of the necessary instruments for home-education, for Christian charity, and for missionary enterprise. The Church, he maintained, ought to supply to Churchmen the organs for these several works of love; and he never shrunk from the responsibility or labor involved in presiding over them. His views on these points met at first with some opposition; but justice has since been generally done to their far-sighted wisdom. "We award,"* says the leading paper of the Methodists in 1835, "to the Episcopalians the priority in the defence of church or denominational, in opposition to national religious societies. We are informed that Bishop Hobart was the first to make a stand. Had others defended this plan with constancy, firmness and discretion, the general Church of God in this country would have been in a much better state."

The effect of the system in New-York was evident. It gathered round the Bishop a band of laymen who felt and acted on the truth that they were indeed one body, of a fixed form, and with spiritual powers which the Lord Himself had marked out and imparted. Nowhere was such a principle more requisite than in the disunited society of democratical America; and here it produced its natural results. The more vigorous life which was awakening was visible on all sides; one measure of its increase is incidentally supplied by the wider circulation of the Book of Common Prayer. Though in 1815 the tide had already turned, only 500 copies were issued from the depository, whilst within two years the sale had risen to 2239.†

· But with this attention to the organic frame-work of the body over which it was his province to preside, the bishop joined a watchful care over the secret fountains of its hidden life. On laity and clergy he pressed, by precept and example, the supreme importance of a truly spiritual

* Quoted in Dr. M'Vickar's Life, p. 383.
† Dr. M'Vickar's Life, p. 387.

religion. In answering the solicitations of affection, which would have persuaded him to lessen his own labors, he revealed the spring of all his conduct. "How," said he, "can I do too much for that compassionate Saviour who has done so much for me."* He reminded his convention† that but little satisfaction could be gathered "from the increasing attachment to their distinctive principles and veneration for their institutions," unless with it were seen "an increase of evangelical piety." His clergy he continually urged "to exert with prudence, fidelity, and zeal, all their talents and attainments in the service of their divine Lord and of the Church which He purchased with His blood," reminding them that "the spirit of the ministry must still be formed in retirement, by study, meditation, and prayer."‡ He cautioned them as plainly against any inclination towards "the gorgeous and unhallowed structure of the papal hierarchy," on the one side, as against "the tumults of schism on the other." He had no shrinking from the title Protestant, and was wholly free from the temper which confounds the maintenance of Church-principles with a secret inclination towards the Romish communion. "God forbid," was his own declaration,§ "that I should say aught against the right of private judgment in matters of religion when properly exercised. The doctrine that every man, being individually responsible to his Maker, and Judge, must, in all those concerns that affect his spiritual and eternal welfare, act according to the dictates of his conscience, is that cardinal principle of the Protestant faith which should be most soundly guarded." And these words came to them from lips they learned to love. He was their friend and their counsellor. To him they turned naturally in sorrow, need or difficulty: and they found him always ready to bear gladly the burden which "came upon him daily, the care of all the churches."

Thus all his visitations told upon them: and with the trees which he loved to plant around the scattered parsonage, and which ever afterwards spoke to them of their

---

* Dr. M'Vickar's Life, p. 568.
† Address to the Convention, 1814.
‡ Dr. M'Vickar's Life, p. 339.   § Berrian's Memoir, p. 226.

bishop's presence and care even for these outer things, there were sowed in many hearts the seeds of better and more enduring produce. Few came thus into his company without receiving some impression; all felt his influence;—from the acute lawyer of the city who watched his public conduct, to the Presbyterian farmer of the backwoods, who declared,* " I at first felt a little afraid of your bishop that you brought to my house; but I soon got over it, for he is the cleverest man I ever saw in my life. He is no more of a gentleman than I am."

Under the rule of such a man we should expect to meet with evident improvement: nor will such hopes be disappointed. The internal progress of the diocese may be marked in the returns of 1835, five years after Bishop Hobart's death. In that year there were reported 2626 baptisms, 10,630 communicants, 198 clergymen, 215 parishes, and 8 new churches consecrated. The total amount of funds raised for religious objects, besides the salaries of clergymen, amounted to 13,500l. The report of two years later shows a still continuing progress. The clergy then were 239, and 55 were candidates for holy orders; the parish churches had increased to 232, and 16 new consecrations had marked the past year; whilst the fund for the support of the Episcopate had risen to 22,890l., a sum which made it thenceforth possible to set the bishop free from any direct pastoral charge.†

By a blessed law of the new kingdom, this internal vigor could not wholly spend itself within; it must bear some good fruit on every side; the welling fountain must water other lands; and the history of the whole Church bears many marks of the change we have been tracing. It may be discerned in all directions. There was a continual increase in the numbers of the Episcopate: in 1812 Dr. Dehon, one of the purest and gentlest spirits ever separated to that work, was consecrated Bishop of South Carolina: in 1814, as we have seen, after a vacancy of two years, Virginia found in the consecration of Bishop Richard Moore the first means of her spiritual revival, and the dis-

---

* Dr. M'Vickar's Life, p. 438. † Caswall's America, p. 151.

puted see of Maryland was filled by Dr. Kemp; whilst in that year the extension of the Episcopate into the wide regions of the west first engaged the care of the general convention. But three years before, there had been, besides Bishop Provoost retired, and Bishop Moore disabled from infirmity, only six acting bishops for the sees of Connecticut, Pennsylvania, New-York, Virginia, Maryland, and the Eastern diocese. Within these sees there were, in Connecticut thirty clergy, twenty in Pennsylvania, in New-York forty-four, in Virginia fifty, five in Maryland, and in the Eastern diocese* fifteen: in all, one hundred and ninety-four.† But since this time a change had passed over the body: its members had begun to understand their own position; higher and more intelligible ground was occupied; their claim to the true succession from the Apostles of the Lord, and the need of such a warrant for His ministers, had been heard, discussed, and remained unrefuted in that land of sects; the hearts of many turned towards it from the confusion and weariness of endless self-multiplying division; its clergy now numbered two hundred and forty, and were so rapidly increasing that they were quadrupled within the next twenty-four years; the vacant seats of the bishops were filled up. In 1815 New Jersey received in Dr. Croes her first spiritual head; in 1818 Dr. N. Bowen succeeded Bishop Dehon, who had been already taken to his rest; and in the following year Dr. Brownell supplied the vacancy of Bishop Jarvis; whilst the first mitre of "the West" was placed upon the manly and enduring brow of Philander Chase.

The life of this prelate brings under our notice a peculiar feature of the Church in America. In the large towns and settled districts of the north and east its growth and increase cannot differ widely from that which we see amongst ourselves,—it is opposed by the same difficulties —it has to subdue them with the same arms. But in the wide wilderness which stretches far behind the settled districts of America, it pursues its work of mercy under new

---

* Composed of Massachusetts, Maine, Rhode Island, Vermont, and New Hampshire.
† Caswall's America, p. 186.

and peculiar conditions. These we must survey more closely, or in this long-settled country we shall never understand how little, without constant domestic missions, the cause of Christ can spread abroad throughout that land.

At this time* in America the tide of civilized life had flowed but a very little westward. Along the sea-coast and near the mouths of the great rivers the white men had long been settled, great cities had grown up, busy multitudes thronged the streets, every acre was possessed and cultivated, and there was little left to show that two centuries before, large forests, where the axe had never rung, had darkened all this coast, amidst the glades of which the cunning Indian hunter might be seen stealthily pursuing his game. But on leaving the sea-board the scene soon changed; the settlers became fewer and fewer; after a time even the backwood farmer disappeared; the roads abruptly ended; the traveller got amongst clearings, where the axe had but just begun its work; and where the stumps of the giants of the forest still stood in their native soil, though mutilated by the strong arm which had felled their glory, or charred by the fire which had been brought in aid of man for their destruction. Here was found the squatter and his family, who had come forth from civilised society, taken up their abode in this far wilderness, cleared the timber, acquired the soil by their own labor, built their log hut, and now with the rifle, which they well knew how to use, provided themselves with food, and maintained against all intruders their title to their " clearing." Beyond these again lay the great forest, with its uniform dark frowning front, its carpet of leaves, its endless shadows, its game, and its red hunters.

In the ranks of those who made up this advanced guard

---

* This account is mainly taken from the interesting work of the Rev. Henry Caswall, M. A., by birth an Englishman, and now a curate in the English diocese of Salisbury, but lately rector of Christ Church, Madison, Indiana, and some time professor in the theological seminary of the diocese of Kentucky,—to whose published volume, and private assistance, the author begs, once for all, to record here his deep obligations.

of civilized society were persons of every condition and character. Amongst them were some who found it convenient to fly from the punishment threatened by the laws which they had broken; others who had contracted debts, from the liability of which they were hopeless of otherwise escaping; whilst the number was completed by men of enterprising spirits or of restless tempers, who found or expected to find in the west an easier provision for themselves and their families than had fallen to their lot amongst the contentions and competitions of more populous districts. This tide was ever rising, and the black line of the forest receded farther and farther as it advanced. The squatter found himself disturbed by neighbors, his wild independence was straitened, and his rifle yielded less for his support; he began to crave after the forest stillness; and having sold his clearing to some farmer, who, having a little more capital and a little less enterprise, was willing to enter into the fruit of his labors, he shouldered his axe anew and cast himself upon the pathless forest. Thus year by year, and almost day by day, the stream of population flowed on; the stragglers multiplied, log huts grew into villages, and before the charred stumps were rotted in the ground, streets and towns had grown up round them, and man with all the multitude of his inventions was there. But amongst those many inventions Christianity was too often forgotten. The mass of such men brought little of it with them, and that little was soon lost. No existing ministry pressed upon them the truths of the unseen world; no village-bells reminded them of worship and of praise; no ancient spire pointed with its silent finger towards the heaven above them. There was for the most part amongst them little sense of the needs of a spiritual life: even if the settler were not one who in the midst of the means of grace had resisted God's goodness and hardened his own heart, yet this careless outward life pressed always upon him. It was all too natural that the making provision for the other life should be postponed until a time of more leisure or greater competence. Thus the last remaining impress of Christianity was worn off, and the children trained in such scenes grew up as heathens, with no faith in Christ or fear of God—unbaptised at birth, and unnurtured from the cradle. Or if there still lingered on amongst these wild men some resemblance of Christianity, or if yearnings after better things sprung up within their hearts, still the Church was not amongst them to seize on and turn to lasting profit the precious opportunity. Sacraments they had none; ministers of God, witnesses for Christ, how should these be found in these far wilds? They were not: and so the rude settler must become his own priest; and this, which was far the best state of things, nourished the seeds of independence; and the religion which sprung up was as when men cast seeds into uncultivated lands,—they grow up, but degenerate, and the ears become thinner, and the fruit becomes scantier, until its first type is almost lost, and it can scarcely be discerned from one of the wild plants around it.

It was in looking on these evils, which were ripening in the western parts of his own diocese of New-York, that the heart of Bishop Hobart was stirred up, and he pressed upon the Church the need of sending forth as of old her army of missionary teachers, who should plant in these young lands, and minister amongst these growing tribes, the knowledge of Christ and the sacraments of His grace. His words were heard—the work was undertaken—and it prospered in their hands. Various were the instruments employed, as God blessed the feeble beginning; but the work was soon proceeding. The pioneer of these labors was often the humble lay reader, who prepared the way for the feet of Christ's ambassadors.

In the life of such a laborer we shall trace the progress of the fertilising stream. Samuel Gunn* was one of these. He was born in Connecticut in 1763, and baptised by one of the missionaries of the Society for the Propagation of the Gospel in Foreign Parts. His early youth was unharmed by the dangers and temptations of the war of independence, and he was amongst the first who presented themselves to receive from Bishop Seabury the blessing of confirmation. His blameless character and holy life recom-

---

* See Caswall's America and American Church.

mended him to the notice of the good bishop, who watched with apostolic zeal over the risings of chastened piety within his infant diocese; and as the parish in which he was settled was without a clergyman, Samuel Gunn was appointed lay reader to a small band of devout Christians who met there to worship God according to the order of the Church liturgy. Now and then a clergyman visited the district, and administered amongst them the especial rites of our religion; but for the most part, during ten or twelve years, they depended chiefly on Samuel Gunn.

At the end of this period, his family having increased, and the soil of Connecticut, naturally somewhat barren, and now much exhausted, not affording them the means of living, he determined to move westward. He settled in the outskirts of the state of New-York, amidst a population made up of moving emigrants. Amongst them he resumed his office of lay reader, until he had gathered together so many that they formed themselves into a parish, and obtained the ministrations of a settled clergyman.

For twelve years he was now stationary; but in the autumn of 1805, finding difficulties gather round him, he determined on a new emigration; and after paying every debt he had contracted, set off again with all belonging to him for the farther west. As he journeyed, one of the sorrows of the early settler fell on him; he lost a child by a sudden and violent death, and had himself to dig its grave and leave in the silence of the leafy forest the mouldering dust which should one day hear the voice of the Son of God, and rise like the long-buried seed out of its place to light and life. In the month of November he reached the banks of the Ohio river, then a wild and comparatively unvisited stream; and embarking on a sort of raft-boat, he floated with his family and goods down the stream until he came to the neighborhood of a small settlement of ten or twelve houses, which seemed suited to his purpose.

Here he settled; and the voice of prayer and praise in the language of the liturgy was soon afterwards heard on the banks of the Ohio. For years his own family formed all his congregation; but at length a band was gathered out of the village of Portsmouth, who united with him in his holy worship. In the course of the year 1819, he heard that the state in which he was settled (Ohio) had been regularly formed into a diocese, and that a bishop had been elected and consecrated. The heart of the pious Churchman was filled with hope and joy at this announcement; and these feelings were soon afterwards increased by his learning that his new bishop was no stranger to him, but one whom as a missionary he had frequently received under his humble roof whilst he acted as lay reader in the western wilds of New-York. As soon as Gunn knew that he was in a regularly formed diocese, he desired to put himself under the direction of its head; and he wrote accordingly to his bishop, announcing the state of things in his village of Portsmouth, and pointing out the blessings which he thought would flow from a visit on the part of their chief shepherd. For a time the bishop could not himself act upon this call; but he sent at once a clergyman to refresh with the consolations of the Gospel those spirits which were fainting in the desert. In about a month the bishop himself arrived. The ground was not fully preoccupied by any existing sect; Gunn's labors had removed some prejudice, and excited some attention, and curiosity as well as better feelings were at work; so that when the court-house of the village was made ready for the bishop's use, numbers flocked to hear him. His simple earnest piety deeply impressed the congregation; and he did not leave the village until he had organised a parish, of which Gunn was elected senior warden, and to which, under the bishop's authority, he ministered as lay reader until it was possible to send a clergyman amongst them. His labors were assisted by the discovery of a set of Prayer-books in the village "store." These, which had long slept as unsaleable commodities, were now in such request, that (money-payments being rare in those back settlements) as many as twenty bushels of corn were sometimes given for a single copy.

For three years Gunn kept together the congregation by these simple services, though they were years of trial and rebuke. Disease, which raged in the village, thinned continually the little flock; and when, in 1823, he procured once a month the services of a clergyman, who came fifty miles to minister amongst them, they were dwindled down so low as often to excite the ridicule of the profane. But few as they were, the seed of life was amongst them, and it only needed the fostering presence of the Church's ordinances to spring up and be seen openly. In 1831 they set apart and fitted up a room in which to worship God according to the manner of their fathers; and in this year the aged lay reader rejoiced to hand over his work to an ordained minister,* who was at length settled amongst them.

But all the good man's work was not yet done. He had to show that he could suffer patiently, as well as labor zealously. Within a few weeks of yielding up his charge, a violent accident, which at first threatened his life, deprived him of the sight of one eye, and enfeebled his health ever afterwards. One service more was left him to perform. In the winter following his accident he called together his neighbors and friends, and earnestly urged them to erect a church in which they might together worship God. He ended his address by saying; "You know, my friends, that I am not rich, and that twice I have lost my all. Yet Providence has given me enough, and my property is now worth a little more than two thousand dollars; of this I will give *one-third* towards the erection of the proposed edifice, on condition that you will contribute the remainder of the necessary amount."

It was well for him, as for David of old, that "it was in his heart to build a house for the Lord his God;" but the good man lived not to worship in it, or even to lay its corner-stone. Before that time came, his warfare was accomplished, and he was received by the Master whom he had so long and so faithfully served into the bright and blessed rest of Paradise.

Such are the labors of the humbler pioneers of the Church in America; and the life of the bishop who thus followed one of them into the wilderness will illustrate that of her missionary clergy. Dr. Philander Chase, then just

---

* The Rev. H. Caswall, from whose work this whole account is taken.

appointed Bishop of Ohio, was born in December 1775,* on the high banks of Connecticut river, a few miles north of Charlestown, which was then the extreme verge of the settled country. The American founder of his race, Aquila Chase, a native of Cornwall in England, settled with his wife and family, in the seventeenth century, at Newbury in Massachusetts. Like all their neighbors, they were Independent Congregationalists, and like very many of them, they were truly right-minded godly people. To their descendants after them they handed on their religious creed and their personal piety ;† and Philander Chase was born of parents who had first ventured amidst the shadows of the mighty forest, supported only by their own stout hearts, and an unshaken confidence in their covenant God. The youngest of fourteen children, most of whom had left their father's tent in the forest for the various walks of busy life, Philander's early aspirations pointed to the patriarchal life, of which the grey-haired man before him was so encouraging an instance. He would close that father's eyes, and inherit the home-farm his hands had formed out of the forest.

But God had destined him for greater things ; and severe sufferings, first from a maimed and then from a broken limb, were His messengers of good to the young farmer. During his son's long confinement the old man watched by his sleepless bed, and read to him the writing of the hand which had thus come forth for him upon the wall ; " By these sufferings God was calling to Himself His destined servant ; college life and the service of the ministry were plainly his appointed sphere."

To college accordingly he went ; and falling in there

---

* Reminiscences of Bishop Chase, by himself, *passim*.

† The family-records give a passing picture of Puritan life amongst the pilgrims of Massachusetts, in recording that Capt. Aquila Chase, a leading man amongst them, was brought to trial because on his reaching home, from a long voyage, on Sunday morning, his wife had gathered and dressed her first dish of green peas to welcome him. It was in vain that he pleaded the danger of scurvy and necessities of health ; the utmost favor he received was, to escape the infliction of "forty-stripes-save-one" by the payment of a heavy fine.

with the Common Prayer-Book, he was won over by its holy tone, and its exhibition of " the authenticated claims"* of the Episcopal ministry to an apostolic commission ; and he returned to the farm upon the Connecticut, to lead back his aged father into the Church from which he and his had been so long estranged. By their own hands and with entire harmony of feeling, the meeting-house, where his father and his grandfather had officiated as congregational deacons, was pulled down, and a church erected in its stead. Here they welcomed the occasional visits of distant clergy ; and here, in their absence, and under their direction, Philander Chase read, as a layman, prayers and sermons.

He was now twenty years of age, and his heart was set upon the labors of the ministry. But how to obtain ordination he knew not. No theological seminaries then sheltered early piety, and fostered such pious resolutions ; no bishop was at hand to direct and crown his labors. With trembling steps, and all the bashfulness of youth, he set out for Albany to obtain help and guidance " A rebuff would have turned his face another way."

But he met with no such discouragement. He reached Albany, and was directed to the house of the " English dominie." " Is this the Rev. Mr. Ellison's ?" he asked, as the top of a Dutch-built door was opened by a portly gentleman in black, with prominent and piercing eyes, and powdered hair. Having announced his name and errand, he was greeted with a " God bless you, come in !" which fixed his lot for life. After almost three years of study and preparation, he was ordained deacon, in **May 1798**, by Bishop Provoost of New-York.

His first sphere of labor was in the western parts of the diocese of New-York. Here he was employed as a domestic missionary upon the outskirts of civilized life. Over that district, where within a few years afterwards large and prosperous towns abounded, the mighty forest then stretched, and its only inhabitants were the emigrant villagers who were busy in settling these outposts of so-

---

* Bishop Chase's Reminiscences.

ciety. Amongst them the young evangelist labored with his whole heart, thinking nothing of the many toils and privations which such a mode of life entailed. With these he was soon familiar. As he travelled to his own sphere of labor, he fell in with a brother missionary, afterwards known and highly honored. He was living in " a cabin built of unhewn logs, with scarcely a pane of glass to let in light sufficient to read his Bible; and even this was not his own, nor long allowed for his use." Chase arrived at the moment of such a dispossession, and assisted him to carry his articles of crockery to a new abode, " holding one handle of the basket as they walked the road, talking of the things pertaining to the kingdom of God," whilst they bore all his substance into the little one-roomed cabin, the rude door of which hung creaking on its wooden hinges. This man was " the founder of the Church in the Otsego country :" and it was at the cost of such self-denial that the Gospel was planted in the west.

Into these labors Chase entered heartily; and as his work was greatly blessed by God, he had the joy of seeing several flourishing congregations gathered by his hands into settled parishes. In this neighborhood he remained some years, until the need of a milder climate for his wife sent him southward, and, at the advice of his bishop, he settled at New Orleans, near the delta of the Mississippi river. Here, where no minister of the reformed communion had yet appeared, he formed another parish; and, after six years' labor, returned to New England, and was, for six more, rector of a church at Hartford in Connecticut. In this parish he was greatly beloved: but, amidst all the enjoyments of civilized society, his thoughts would often wander to the desolate districts of the West; to the lonely " clearing," and to the growing villages where the name of Christ was daily more and more forgotten; he thought upon his own labors in time past until his heart yearned to be again employed in that high and holy enterprise; and accordingly, in 1817, he set out once more upon his missionary work.

Since the days of his former labors in the back districts of New-York, the mighty tide of civilized life had swept on far to the west. His former desolate stations were now populous towns, and the early seed which he had scattered in the waste had ripened into a harvest; for through his labors, the institutions and influence of Christianity had healed the spring-head of social life amongst the earliest settlers before they had swelled into an irreligious multitude.

As he retraced his steps over his old sphere of duty, he marked the changes, which he thus records:—"I remember these busy villages one dreary salt marsh; except two or three cabins for boiling salt—most unsightly and uncomfortable, because only tenanted in winter—there were no appearances of civilized men."* "Where," he asked of one of his old flock, "was the cabin in which I baptised your family?" "I will show you," said he, taking his hat and a great key; "but we must stop at the church as we go along." And so they did. There it stood where the tall tree so lately occupied the ground. It was a beautiful, well-finished edifice. "This is the tree which you planted; may it bear fruit acceptable to the heavenly Husbandman!" The site of the old cabin was found occupied by the "bustle of business; coaches passing, warehouses on each side lofty and well supplied, streets paved, and sidewalks flagged." Such is the rapid upgrowth of civilized life in the ancient domain of the western forest.

To the difficulties and the blessing of planting the Church in the waste, the heart of Chase was still drawn, and he sought, therefore, his new field of labor in yet remoter districts. He passed on to the state of Ohio, where the straggling villages of the distant settler were beginning to stud the long unbroken forest. All his soul was in his work, and again he was greatly prospered in it. One by one other clergymen came to his aid; parishes were formed; and in the very year after his coming amongst them, the new diocese of Ohio was organized. At its second diocesan convention, he who had brought to them the message of salvation was, by the votes of both laity and clergy, elected as their bishop. In February 1819 he was consecrated in

* Bishop Chase's Reminiscences, vol. i. p. 53.

the town of Philadelphia by the good old Bishop White, assisted by Bishops Hobart, Kemp, and Croes, and entered directly on his work. Anxiously did the new bishop watch over his rising diocese; he was still in heart what he had ever been; and though now a ruler of Christ's Church, he was, as of old, a devoted missionary, constantly engaged in seeking to carry on, in every direction, the work in which he had so diligently labored.

In effecting this he spared himself no exertion. His diocesan labors involved "vast distances of journeyings on horseback, under the burning sun and pelting rain, through the mud and amid the beech-roots, over log bridges and through swollen streams." It was no wonder that he reached the end of his circuit of "1279 miles on horseback with his constitution impaired and his voice almost gone."* Fresh cares met him at the threshold of his home. "Three parishes were to be supplied," (lay readers being often his only substitute during his necessary absence,) "two of them nearly fifteen miles distant from his residence." In spite of close economy, there was within doors "but a poor prospect for the coming winter;" with a sickly wife, and this press of Episcopal and pastoral care, "there was not a dollar left, after satisfying the hired man for the past, wherewithal to engage him for the future; and as for the making promises when there was no prospect of making payment, such had ever been regarded as a sin. The hired man was then, from a principle of duty, discharged. The result was inevitable;" the bishop "must do what the man would, if retained, have done; *i. e.* thrash the grain, haul and cut the wood, build the fires, and feed the stock."

With such anxieties would mingle doubts whether he had done rightly in accepting the arduous trust of such an episcopate. But these dark clouds seldom settled on his mind. They are commonly dispersed by active exertion, and Bishop Chase was always active, Wherever an opening appeared, he was ready to attend, to show the fair front of the Church's goodly order, and plant the standard of his Master; and for this work his zeal and earnestness fitted him remarkably.

* Bishop Chase's Reminiscences, p. 192.

His journey, at the call of Samuel Gunn, is an example of his labors; for such calls were continually arising. In these cases the ground was happily prepared, and the bishop's main work was to foster the weak beginnings of the apostolical communion, and to provide pastors for its ministry. But he did not confine himself to these more favored spots; all through his diocese, wherever the flow of civilised life carried the settler from the means of grace, there was turned the attention of the bishop, and there, if it was possible, was soon seen his fatherly presence. In the year 1820 these objects took him on horseback through his diocese (carriage-roads not having yet been made), a distance of almost 1300 miles.

But all his personal energy could not supply the want of instruments. To "ordain elders in every district" was his earnest desire. To commit the flock to a regular ministry, who should daily cement and carry on to perfectness the goodly building, the foundations of which he, as a wise master-builder, had laid,—this was the longing of Bishop Chase's heart. The want was pressing and weighed like a heavy burden on his soul. He saw "the whole community of those western settlements sinking fast in ignorance and its never-failing attendants, vice and fanaticism. "Our own Church," he declares, "is like a discomfited army seeking for strange food in forbidden fields, or sitting in solitary groups by the way-side fainting, famishing, and dying. . , . , No missionaries make their appearance. . Those who transiently visit us pass like meteors, leaving behind little or no salutary effect."* Fixed and settled pastors were what the people required.

But the work of the ministry amongst the wild and straggling settlers of the West required peculiar gifts and habits. Clergy who had been accustomed to labor in more civilised districts were in a great measure unfitted for the charge; and the bishop saw, therefore, the necessity of founding a college in his own diocese to prepare proper instruments for this peculiar service. He laid his plans before his diocesan convention, and with their concurrence

* Reminiscences.

resolved to visit England, and collect subscriptions for the endowment of his college. In urging his cause here, he had not only the general claim of spiritual relationship to which the Church of the mother country has ever gladly answered, but a further title to assistance in the fact, that about one-third of all the population of his diocese were British emigrants. Difficulties of various kinds opposed his resolution. He left behind him a dying son; his resources would not prudently warrant the excursion; and the bulk of Churchmen east of the Alleghany mountains discouraged, whilst some openly opposed, his undertaking. All this made his heart ache, but it could not turn back his steps. After appointing a day for fasting and prayer in his own diocese, and seeking the intercession of the Church throughout the west, he sailed for England in October 1823; and there, after bravely making head for a season against a repetition of the same difficulties which had often met him in America, he collected more than six thousand pounds for his noble object. This enabled him, on his return, to purchase 8000 acres of good land, and begin to build a college and village, to which, in remembrance of two of his most active friends in England, he gave respectively the names of Kenyon and Gambier.

In erecting these all the bishop's energy of character was seen. Not content with undertaking the office of post-master, that he might have the privilege of franking the multitude of letters which his enterprise required him to circulate, he acted as chief builder also. "He rises,"* says his friend and coadjutor, "at three every morning, and is engaged till night in superintending the workmen on the college buildings." The results were commensurate with these exertions. The college was soon in full operation. "Within two years from the time when the lowest story was yet incomplete, and tall trees covered the face of the ground, whilst the students occupied temporary wooden houses, in which the frost of winter and the heat of summer alternately predominated, and the laborious bishop inhabited a cabin of rough logs, the interstices of which were filled with

* America and the American Church, p. 26.

clay,—the massive stone walls of the college, four feet thick and four stories in height, lifted themselves almost to the elevation of the surrounding woods, and a tall steeple indicated its situation to the distant wanderer." Around it also all was changed. The clearing had proceeded rapidly; " several hundred acres of rich land supplied grain in abundance, and pasture for numerous cattle. A printer inhabited the bishop's former domicile, and published a religious newspaper, denominated the ' Gambier Observer ;' while the students were in part provided with commodious dwellings, and in part supplied with lodgings in the college beneath the same roof with the bishop and the professors."

Of these students, many were destined for the different walks of ordinary life ; but a considerable number also were here trained, under the bishop's eye, for the peculiar services of a far-western clergyman. To these they were here accustomed even during the time of their college life ; and they therefore entered upon the discharge of their ministry with the habits already formed which they afterwards needed. They maintained Sunday-schools, and in other ways supplied the religious wants of the settlers within a circuit of some miles around the college. We may follow one of them* in his accustomed labors. "We rise early (on a summer morning), and sally forth with a few books and some frugal provision for the day. We proceed about half a mile through the noble aboriginal forest, the tall and straight trees appearing like pillars in a vast Gothic cathedral. The timber consists of oak, hickory, sugar-maple, sycamore, walnut, poplar, and chesnut, and the wild vine hangs from the branches in graceful festoons. Occasionally we hear the song of birds, but less frequently than in England. Generally deep silence prevails, and prepares the mind for serious contemplation. We soon arrive at a small clearing, where a cabin built of rough logs indicates the residence of a family. Around the cabin are several acres upon which gigantic trees are yet standing, but perfectly deadened by the operation called 'girdling.' Their bark has chiefly fallen off, and the gaunt

---

*America and the American Church, p. 35, &c.

white limbs appear dreary, though majestic in decay. Upon the abundant grass which has sprung up since the rays of the sun were admitted to the soil, a number of cattle are feeding, and the tinkling of their bells is almost the only sound which strikes the ear. We climb over the fence of split rails piled in a zigzag form, cross the pasture, and are again in the deep forest. The surface of the ground is of an undulating character, while our pathway carries us by a log-hut surrounded by a small clearing. After an hour we arrive at a rudely constructed saw-mill erected on a small stream of water. The miller is seated at his cabin-door in his Sunday clothes, and is reading a religious book which we have lent him before. We now talk to him; his interest in the Church is growing, and he offers us his horse for our future expeditions; we accept it, and proceed with its assistance on our course. After another hour we reach a village of log-cottages, at the end of which is a schoolroom, around which a temporary arbor is constructed, covered with fresh boughs. In this the children of the neighbors soon gather round us, and with them often come their friends and parents. When a goodly company is thus assembled, a hymn is given out and sung; then all kneel for prayer, and a large portion of the Church-service is repeated from memory, from a tender regard to the prejudices of many who, until they have learned a better lesson, would turn away if they were told that they listened to the Church's voice. Then, under the sanction of the bishop, a few words of exhortation are added where the student is a candidate for holy orders. We then instruct the children, and, having finished this, set out upon our journey homeward."

The reception of these messengers of peace was widely various. In all cases, indeed, they appear to have received from the settlers that hospitality which is the uniform accompaniment of imperfect civilization. But while they were welcomed by some as spiritual guides, by others they and their objects were looked at with the most watchful suspicion. Thus one backwood farmer received gladly the wandering students, and lavished upon their reception all the stores of his rude hospitality; but when he found that they were inhabitants of Gambier, and emissaries of Kenyon College, his countenance fell, and, with the sincerity of a backwood freeman, he at once expressed his apprehensions of such visitants.* "I have fought the British," he told them, "in the revolutionary war, and I have again encountered them in the last war, and I know something of their character. I know that they would not contribute so many thousand pounds to build a college in Ohio without some sinister object. I am, therefore, convinced that Bishop Chase is an agent employed by them to introduce British domination here. The college is, in fact, a fortress; all you students are British soldiers in disguise; and when you think you have the opportunity, you will throw off the mask and proclaim the King of England." No explanation or assurance could dispel the scruples of the old man, who was a Calvinistic Anabaptist in religion, and probably a fiery democrat in politics.

At other times, this is the narrative of their reception: "We have scarcely left the village, when a blacksmith runs after us and requests us to stop. He tells us that he has felt deeply interested in the services, that he desires more information, and that he wishes us always to dine with him on Sundays in future. We accordingly return to his cabin; and his wife sets before us a plentiful repast of chickens, potatoes, hot bread, apple-pies, and milk. After some profitable conversation we depart, and at about three o'clock arrive at the miller's house, almost overcome by the excessive heat. When we have somewhat recovered from our fatigue, we proceed to a spot on the banks of the stream where the grass is smooth and the thick foliage produces a comparative coolness. Here we find about one hundred persons collected in the hope of receiving from us some religious instruction. We conduct the service much in the same way as in the morning. The effect of the singing in the open air is striking and peculiar; and the prayers of our liturgy are no less sublime in the forests of Ohio than in the consecrated and time-honored minsters of York or Canterbury."†

* Caswall's America and the American Church, p. 45.
† America and the American Church, p. 38.

In such natural sanctuaries are sometimes celebrated all the rites of our most holy faith. One such in Delaware County, Ohio, is thus described by an eye-witness: "The place of worship was a beautiful orchard, where the abundant blossoms of the apple and the peach filled the air with their delicious odor. A table for the Communion was placed on the green grass, and covered with a cloth of snowy whiteness. Adjoining the rustic altar, a little stand was erected for the clergyman, and a number of benches were provided for the congregation. A large number attended, and behaved with the strictest propriety. Besides the service for the day, baptism was administered by the missionary to three or four adults, a stirring extempore sermon was delivered, and the Lord's Supper completed the solemnities."*

But to return to our Kenyon College students, whom we must follow home: "The service concluded, we return on foot; and as we approach the college with weary steps, the fire-flies glisten in the increasing darkness. We arrive at our rooms fatigued in body, but refreshed in mind, and encouraged to new efforts."

By such exertions as these the Church was widely spread throughout the West. From them the sound of the Gospel reached the settler's family; by them, under God's blessing, was formed first the struggling parish, and afterwards the ill-endowed but laborious diocese, extending over its fifty thousand square miles, and carrying into the waste the germ of civilization and of order,

The want of funds proved the great hindrance to these domestic missions. Years must commonly pass before the spiritual laborer saw gathered round him a flock sufficient to maintain him in his work. This, therefore, was one great demand of Christian charity, and efforts were made in various places to respond to it. Thus in Philadelphia, as early as 1812, there was a movement in this direction, begun by the zeal and earnestness of Jackson Kemper, then a deacon there. In New-York also, which was soon to be the centre of the Christian charity of North America,

---

* America and the American Church, p. 286.

Bishop Hobart took, in 1813, an important step in the same cause. He proposed and carried through a canon which made it imperative on every congregation in the diocese once a year to collect funds for this specific object. This was the beginning of great things. The cause grew under his hand, and the noble aspect it assumed a few years later may be traced to this as its beginning.

But this was not the only species of domestic missions which engaged his attention. There was another race of men who had the strongest claims on all Americans; these soon attracted the attention of the Bishop of New-York. In surveying the teeming multitudes of European origin who now fill the shores of the great western continent, the question often recurs sadly to the mind, Where are those who were its former tenants? where are the red men, to whom the God of heaven had apportioned out by lot the hunting-grounds and forests on whose site now stand the busy cities of the West? The answer is a mournful one to every thoughtful mind. Scarcely one of them remains. War, treachery, famine, and, above all, diseases of European growth, have mowed down whole nations of Indians, until they are not upon the face of the earth. A few remain; and as these have rarely become mingled with their white invaders, they have been continually beaten back farther and farther into the interior, as the tide of civilised life gradually rose upon them.

At length the government of the United States has taken upon itself to confer titles to their land, and to remove them to certain "reserves," of which it guarantees to them the undisturbed possession. The whole subject must give rise to bitter reflections. But this surely is the first question which rises on the mind, What has the Church of Christ done for this unhappy race? Has it, according to its chartered rights, received into itself these children of the human family, and, by its greater boons of heavenly light and everlasting life, turned all their other losses into gain? The answer to this question also involves a catalogue of fearful facts. It is therefore with peculiar pleasure that we light here and there upon plans and efforts devised in the spirit of those times when apostles bore to men of every blood the message of salvation. To some such we are led in surveying the course of Bishop Hobart's episcopate.

In the year 1815 his attention was called to the condition of a portion of the tribe of the Iroquois, distinguished as the Oneidas, who, to the number of four thousand, were settled on some "reserved" lands known by the name of "the Oneida country." His first object was to find a proper instrument for carrying out amongst them his purposes of Christian love. His search was not in vain; he was guided to one of their own blood who had received a Christian education, and could speak to them of the name of Jesus in the beloved accents of their fathers' tongue.

The history of Eleazer Williams, whom he now sent to them, is full of that romance by which Indian life is so frequently distinguished. Amongst the last inroads of the Indian tribes upon the white men's settlements, was one against the frontier village of Deerfield in Connecticut. It proved so far successful that the red men returned to their trackless forests loaded with all kinds of booty. Amongst their various prey they carried off the wife and children of the rector of the village, the Rev. Mr. Williams, who was absent at the time. He returned home to learn the full extent of his calamity; and with a bleeding heart, set out at once to seek for those with whom his life was thus bound up. Years passed over him in his fruitless and heart-sickening toil; but still he desisted not until he was at last guided to their haunt in the distant prairie. But when he had found them, all would not return. One daughter of his house had wedded an Indian chief, and she refused to leave the land of her adoption. Little could the pious father forecast the blessing which was thus in store for his despoilers: for from this marriage sprung, amongst others, the son who was now the bearer of the message of salvation to his red brethren of the forest. He went forth as catechist and schoolmaster, taking with him portions of the Gospels and the Psalms, which, through the bishop's care, had been translated into their native dialect.

The blessing of God rested on his labors; and some of their fruits may be found marked in the following touching words addressed to the bishop three years afterwards, in the name of his brethren, by a young Indian communicant:—

"Right Rev. Father,—We salute you in the name of the ever-adorable, ever-blessed, and everlasting sovereign Lord of the universe; we acknowledge the great and almighty Being as our Creator, Preserver, and constant Benefactor.

"Right Rev. Father,—We rejoice that we now, with one heart and mind, would express our gratitude and thanksgiving to our great and venerable father for the favor which he has bestowed upon this nation, viz., in sending brother Williams among us to instruct us in the religion of the blessed Jesus. When he first came to us we hailed him as our friend, our brother, and our guide in spiritual things, and he shall remain in our hearts and minds as long as he shall teach us the ways of the great Spirit above.

"Right Rev. Father,—We rejoice to say, that by sending brother Williams among us a great light has risen upon us; we see now that the Christian religion is intended for the good of the Indians as well as the white people; we see it and do feel it, that the religion of the Gospel will make us happy in this and in the world to come. We now profess it outwardly, and we hope, by the grace of God, that some of us have professed it inwardly. May it ever remain in our hearts, and we be enabled by the Spirit of the Eternal One to practise the great duties which it points out to us.

"Right Rev. Father,—Agreeable to your request, we have treated our brother with that attention and kindness which you required of us; we have assisted him all that was in our power as to his support: but you know well that we are poor ourselves, and we cannot do a great deal. Though our brother has lived very poor since he came among us, but he is patient and makes no complaint, we pity him, because we love him as we do ourselves. We wish to do something for his support, but this is impossible for us to do at present, as we have lately raised between three and four thousand dollars to enable us to build a little chapel.

"Right Rev. Father,—We entreat and beseech you not

to neglect us. We hope the Christian people in New-York will help us all that is in their power. We hope our brother will by no means be withdrawn from us. If this should take place, the cause of religion will die among us, immorality and wickedness will prevail.

"Right Rev. Father,—As the head and father of the holy and apostolical Church in this state, we entreat you to take a special charge of us. We are ignorant, mean, poor, and need your assistance. Come, venerable father, and visit your children, and warm their hearts by your presence in the things which belong to their everlasting peace. May the great Head of the Church whom you serve be with you, and His blessing ever remain with you!

"We, venerable father, remain your dutiful children."

The bishop's answer breathes an apostolic spirit :—

"My children,—I have received your letter by your brother and teacher, Eleazer Williams, and return your affectionate and Christian salutation, praying that grace, mercy, and peace from God the Father and from our Lord Jesus Christ, may be with you.

"My children,—I rejoice to hear of your faith in the one living and true God, and in His Son Jesus Christ whom He has sent, whom to know is life eternal : and I pray that, by the Holy Spirit of God, you may be kept steadfast in this faith, and may walk worthy of Him who hath called you out of darkness into His marvellous light.

"My children.—It is true, as you say, that the Gospel of our Lord and Saviour Jesus Christ is intended for Indians as well as white people. For the great Father of all hath made of one blood all the nations of the earth ; and hath sent His Son Jesus Christ to teach them all, and to die for them all, that they may be redeemed from the power of sin, and brought to the acknowledgment of the truth, and to the service of the living God.

"My children,—It is true, as you say, that the religion of the Gospel will make you happy in this world, as well as in the world to come ; and I join in your prayer, that you may profess it inwardly as well as outwardly ; that, by the power of the Holy Spirit, you may be transformed by the renewing of your minds, and acquire holy tempers, and practise the holy duties which the Gospel enjoins. And for this purpose I beseech you to attend to the instructions of your faithful teacher and brother, Eleazer Williams : to unite with him in the holy prayers of our apostolic Church, which he has translated into your own language ; to listen with reverence to the Divine word which he reads to you ; to receive, as through grace you may be qualified, and may have an opportunity, the sacraments and ordinances of the Church ; and at all times, and in all places, to lift up your hearts in supplication to the Father of your spirits, who always and every where hears and sees you, for pardon and grace, to comfort, to teach, and to sanctify you, through your divine Mediator, Jesus Christ.

" My children,—Let me exhort you diligently to labor to get your living by cultivating the earth, or by some other lawful calling; you will thus promote your worldly comfort, you will be more respected among your white brethren, and more united and strong among yourselves. And when you are thus engaged, you will be saved from many temptations ; and you will prove yourselves to be good disciples of Him, who, by His inspired apostle, has enjoined, that while we are ' fervent in spirit,' we be ' not slothful in business.'

" My children —Continue to respect and to love your brother and teacher, Eleazer Williams, and to treat him kindly ; for he loves you, and is desirous to devote himself to your service ; that, by God's grace, he may be instrumental in making you happy here and hereafter. It is my wish that he may remain with you, and may be your spiritual guide and instructor.

" My children,—I rejoice to hear that your brethren, the Onondagas, are desirous of knowing the words of truth and salvation. I hope you will not complain if your teacher, Eleazer Williams, sometimes visits them, to lead them in that way to eternal life, which, from God's word, he has pointed out to you. Freely ye have received, you should freely give ; and being made partakers of the grace of God through Jesus Christ, you should be desirous that all your red brethren may enjoy the same precious gift.

"My children,—It is my purpose, if the Lord will, to come and see you next summer; and I hope to find you as good Christians, denying ungodliness and worldly lusts, and living righteously, soberly and godly in this present world. I shall have you in my heart, and shall remember you in my prayers, for you are a part of my charge, of that flock for whom the Son of God gave Himself even unto the death upon the cross, and whom He commanded His ministers to seek and to gather unto His fold, that through Him they might be saved for ever.

"My children,—May God be with you and bless you.

(*Signed*) JOHN HENRY HOBART,
Bishop of the Prot. Epis. Church in the State of New-York.

Dated at New-York, the 1st day of February, in the year of our Lord 1818, and in the seventh year of my consecration."

From this promised visit no other engagements could divert him. In the following summer he penetrated to the Indian reserves. The scene he witnessed filled him with deeper interest for his red children.

Their wide extended domains were lying in common, the property of the tribe, not of individuals; some little of it cultivated, more in open pasture, but most in its state of native wildness, and reserved for hunting-ground. Through these forests, paths there were many, but roads none; and the generally rude, though sometimes neat and rustic dwellings of these sons of the forest lay scattered in wild but picturesque confusion—some upon gentle eminences, others in rich valleys; some open to the sun, others embosomed in shade; and exhibiting here and there traces of a taste for natural scenery which recommended them still further (at least as objects of interesting inquiry) to such a lover of nature as Bishop Hobart. Among those who flocked around him on this occasion, as he stood in the recesses of their primeval forests, was one aged Mohawk warrior, who, amid his heathen brethren, had for half a century held fast by that holy faith in which he had been instructed and baptised by a missionary from the society in England, while these states were still colonies. Through the catechist as interpreter, he now recounted the event in the figurative language of these children of nature, and pointed out to his admiring auditor, with as much feeling as belongs to that imperturbable race, the very spot where this early missionary had been accustomed to assemble them, and preach to a congregation which, as it afterwards appeared, had listened to him rather from curiosity than conviction.

It was, as the bishop in conversation described it, an open glade in the forest, with a few scattered oaks still vigorous and spreading; and within view, as if to perpetuate the association, now arose the tower of the neat rustic church, which the Christian party among them had recently erected. To his next convention Bishop Hobart gave his own account of this visit to the forest and its red inhabitants:—

"It is a subject of congratulation, that our Church has resumed the labors which, for a long period before the revolutionary war, the society in England for Propagating the Gospel in Foreign Parts directed to the religious instruction of the Indian tribes. These labors were not wholly unsuccessful; for on my recent visit to the Oneidas, I saw an ancient Mohawk, who, firm in the faith of the gospel, and adorning his profession by an exemplary life, is indebted, under the Divine blessing, for his Christian principles and hopes, to the missionaries of that venerable society. The exertions more recently made for the conversion of the Indian tribes have not been so successful, partly because not united with efforts to introduce among them those arts of civilisation without which the gospel can neither be understood nor valued; but principally because religious instruction was conveyed through the imperfect medium of interpreters, by those unacquainted with their dispositions and habits, and in whom they were not disposed to place the same confidence as in those who are connected with them by the powerful ties of language, of manners, and of kindred. The religious instructor of the Oneidas employed by our church enjoys all these advantages. Being of Indian extraction, and acquainted with their language, dispositions, and customs, and devoting himself unremittingly to their spiritual and temporal welfare, he enjoys their full confidence, while the education which he has received has increased his qualifications as their guide in the faith and precepts of the gospel. Mr. Eleazer Williams, at the earnest request of the Oneida chiefs, was licensed by me about two years since, as their lay reader, catechist, and schoolmaster. Educated in a different communion, he connected himself with our Church from conviction, and appears warmly attached to her doctrines, her apostolic ministry, and her worship. Soon after he commenced his labors among the Oneidas, the Pagan party solemnly professed the Christian faith. Mr. Williams repeatedly explained to them, in councils which they held for this purpose, the evidences of the divine origin of Christianity, and its doctrines, institutions, and precepts. He combated their objections, patiently answered their inquiries, and was finally, through the Divine blessing, successful in satisfying their doubts. Soon after their conversion, they appropriated, in conjunction with the old Christian party, the proceeds of the sale of some of their lands to the erection of a handsome edifice for divine worship, which will be shortly completed.

"In the work of their spiritual instruction, the Book of Common Prayer, a principal part of which has been translated for their use, proves a powerful auxiliary. Its simple and affecting exhibition of the truths of redemption is calculated to interest their hearts, while it informs their understanding; and its decent and significant rites contribute to fix their attention in the exercises of worship. They are particularly gratified with having parts assigned them in the service, and repeat the responses with great propriety and devotion. On my visit to them, several hundred assembled for worship; those who could read were furnished with books, and they uttered the confessions of the liturgy, responded its supplications, and chanted its hymns of praise, with a reverence and fervor which powerfully interested the feelings of those who witnessed the solemnity. They listened to my address to them, interpreted by Mr. Williams, with so much solicitous attention, they received the laying on of hands with such grateful humility, and participated in the symbols of their Saviour's love with such tears of penitential devotion, that the impression which the scene made on my mind will never be effaced. Nor was this the excitement of the moment, or the ebullition of enthusiasm. The eighty-nine who were confirmed had been well instructed by Mr. Williams; and none were permitted to approach the communion whose lives did not correspond with their Christian professions. The numbers of those who assembled for worship, and partook of the ordinances, would have been greater, but from the absence of many of them at an Indian council at Buffalo.

"I have admitted Mr. Williams as a candidate for orders, on the recommendation of the standing committee; and look forward to his increased influence and usefulness, should he be invested with the office of the ministry.

"There is a prospect of his having, some time hence, a powerful auxiliary in a young Indian, the son of the head warrior of the Onondagas, who was killed at the battle of Chippewa, and who, amiable and pious in his dispositions, and sprightly and vigorous in his intellectual powers, is earnestly desirous of receiving an education to prepare him for the ministry among his countrymen. I trust that means will be devised for accomplishing his wishes. We ought never to forget that the salvation of the gospel is designed for all the human race; and that the same mercy which applies comfort to our wounded consciences, the same grace which purifies and soothes our corrupt and troubled hearts, and the same hope of immortality which fills us with peace and joy, can exert their benign and celestial influence on the humble Indian."

CHAPTER XI.

FROM 1820 TO 1836.

American education—Temper of American youth—Jealousy of high education—Absence of theological training—Foundation of the General Theological Seminary—Its success—Bishop Hobart's connexion with it—His death—And character—Bishop B. T. Onderdonk succeeds—Increase of the episcopate—Bishops Ravenscroft and Ives of North Carolina—Bishop Meade of Virginia—And H. U. Onderdonk, assistant bishop of Pennsylvania—Bishop Chase of Ohio—Resigns his bishopric—Consecrations of Bishops M'Ilvaine of Ohio, Hopkins of Vermont, Smith of Kentucky, and Doane of New Jersey—Change of feeling as to the episcopate—Convention of 1835—Bishop Chase of Illinois—Division of dioceses—New organization of missionary board—The missionary bishop—Bishop Kemper consecrated—Success of the new plan—Subsequent growth of the Church—Bishop White's illness—Death and character.

AMIDST the various subjects which occupied the mind of Bishop Hobart, one had constantly recurred. None, indeed, more deeply concerned North America than the influence of the Church on education. This, at present, is more widely spread and of a lower standard than in the older nations of Europe. Throughout the eastern states, reading, writing, geography, and arithmetic, are almost universal; and even some measure of classical attainment is by no means rare. In New-York, in 1832, out of a population of two millions, half a million, or one in four, were at school.* It is asserted, but without any grounds being given to justify the calculation, that of the whole population of the United States, one in five are under education.†
In the slave-states of the south, the diffusion and character

---

* Caswall's America, p. 197.
† J. S. Buckingham's America, vol. ii. p. 366.

of education falls greatly lower than this level; whilst in Ohio and some of the newer north-west states, lands for the support of education have been set aside from their first settlement; and these bid fair, ere long, to rival the "empire"* state. But with all this wide spread of education, it nowhere reaches to the high measure of the Old World. For this there is as yet neither provision nor demand. This must be more or less the case where there are no classes born to hereditary wealth; and this tendency is increased by the peculiarities of American character, which is eminently busy and practical; urging men to acquire money, immediate influence, and direct results in all things. Even childhood is moulded by these feelings. "Boys are men before they are loosed from their leading-strings. They are educated in the belief that every man must be the architect of his own fortune. There is, to be sure, a limited class who look forward to the decease of parents as the commencement of an era in which they will have no duty to do but to enjoy the property bequeathed to them; but, as a class, it is too small to be considered in the estimate of national character. The great majority look forward to manhood as the time to act, and anticipate it by juvenile participation in the events of busy life. Boys argue upon polemics, political economy, party politics, the mysteries of trade, the destinies of nations. Dreams of ambition or of wealth nerve the arm which drives the hoop. Toys are stock in trade; barter is fallen into by instinct."

This is an American estimate† of the character of boyhood there: and with this the highest measure of education is manifestly incompatible. It is valued only as it fits men to act successfully their immediate part in the busy scene before them. Whatever rises above this level is looked at rather with suspicion than good will. Like great wealth or distinctions of rank, it cannot harmonize entirely with republican institutions. It is the assertion of superiority. "The multitude in this country," says an

---

* An American name for New-York.
† Extracted by J. S. Buckingham, vol. i. p. 170, from a leading New-York journal.

address delivered in an eastern state to a collegiate institution,* "so far from favoring and honoring high learning and science, is rather prone to suspect and dislike it. It feareth that genius savoreth of aristocracy! Besides, the multitude calleth itself a *practical man*. It asketh, what is the use? It seeth no use but in that which leads to money or the material ends of life. It hath no opinion of having dreamers and drones in society. It believeth, indeed, in railroads; it thinketh well of steam; and owneth that the new art of bleaching by chlorine is a prodigious improvement: but it laughs at the profound researches into the laws of nature, out of which those very inventions grew; and with still greater scorn it laughs at the votaries of the more spiritual forms of truth and beauty, which have no application to the palpable uses of life. Then, again, the influence of our reading public is not favorable to high letters. It demands, it pays for and respects, almost exclusively, a lower style of production; and hence a natural influence to discourage higher labors."

In such a state of feeling the best hope was in the institution of theological seminaries of a high caste. Though the clergy had too commonly been engrossed by the incessant claims of pastoral duty, yet amongst them there was the best chance of forming a set of thoughtful, highly cultivated minds: and if once the standard were raised anywhere, discontent with the general poverty of attainments would soon be widely felt. To these motives for exertion must be added the absolute deficiency of theological instruction. Hobart himself was trained in a Presbyterian college: and while such a course of education might endanger the principles of weaker minds, it certainly deprived the stronger of the blessing of strict theological instruction. To this want, therefore, his attention was early called: he longed to see such institutions founded; but his first care was, that their principles should be so firmly fixed as to preserve them from the passing influence of the day. They were to impart a character; not to adopt that of others. For otherwise they would fail of their highest purpose, and instead of teaching the student

* Quoted in Caswall's American Church.

> "How patiently the yoke of thought to bear,
> Subtly to guide its finest threads along."*

they would soon degenerate, under another name, into the common run of ordinary schools. From fear of this, he opposed, at the cost of much misrepresentation, the earliest proposals for founding a general theological seminary; though none felt more strongly the need of such an institution, or labored more diligently in its formation, when the temper of the Church seemed to justify the undertaking.

In the convention of 1817 this scheme was adopted; and in that of 1820, and in one specially held in 1821, it received its perfect form. The general seminary was established in New-York; it was placed under the control of the whole Church, her bishops being officially trustees, in common with a body elected by the several states from residents within their own borders. Each state chooses one trustee, and one more for every eight of its clergy; and, besides these, it may elect one trustee for every two thousand dollars it contributes to the common fund, with a proviso that when one state already possesses five such trustees, its further contributions must amount to 10,000 dollars for an additional trustee. Thus founded, "the General Theological Seminary" soon struck its roots firmly in the soil. In 1836 eighty-six students were upon its books, at an annual expense of 24*l.* each.† It has already greatly raised the standard of clerical attainments, and its future influence may be more momentous still. Already it has gathered to itself various important endowments, and gives promise of assuming and maintaining something of that high character which for centuries the mother-country has identified with the very names of her "two famous universities." In 1841, though still greatly needing further exertions, it possessed twelve scholarships, endowed with sums varying from 450*l.* to 660*l.*, and professorships, for which endowments of 4,500*l.* and 5,625*l.* had been obtained.‡ It had received since its foundation,

---

* Wordsworth's Ecclesiastical Sketches.
† Caswall's America, p. 155.
‡ Appendix A. to Report of Convention of 1841.

by voluntary contributions, the sum of 228,420 dollars, or about 50,770*l*.; its library at the close of 1837 numbered 6011, and in 1843, 7500 volumes; and, besides the additions made by benefactors, was increasing yearly from the interest of 6000 dollars held as a permanent investment for its benefit.

It was mainly to Bishop Hobart that this institution, so full of promise for America, owed its origin; but he scarcely lived to see it in active operation. The convention of October 1829 filled up the requisite number of trustees, and in the September of the following year he was taken to his rest. He died at his work at Auburn, whilst on the visitation of the western district of his diocese. Worn out by the combined labors of a pressing pastoral charge and an exhausting bishopric, he sunk upon the threshold of his 56th year. His memory will long endure in the grateful remembrance of the churchmen of the west. He left an impression of his well-ordered zeal deeply traced upon many minds and many institutions round him. This he had the joy of witnessing before his dismissal. He was the centre to which men of active and high-principled exertion naturally turned. He lived long enough to survive the clamor which broke in so rudely upon his opening episcopate; and whilst he never receded from a principle, so greatly did his straightforward honesty of character win on all men, that in a contested election of governor of his own state, it was commonly asserted, " that were Bishop Hobart to stand, he would be the only candidate who would carry the vote of both parties."*

In the next convention (Oct. 1832) Bishop B. T. Onderdonk, who had been consecrated two months after Bishop Hobart's death, took his place in the general council of the Church. The episcopate was greatly strengthened since the time when the consecration of Dr. Hobart was a matter of doubtful possibility. In 1823 North Carolina was placed under the care of Bishop Ravenscroft. He administered that diocese in Hobart's spirit. " The situation of this southern country," he tells the Bishop of New-York,

* M'Vickar, p. 485.

"surrendered for the last forty or eighty years to the exclusive influence of dissenters, left me no alternative, but either to increase that influence by adopting half-way measures, or by a decided course to call into action what was left of predilection for her, and to rally her real friends around her."* There were not wanting those who predicted failure from these efforts, which to them seemed premature. But the conclusion, says the bishop, justified his expectations. His course was far shorter than that of his friend and brother in authority. Since the convention of 1829 he, too, had been gathered in amongst the perfected; and in September 1831, Dr. L. S. Ives was consecrated in his room. Others too had been added to the apostolic college. Dr. Meade, as we have seen, had been appointed assistant-bishop of Virginia; Dr. Stone,* after a two-years' vacancy, occupied the place of the late Bishop Kemp of Maryland; whilst three years before, in Pennsylvania, Dr. H. U. Onderdonk had been associated with the aged Bishop White. His election had allayed a strife which threatened to molest the last years of the mild patriarch of the Western Church, and the assistant-bishop strengthened with zeal and judgment his venerable principal. Though now bearing the burden of eighty-four winters, Bishop White was still a constant attendant at the meeting of convention, and imparted to its councils the wisdom and the meekness of his old experience. These were called for at this time by difficulties which had arisen in the state of Ohio. Dr. Philander Chase, whom we have followed through his missionary life to his consecration as its bishop and the founder of Kenyon College, now desired, under trying circumstances, to resign his bishopric. This had been made inseparable from the headship of the college, and between himself and its professors irreconcilable variance had arisen. After long debates, the convention allowed his resignation, and proceeded to act on the choice of a successor, which his diocese had made. On the 31st of October, forty-six years (within two days) from the time of his embarking from the same city to receive consecration

---

* Letter to Bishop Hobart,—Dr. Berrian's Life, p. 366.
† Consecrated Oct. 1830.

from the English archbishop, Bishop White laid his aged hands upon the heads of four more who were severed to bear onward their Master's witness. Dr. M'Ilvaine was consecrated Bishop of Ohio ; Dr. John H. Hopkins of Vermont, now parted from the eastern diocese ; Dr. B. B. Smith of Kentucky, which had been organised three years before ; and Dr. G. W. Doane of the old diocese of New-Jersey. "What a wonderful change,"* says the aged bishop, "had he lived to witness in reference to American episcopacy ;" he who now thus peacefully filled up the vacant seats of rule, "remembered the ante-revolutionary times, when the press profusely emitted pamphlet and newspaper disquisitions on the question, whether an Amerioan bishop was to be endured, and when threats were thrown out, of throwing such a person, if sent, into the river."

Still more important matters marked the next assembly of convention. It met in 1835 at the city of Philadelphia, and would have been marked amongst the synods of that Church, if by nothing else, yet by being the last at which the aged Bishop White was present. But besides this, enduring consequences resulted from its sittings. These appropriately opened with the readmission of Dr. Philander Chase to the upper house as Bishop of Illinois, which under his care had been organised as a diocese since the meeting of the last convention. During that interval he had been laboring as an indefatigable missionary in Michigan, Indiana, and Illinois : and now "a veteran bishop, a soldier of the cross, whom hardships never have discouraged, whom no difficulties seem to daunt, and who entered upon his new campaign with all the chivalry of thirty-five, was cordially welcomed to his seat amongst the counsellors of the Church."†

Early in the session a committee was appointed to take into consideration such an alteration of the constitution as should allow of the division of any diocese which had outgrown the powers of one bishop. "The prosperous and powerful diocese of New-York" gave occasion for this sug-

* Notes to page 63 of Bishop White's Memorial, p. 266.
† Appendix to "Missionary Bishop," p. 37.

gestion; and the canon adopted in committee has since become a part of the constitution, and under it New-York was parted into the eastern and western diocese. This was scarcely arranged, when the whole missionary operations of the Church were brought into discussion. Since the year 1820 these had come under the consideration of convention; before that time they had been left to the voluntary zeal of self-constituted societies; but in that year "a board of missions" was authoritatively organised. The constitution then formed was not, indeed, long retained. It was hastily adopted on the last day of the sitting of convention, and was quickly found to be as inconvenient in practice as it was undoubtedly unsound in principle, since the Bishops of the Church were scarcely recognized, in this their especial function. In 1823, 1829, and 1832, it came again under review, until in 1835 it received its last alterations and permanent organisation.

The importance of this matter requires a more detailed relation of its progress, and this shall be mainly given in the words of those who conducted it, because these will bring more vividly before us the views and feelings which guided the framers of this new arrangement.

The moral and religious state of the vast population which was springing up along the great valley of the Mississippi had grown into a matter of political as well as spiritual moment. The attention of the Church was loudly called to its condition. In a sermon preached at Brooklyn,* the suburbs of New-York, in the year 1835, and published at the request of those who heard it, the preacher asks,† "Can any Christian look without concern upon the movements at the west—the rush of foreign population, the rapid growth of cities and villages, and the astonishing rise in the value of land—without inquiring who is taking possession of this finest part of our country? What are the habits, the intelligence, and the religion of the people? Have they our sacred institutions? Are they an educated people? Are they a religious people? Will they carry with them the 'ark of the covenant' into the wilderness?

---

* By Dr. Benjamin C. Cutler.   † Sermon, p. 9.

Suppose, in answer to these questions, it should be told you, that they were coming to this country without the means of education or religious instruction, or if they have the latter, so closely connected with a foreign political power, and having so little relation to our modes of thinking and feeling, that to the most charitable they promise little or no aid in the great work of enlightening the mind, and to others they are the most alarming accompaniement of the emigration—could you sit quiet and at ease?

" And while you proudly traversed with your eye the majestic map, or beheld the swelling columns of your numerical strength; while the rivers of the west are rolling down their rich harvests, and you by them are enabled to build stately habitations and to dwell in them,—could you forbear to think of the *future?* The more you magnify the wealth and population of the west, unless that population is enlightened and religious, the more should your fears be magnified.

" Cities and villages, governments and maxims of government, opinions, principles, and habits, are all now struggling for existence amid that peculiarly selected, vigorous, and independent population. And while the comparative poverty of the eastern part of our national domain, and the impassable barrier of the Atlantic Ocean, is hemming in and limiting for ever the influence of the eastern and Atlantic states, the horizon towards the west is illimitable.

" States and nations may in future times date their origin back to the millions which have now taken possession of that most fertile part of the American continent. Nor is this all. While the population is increasing and rolling westward, that which is now denominated the east will be compelled into entire subjection to its own offspring. The time cannot be far distant when, contrary to the course of heaven, light and authority will proceed from west to east.* But oh, will it be the pure light of heaven, or the lurid fires of superstition, cruelty, and crime

---

* One state at the west now has more votes and more voices on the floor of congress than four of the New-England states.

"Upon *us* most certainly devolves the duty of directing the destiny of the west, and that is the destiny of both east and west. . . . There is now a crisis in the affairs of the American people. . . . . (much is needed) to retain our prosperity, our liberty, and our religion. . . . On two or three important places has our Church commenced this work. Ohio and Kentucky, at the head of the great valley, have now in the centre of each an institution for extending the influence of religion and learning. Further on, Tennessee and Illinois are organising for this purpose; Missouri and the fertile states at the south through which the riches of the west are passing, will not be long unoccupied. . . . . Whether we shall push our own principles of liberty and religion on to the great battle-ground, and effectually establish them against all opposition, or whether we shall there be met and resisted, and crowded back to the mountains and rocks, where the first great battles of our independence were fought, upon the present generation of American Christians or upon that which shall immediately succeed them, it must under God depend."

Under such a sense of responsibility as regarded the work of domestic missions did the Church engage in reconstructing her missionary constitution. A few extracts from the sermon preached by Dr. Doane, the bishop of New Jersey, at the consecration of Bishop Kemper, on his election by this convention as first missionary bishop, will show the ground taken and the principles affirmed throughout this whole institution. They differ widely from that earlier temper which depressed as low as possible the office and authority of bishops, which restrained the Church from their election, and looked upon them with a watchful jealousy. In answer to the question, "What is a missionary bishop?" he observes: "As the Church obeying the mandate of her divine Head sends presbyters and deacons 'to go into all the world and preach the Gospel to every creature;' so may she, and so should she—emulating that divine compassion which yearned over the fainting multitudes that roamed untended and unfed amongst the mountains of Judæa—send bishops to them, to seek the wandering flocks, to lead them to the sacred fold, to appoint them under-shepherds, to oversee and govern them with due authority and godly discipline, and 'warning every man and teaching every man in all wisdom,' to do all that in them lies 'to present every man perfect in Christ Jesus.' And this is what is meant by a missionary bishop: a bishop *sent forth by* the Church, not *sought for of* the Church ; going *before* to organise the Church, not waiting till the Church has been partially organised ; a leader, not a follower, in the march of the Redeemer's conquering and triumphant Gospel; sustained by their alms whom God has blessed both with the power and will to offer to Him of their substance, for their benefit who are not blessed with both or either of them ; sent by the Church, even as the Church is sent by Christ, not to such only as have knowledge of His truth and desire Him for their King, but to the ignorant and rebellious, to them who know not of His name, or will not have Him to reign over them."

He then goes on to show from holy Scripture that " the *office* of apostle or—the inspiration and the power of miracles ceasing with the necessity for them—of *missionary bishop* was confirmed by Jesus Christ Himself with perpetuity of succession to the end of time;" and then points out " why the times especially require such efforts." Having shown the needs and openings of heathen lands, he points their attention to their own. " Do we look homeward? Through the regions of our own unbounded west see how the stream of life sets onward. Behold, in arts, in wealth, in power, a progress such as earth has never seen, outrunning even fancy's wildest dreams ; but with no provision that at all keeps pace with it for the securing of man's nobler and immortal interests. Observe with what a keen and shrewd regard the Church of Rome has marked that region for her own, and with what steadiness of purpose she pursues her aim, and seeks to lay the deep foundations of a power which is to grow as it grows, and to strengthen as it gathers strength." Further on he reminds them where they are to labor. " THE FIELD IS THE WHOLE WORLD. To every soul of man in every part of it the Gospel is to be preached ; everywhere the Gospel is to be preached, *by, through*, and *in* the Church. To bishops, as the successors of the Apostles, the promise of the Lord was given to be with His Church 'alway to the end of the world;' upon bishops, as successors of the Apostles, the perpetuation of the Christian ministry depends; to bishops, as successors of the Apostles, the government of the Church, the preaching of the word, the administration of the sacraments, the care of souls, has been entrusted. Without bishops, as successors of the Apostles, there is no warrant, and for fifteen hundred years from Christ there was no precedent, for the establishment or the extension of the Church. Possessing these things, act accordingly. Freely ye have received, freely give. Open your eyes to the wants, open your ears to the cry, open your hands for the relief, of a perishing world. Send *the Gospel*, send it as you received it, *in the Church;* send out to preach the Gospel and to build the Church—to every portion of your own broad land—to every stronghold of the prince of hell, to every den and nook and lurking-place of heathendom—a missionary bishop."

Further, he enforces on them the discharge of this their duty by the consideration of the very "genius and order of the Church." "It is of the nature of a *trust* that there be always given with it authority and power for the due execution of all its proper uses. It is still farther of the nature of a trust, that on its acceptance there devolves on the trustee the bounden duty to secure as much as in him lies its full and faithful execution. Now the Gospel is God's gift in trust for the conversion and salvation of lost man. The Church is his trustee. . . . To discharge the duties of a continual trust, the trustee of necessity must have continuance. The Church is by divine appointment *perpetual by succession* in the highest order of her ministry. 'All power is given unto me in heaven and in earth;'* 'As my Father hath sent me, so send I you;'† 'Lo, I am with you always, even unto the end of the world.'‡ . . . . Hence of necessity flow out resulting *trusts*, immense in value and of infinite responsibility. She is to be a *missionary Church*. . . . . Her *bishops* are *Apostles*, each in his proper sphere sent out to 'feed the Church of

---

* St. Matt. xxviii. 18.   † St. John xx. 21.   ‡ St. Matt. xxviii. 20.

God;' jointly and in agreement with established principles of order in the Church, they have the power which Christ imparted to the twelve—'As my Father hath sent me, so send I you'—to send Apostles in His name. Her ministers are all evangelists, to go wherever God shall call them through His Church to bear the blessed tidings of salvation, through the blood of Jesus, for a ruined world. Her *members*, baptised into the death of Jesus, and so purchased by His blood, are missionaries all in spirit or intent, to go, or —if themselves go not—to see that others go, and to contribute faithfully and freely of the ability which God shall give them to sustain them while they go and 'preach the Gospel unto every creature.' Such, as the Scripture teaches, is the original, the permanent, the immutable constitution of the Christian Church; such, by the solemn act of its highest legislative council, is declared to be the constitution of this Church. Baptised into her in the name of the eternal Three in One, you become a *party to the trust* with which she is honored by her heavenly Head to preach the everlasting Gospel. It is a trust which no man who has once assumed can put off; for his baptisimal vow is registered in heaven, and will go with him in its consequences of unmingled bliss or woe throughout eternity."

For the discharge of this trust by her children, he goes on to show them that the Church, after her Lord's example, had now made a fit provision. "It is recorded of the Holy Saviour, as He went out amongst the cities and villages of Judæa preaching the Gospel of the kingdom, that when He saw the multitudes He was moved with compassion on them, because they fainted and were scattered abroad as sheep having no shepherd. 'Then saith He unto His disciples, the harvest truly is plenteous, but the laborers are few; pray ye therefore the Lord of the harvest, that he will send forth laborers into his harvest'.
Behold, brethren, in the service which assembles us this day, the result of God's especial blessing on the Church's holy emulation of her Savior's love. Like Him and on the pathway which His blessed footsteps traced with tears and blood, the Church has gone about amongst the villages and and cities of this broad and sinful land. Everywhere has

she found ignorant to instruct, mourners to comfort, rebels to reclaim, sinners to save; but the west, the vast distant and unsettled west, has fixed her eye and agonised her heart. There, indeed, has she saved great multitudes that fainted with the burden of the weary way, and wandered cheerless and uncared for as 'sheep that have no shepherd.' There, indeed, has she beheld the wily serpent and the prowling wolf, and regretted with bitter tears that she could do no more to guard her Savior's lambs. Encouraged by the divine assurance, she betook herself to prayer . . . she supplicated the gracious Lord of that abundant harvest, that he would 'send forth laborers into His harvest.' He graciously inclined His ear and heard her prayer. . . . . He was present by His divine and Holy Spirit in the council of His Church, as He had been in the councils of the Apostles. He harmonized all hearts. He suggested wisdom, He imparted courage, He communicated thoughts; above all, He sent His Holy Ghost, and poured into their hearts 'that most excellent gift of charity, the very bond of peace and of all virtues,' and so enabled them as but one man to contrive, digest, mature, propose, accomplish, and carry into practice the great missionary work, that here, this day, ... we have come up before His altar, to present the first fruit of the Saviour's answer to His Church's prayer for her lost sheep in the vast west—her first—God grant that it need not long be said—her only missionary bishop."*

Such were the principles on which the new missionary constitution of the American Church was founded; and they are consistently maintained throughout all its details. The report of the committee to which its organization was entrusted, and who agreed " as one man" in their conclusions, was thus explained by their chairman, Bishop Doane (of New Jersey) to the convention. " He showed† that by

---

* Bishop Doane's Sermon.
† Appendix to a sermon preached at the consecration of the Right. Rev. Jackson Kemper, D.D., Missionary Bishop for Missouri and Indiana, in St. Peter's Church, Philadelphia, by G. W. Doane, D.D., Bishop of the diocese of New Jersey, Sept. 25, 1835. The italics, &c., in the text, are copied from the original.

the original constitution of Christ, THE CHURCH, as the Church, was the one great missionary society; and *the Apostles and the Bishops their* SUCCESSORS. *His perpetual trustees; and that this could not and should never be divided or deputed.* The duty, he maintained, to support the Church in preaching the Gospel to every creature, was one which passed on *every Christian by the terms of his baptismal vow*, and from which he could never be absolved. The *general convention* he claimed to be the duly constituted representative of the Church; and pointed out its admirable combination of all that was necessary to secure, on the one hand, the confidence of the whole Church, and, on the other, the most concentrated and intense efficiency. He then explained the constitution of the *board of missions*, the permanent agent of the Church in this behalf; . . . and in subordination to it the two *executive commitees* for the two departments, foreign and domestic, of the one great fold. . . Each having its *secretary* and *agent*, some strong and faithful man, embued . . . with the missionary spirit, the *index-finger*, as it were, of the committee. . . . For the effectual organization of the body in the holy work to which the Saviour calls them, he indicated the *parochial relation* as the most important of all bonds, calling on every clergyman, as the agent of the board, for Jesus' sake to use his utmost efforts in instructing first, and then interesting his people, then in engaging their free-will offering of themselves in its support, upon the apostolic plan of *systematic charity*, laying up in store on every Lord's day as God should prosper them; and when the gathering was made, transmitting to the treasury of the Church the consecrated alms."

This report being received by the convention, a "constitution" in accordance with it was prepared, and adopted with remarkable unanimity. Nothing could show more clearly the general change of feeling in the body than the unanimous adoption by clergymen and laity of this report. Instead of doubtfully and timidly maintaining Episcopacy, amply contented with a cold toleration from others, and deeming apology for her peculiarities continually needful, the Church now declared herself to be indeed Christ's messenger, resolved in His strength to bear his message. Instead of watching jealously the bishop's authority, and restraining it under the merely human machinery of committees and the like, she boldly avowed that in it was the secret of administrative strength, of vigor combined with unity, as well as the principle of ministerial reproduction, and therein the great external instrument for the perpetuity of her own witness. This new and vigorous conduct was the fruit of God's blessing upon their labors who lived not to see on this earth their reward. It was that at which Bishop Hobart had aimed when, as by a trumpet's voice, he had roused her slumbering watchmen. It filled with humble joy the hearts of those who witnessed it. "For ourselves," says an American publication* of the day, "we consider it a measure of far greater promise to the Church of Christ than any which in our day has been effected. In its adoption the Protestant Episcopal Church in the United States has placed herself on primitive ground. She stands as a Church in the very attitude in which the apostolic Church at Jerusalem, when the day of Pentecost had brought the Holy Spirit down to guide and bless it, set out to bear the Gospel of its heavenly Head to every soul of man in every land. As the Church she undertakes, and before God binds herself to sustain the injunction of her Lord, to go and 'make disciples of all nations, baptising them in the name of the Father, and of the Son, and of Holy Ghost.' Upon every one who, in the water of baptism, has owned the eternal triune Name, she lays, on peril of his soul if he neglect it, the same sacred charge. Her bishops are apostles all; her clergy, all evangelists; her members,—each in his own sphere and to his utmost strength—are missionaries every man: and she—that noblest of all names—a *missionary Church*, ' to the intent that now unto the principalities and powers in heavenly places may be made known, by the Church, the manifold wisdom of God.'

"The constitution, as amended, having passed both houses on Friday the 28th, and the committee to nominate

---

* See Appendix to "Missionary Bishop," p. 46.

the board of missions having, on Saturday, been elected by ballot, they reported, on Monday, the persons nominated, who were at once unanimously confirmed. Then, for the first time, was the Church enabled to act to the full limit of her divine commission. Hitherto she had worked to disadvantage in sending out and sustaining, in her missionary field, deacons and presbyters, without the benefit of Episcopal influence and Episcopal supervision. Her flocks were thus without a shepherd; and she stood before the world, so far as she was a missionary Church, an anomaly, a self-contradiction; professing to 'do nothing without a bishop,' and yet planting churches everywhere, which owed allegiance to no bishop, and could claim no bishop's blessing. By the new organization, the missionary authority and the missionary means come into the same hands. Before, the Church ordained missionaries who were to go out under the protection, and rely on the patronage, of a society which the Church could not control; now, the Church herself, by her constituted representative, collects from all her members the offerings of their love; and from the sacred treasure clothes and feeds the servants, whom, in Jesus' name, she sends. She is free now to send; she is able to send; she is entirely safe in sending, as her divine Lord sent at first, the overseer as well as the servant; the elders of the Church not only, but the apostle, 'to ordain elders in every city,' and to 'set in order the things which are wanting.' Accordingly, the board of missions was no sooner organized, than the canon 'of missionary bishops,' which had occupied for several days the attention of the house of clerical and lay deputies, was passed unanimously, providing not only that apostles should be sent to gather in the scattered sheep throughout our own broad land, but to preach the Gospel, and to build the Church, 'where'er the foot of man hath trod.' A canon worthy to be inscribed in golden letters over every altar—let us say more of it than that, *a truly apostolic canon.*

"But Tuesday, Sept. 1st, as it was the last day of the convention, so was it, by eminence, the day of glorious issues for the Church. The board of missions, at the call of the venerable presiding bishop, held its first meeting, and appointed its two committees; that for domestic missions to be located in the city of New-York, and that for foreign missions in the city of Philadelphia. The important business of the session was tending to a close; the whole day had been diligently occupied in the most solemn duties. The canon 'of missionary bishops' had received the final sanction of both houses. Two over-shepherds were to be sent out, the messengers of the Church, to gather and to feed, under the direction of the house of bishops, the scattered sheep that wander, with no man to care for their souls, through all the wide and distant west. It was an act in this Church never exercised before, and yet, upon its due discharge, interests depended which outweigh the world, and will run out into eternity. In the church (St. Andrew's) the representatives of the diocese are assembled. They wait, in their proper places, the eventful issue, while expectation thrills the hearts of all the multitude which throngs the outer courts. In a retired apartment, the fathers of the Church are in deep consultation. There are twelve assembled. They kneel in silent prayer. They rise. They cast their ballots. A presbyter, whose praise is in all the churches, is called by them to leave a heritage as fair as ever fell to mortal man, and bear his Master's cross through the deep forests of the vast south-west. Again the ballots are prepared. They are cast in silence. They designate to the same arduous work, where broad Missouri pours her rapid tide, another, known and loved of all, whom, from an humbler lot, the Saviour now has called to feed His sheep. A messenger bears the result to the assembled deputies. A breathless silence fills the house of God. It is announced that Francis L. Hawks and Jackson Kemper, doctors in divinity, are nominated the two first missionary bishops of the Church; and all the delegates, as with a single voice, confirm the designation.

"One scene remains. The night is far advanced. The drapery of solemn black which lines the church seems more funereal in the faint light of the expiring lamps. The congregation linger still, to hear the parting counsels of their fathers in the Lord. There is a stir in the deep chancel. The bishops enter, and array themselves in their appropriate seats. The aged patriarch, at whose hands they all have been invested with the warrant of their holy trust, stands in the desk—in aspect meek, serene, and venerable, as the beloved John at Ephesus, when, sole survivor of the apostolic band, he daily urged upon his flock the affecting lesson, ' Little children, love one another !' Erect and tall, though laden with the weight of almost ninety winters, and with voice distinct and clear, he holds enchained all eyes, all ears, all hearts, while with sustained and vigorous spirit, he recites, in the behalf and name of all his brethren, the pastoral message, drawn from the stores of his long-hoarded learning, enforced by the deductions of his old experience, and instinct throughout with the seraphic meekness of his wisdom. He ceases from his faithful testimony. The voice of melody, in the befitting words of that delightful Psalm, ' Behold, how good and pleasant it is for brethren to dwell together in unity,' melts every heart. And then all knees are bent, to ask once more, as something to be borne and cherished in all after-life, the apostolic benediction of that good old man."

It was indeed a goodly progress which God had permitted this aged man to witness since eight and forty years before (February 1787) he had kneeled in the chapel at Lambeth, and received the gift of consecration from the English primate. Great had been God's goodness to the infant western Church ; and now, at last, in the spirit of love and of a sound mind which He was pouring out upon her, that goodness seemed to be fulfilled. The old man might well take up the song of holy Simeon, and declare his readiness now " to depart in peace."

The direct consequences of the new missionary organization were soon visible in the Church. They might be traced in a general increase of healthful energy, the natural consequence of the consciousness of having taken rightfully high ground. Funds, which had been sparingly supplied whilst the missionary cause was trusted to occasional appeals, and sacrifices made under excited feelings, now flowed in steadily and abundantly, when every baptised man was summoned in right of his vow at baptism to the duty of making systematic offerings to His Master's cause.

The whole machinery of meetings, and sermons, and auxiliary societies, had only raised the missionary income to 337*l*. per annum from the year 1820, when the society was founded, until 1829. Then a new spirit began to awaken, and in the three next years it had reached more than ten times that amount, exceeding 3000*l*. But it did not rest here. In the very year which followed the amended constitution, the missionary income of the Church was raised at once by the principles, now brought to bear upon the whole community, to a sum exceeding 12,000*l*. The main cause of this vast increase is to be found in the one simple principle of calling upon all to give something to the work, as God hath prospered them, upon the first day of the week, because they are Christian men. This was first warmly pressed upon the Church by the present Bishop (G. W. Doane) of New Jersey, and its immediate pecuniary consequences (far, indeed, the smallest in importance) may be seen in the following statement* of the comparative sums raised in six parishes within his diocese, on an average of five years on the old plan and one of the new.

Parishes.	Average of 5 years under the old plan.			Offerings of the Church for the first year		
	Doll.	Cts.	£. s.	Doll.	Cts.	£ s.
St. Mary's, Burlington	76	94	17 7	271	59	61 4
Trinity Church, Newark	49	52	11 3	149	20	33 1
Christ Church, New Brunswick	13	46	3 0	79	98	18 0
Christ's Church, Newton	5	0	1 2	50	0	11 5
St. Mark's, Orange	7	54	1 15	49	15	11 1
St. Peter's, Morristown	12	36	2 15	32	6	7 4
Total	Under the old		37 2	Under the new		141 16

Nor was this the only evident advance. Men, for the work of the ministry, are more needed in America than money for its conduct. So it must ever be to a great degree; for personal service is a far harder sacrifice than any gifts of substance, and one, therefore, which requires a much stronger faith in him who offers it. Nor can anything more effectually repress this high spirit of self-sacrifice than conducting missionary exertions on a contracted scale, or em-

---

* Taken from Caswall's America and American Church, p. 264.

ploying in the work the lower orders only of the ministry, as if it were unworthy of the higher. On this account the move now made in America promised the happiest results. The sending out the missionary bishop; the attitude assumed by the whole Church; the new responsibility so solemnly professed; all of these awoke attention to the real greatness of the undertaking, and so called forth minds of the highest temper to their appropriate work. The first fruit of the new system may be found in Bishop Kemper's labors, who at once undertook that office for the due discharge of which he was admirably qualified. Wise, courteous, and conciliating, he was at the same time unwearied in energy and unsparing in exertion. The scattered settlers of his missionary diocese have seen and heard the Witness for Christ, who has followed them into the moral wilderness; and to the red man of Indian blood the same blessed message has been borne by the same chief minister of Christ. The band of presbyters is gathering around him. When he was consecrated there was but one in all Indiana; in 1838, eight clergymen were laboring amidst growing congregations. In Missouri, a college under the bishop's eye will soon spread more widely still the daily advancing influence of the Church. Every where life is present and growth visible. In most of the older dioceses there is a marked and even rapid increase. Virginia can again show eighty-four presbyters amongst her pastors, and, which she could not do of old, two bishops at their head. Vermont, which had long formed a part of the eastern diocese, elected, in 1832, its separate bishop, and under his able and vigilant superintendence has been steadily growing in strength and vigor. The other members of the eastern diocese are looking on to a like partition, and like separate existence under their own bishops. New-York is dividing under the provisions of the general convention, into two independent sees. The clergy of Ohio, whose infant beginnings Bishop Chase had fostered, in 1838 numbered almost sixty. In Kentucky diocese they had multiplied from eight to twenty-one between 1832 and 1838; whilst in the same space, in Tennessee, three scattered presbyters have been exchanged for a resident diocesan, twelve settled clergymen, and an infant college for theological instruction. In 1836, Michigan received its bishop, and has since flourished greatly under his exertions; while, in 1838, a diocese was organised in the far southern state of Florida.

Such have been some of the immediate results which have followed the awakening of the Church to the sense of her high duties and entrusted powers. That she may thus go on and prosper, must be the earnest prayer, not only of every English Churchman, but of every one who loves in truth the honor of His Master's name.

For the work of foreign Missions she is eminently qualified. For this peculiar service she is rendered fitter even by her separation from the state; unfettered by political connection, she may multiply at need her bishops, whilst the energy and maritime adventure of her anglo-Saxon race promise to secure admission for her sons to every nation of the earth. It may be that for this work specially her witness has been thus raised up in the west; it may be that for this the providence of God was over-ruling that want of faith, or that indolence, at home which never suffered her to grow into a perfect Church whilst her connection with the mother-people lasted;—that so she might spring at length into a sudden maturity, rich in hopes, rich in expectations; in the first possession of her powers, when she could thus use them without let or hindrance for the evangelizing of the world.* From us she must have learned a

---

* It is impossible to omit here all mention of the noble efforts made in this great cause at Athens, by the Rev. Mr. and Mrs. Hill. I have now before me, through the kindness of a friend, a letter from one well qualified to judge, written from Athens in October 1844, and which contains the following sentences:—" Mr. Hill is the next man in Athens to King Otho. .... An able and successful diplomatist here told me, that he was firmly persuaded that Mr. and Mrs. Hill had conferred far more signal benefits upon Greece than all the allied powers put together. His praise of Mrs. Hill was scarcely bounded; he said that she was a woman of the rarest qualities of excellence, and that her heart, especially for goodness and stoutness (and it had been severely tried in both respects), could scarcely be equalled. He believed that they had been the cause of the education of more than 20,000 Greeks. They taught and they sent forth those prepared to instruct; and their example has been followed, and is working a wonderful reformation.

slower and more cautious policy; and even the achievement of her national independence might not have broken through old habits, or set her free to labor in the ardor of her first love for every race which yet sits in darkness.

May this, then, be her course; may she be stirred up to earnest prayer, to high gifts of self-sacrifice, to untiring and well-ordered labors, and the grace of God will go along with her. Great achievements lie before her. An open field for noble and unlimited service invites all her energies. In her, too, is the "salt of the earth" for the preservation of her own busy and restless people. The unbounded western frontier, her fertile soil, her enterprising citizens, her mighty forests, her harbors, her traffic, and her merchandise—these may make America rich and luxurious, and for a season mighty among the people of the earth; but in the Church of Jesus, thus planted in the midst of her, and in that alone, is to be found the pervading, elevating, and enduring influence, which can make her truly great.

This important convention rose on the 1st of September, 1835. It was the last, as has been said, over which the venerable Bishop White presided. Long as it had been delayed, to him also the last summons was now sent. Throughout this year and until the following June, he continued as usual to officiate in his parish duties. Then severe illness bowed down his aged frame. Still his strength endured. He rallied from his sickness, and appeared to be again possessed of renovated vigor; and it was hoped he might preside at the approaching consecration of Dr. M'Coskry, elected bishop of Michigan. But his sands were fast running out. No violent disease re-appeared; but the fountains were broken up, and his life ebbed gently from him. Surrounded by his family, and attended by Bishop Doane and Dr. M'Coskry, "in full reliance on the alone merits of his Saviour, and blessed in realizing God's protecting care in life and death,"* he meekly breathed his last, during the morning service of the Church he loved, on Sunday, July 17, 1836.

* Life of Bishop White, by Dr. Bird Wilson, p. 267.

Of the character of this good man, little can be added to what has been already said in tracing the history with which his life is intertwined. He was doubtless an eminent instrument of God in laying the foundations of the western Church. For this his meek wisdom greatly fitted him; probably with any other cast of character he could not have done what he now was able to effect. Though classed by his biographer with "the low-church divines, as they are called, of the Church of England," he yet maintained firmly the distinctive features of Church doctrine. Speaking of a sermon preached by Bishop Moore before the convention of 1820, and of the offence given to some of the house of deputies by its maintaining the doctrine of baptismal regeneration, he admits that on such an occasion "all questions should be avoided in which the sense of the episcopal Church is doubtful." "But," he continues, "it is to be lamented that there should be brought under this head a doctrine which we have been taught to lisp in the earliest repetitions of our Catechism, which pervades sundry of our devotional services, especially the baptismal, which is affirmed in our Articles also, which was confessedly held and taught during the ages of the martyrs, and the belief of which was universal in the Church until it was perceived to be inconsistent with a religious theory, the beginning and the progress of which can be as distinctly traced as those of any error of popery"*

He was not less distinct as to the ministry of the Christian Church. In his "Lecture on the Catechism," he lays it down that bishops, priests, and deacons, are of divine appointment;† that succession is the only mode of transmitting the ministry which is of divine institution; and that the door of entering opened by the Head of the Church is the only one through which the character of a pastor in the Church can be obtained.‡

It is true that it is difficult always to reconcile his

---

* Life by Dr. Bird Wilson, p. 229.
† Ibid. p. 157, 158.
‡ Vide letter of Bishop Hobart to Bishop White—in M'Vickar's Life, p. 413.

practical concessions with the strictness of the principles he here lays down; but, as we have seen, this very temper made him probably the fitter instrument for his own peculiar task. God works by various hands; and the soft and yielding, so that they be faithful to His truth, have their own appointed task, even as to the sterner and more rugged, if his grace dwell in them, is allotted theirs. And to his light this venerable man would seem to have been always true. He was bred, indeed, in a lower school both of faith and Christian feeling than that which was afterwards vouchsafed to the Church; and from this cause there seems, to a certain extent, to have always hung about him a want of distinctness as to the higher Christian doctrines, and a corresponding want of warmth of spiritual character: but he was a truly humble man, and the blessing of the meek was his. His trust was only in his crucified Redeemer, and he did seek for the sanctifying presence of the Holy Spirit. The rock was under him; and throughout a long life he never shrunk from any known duty.

When, in the autumn of 1793, the yellow fever first appeared in Philadelphia, it spread a panic terror through all classes. The curse of a plague-struck city was upon the population. Along the deserted streets, amidst the vultures which prayed upon the offal, roamed only those fiends in human garb, who seek at such a moment for plunder amongst the dying and the dead. Three-fourths of all the inhabitants had fled from the place. The outcast, the infected, the dying, and the few whom love kept still around their beds,—these only remained. Dr. White was strongly urged to join the flying throng. The specious argument, that his single life was eminently precious, assailed him from the lips of those whom he esteemed for piety and loved with the simple warmth of family affection. But he listened not to such suggestions. Where should the pastor be at such a time but with the sick and dying? where the bishop but at the head of his flock? Removing his family into the country, he remained at his own house, spending days and nights with the victims of the pestilence. One servant, who resolved to remain with his master, died in his sight; but his faith was not shaken; and the plague passed off without his receiving any injury.

Once again, thirty-nine years later, he was tried in the same way. The Asiatic cholera appeared at Philadelphia with all the terror of its appalling character and unknown course. His advanced years would then have furnished an easy excuse for one who sought to escape the supposed danger of intercourse with the infected. But the aged bishop was a man of another stamp; and in his eighty-fifth year he might be seen daily in the cholera-hospital, praying by the bedside of the dying patient.

Nor, with so much that was naturally yielding in his temper, did he fail, when his judgment was decided, boldly to resist those with whose political opinions he was most predisposed to sympathise. In his later years a large sum of money was bequeathed by a wealthy Philadelphia merchant to the corporation of the city, for the foundation of an orphan college, on the sole condition that the boys should be kept without any instructions in any religious creed, from six to eighteen, that they might then "adopt such religious tenets as their matured reason should enable them to prefer." But the good bishop was not to be led away by this specious liberality. He at once condemned the conditions of the will, and addressed to the corporation an uncompromising and powerful appeal, in which he urged them "to a respectful but determined rejection of the trust." "It is," he allowed, "a great sacrifice; but it cannot be too great when the acceptance of it would be an acknowledgement that religion, even in its simplest forms, is unnecessary to the binding men to their various duties."*

---

* Life of Bishop White, p. 244. The speech of D. Webster, when, in 1844, the question came, by appeal from the local jurisdiction of Philadelphia, before the supreme court of the United States, is full of a noble eloquence: "Would any Christian parent," he asks, "consider it desirable for his orphan children after his death to find refuge in this asylum . . . under all the circumstances and characteristics which belong to it? . . . . . Poor as children can be left, who would not rather trust them to the Christian charity of the world,

Diocese.	Connecticut.	Pennsylvania.	New-York.	Virginia.	Maryland.	South Carolina.	New Hampshire and Massachusetts.	New Jersey.	Ohio.
1784. Nov. 14	Dr. S. Seabury.*								
1787. Feb. 4.		Dr. W. White.							
1790. Sep. 19			Dr. S. Provoost.						
1792. Sep. 12				Dr. J. Madison.					
1795. Sep. 14					T. J. Claggett, D.D.				
1797. May 7						R. Smith, D.D.			
— Oct. 18	Abraham Jarvis, D.D.						E. Bass, D.D.		
1801. Sep. 11			Benj. Moore, D.D.*						
1804. Sep. 14							Samuel Parker, D.D.*		
1811. May 29			J. H. Hobart, D.D.†				A. V Griswold, D.D.†		
1812. Oct. 15						Theo. Dehon, D.D.			
1814. May 18				R. C. Moore, D.D.*					
— Sep. 1					— Kemp, D.D.*				
1815. Nov. 10								John Croes, D.D.	
1816.	Vacant by the death of Dr. Jarvis.								
1818. Oct. 8						N. Bowen, D.D.*			
1819. Feb. 11									Philander Chase, t.D.
— Oct. 27	T. C. Brownell, D.D.								
1823. May 23					Vacant by the death of Dr. Kemp, 1827.				
1827. Oct. 25		H. U Onderdonk, D.D.*							
1829. Oct. 19				W. Meade, D.D.†					
1830. Oct. 21			B. T. Onderdonk, D.D.		W. M. Stone, D.D.				
— Nov. 26									J. S
1831. Sep. 59.									
1832. Oct. 31								G. W. Doane, D.D.	C. P. McIlvaine, D.D.
1834. Jan. 14									L. S. I
1835. (consecrated 1819)									
1835. Sep. 23									
1836.									
Joined the general convention as "organised Churches."	1789	1785	1785	1785	1785	1785		1785	1819

* Bishop Seabury died in 1796.
† Assistant bishop to Bishop White

* Dr. Provoost resigned.
† Assistant bishop.

* After a vacancy of two years
† Assistant bishop.

* Vacant by the death of Dr. Smith.

* Suffragan to Bishop Claggett till 1818.
† After a vacancy of three years.

* Succeeded Dr. Dehon, who died August, 1817.

* On the death of Dr. Bass, Vermont and Rhode Island were associated with Massachusetts and New Hampshire, called henceforth "the Eastern Diocese."

He died, as he had lived for eighty-eight years—without an enemy ; and, the first of that order which had been the subject of such fierce suspicions, he was followed to the grave, through streets from which ordinary business had been spontaneously banished, by the public authorities, by the various literary and charitable bodies, and by thousands of unpurchased mourners.

The thread of our history has brought us down to living men, and scenes in the great drama which are not yet acted out. Here it seems meet to pause, remembering the caution of the wise historian, who, for safety's sake, would not " follow even truth too closely by the heels." We have brought down the history of the Church from its ambiguous colonial existence, through the struggles of the war of independence, to its firm and general establishment in the wide regions of the western continent. The table which concludes this chapter will show at one view the dates and order of the foundation of the various dioceses, and the consecrations of the different bishops of America.

It remains only, in the concluding chapter, to estimate the present position, and, as far as may be, the yet distant prospect, of the body the history of which thus lies before us.

however uncertain it has been said to be, than place them where their physical wants and comforts would be abundantly attended to, but away from the solaces, the consolations, the graces, and the grace of the Christian religion ?"

CHAPTER XII.

Present influence of the Episcopal Church—Rapid extension—Estimated numbers—Clergy—Extent and population of dioceses—Influence on the moral character of the people—Favorable symptoms—Sects—Revivals—Socinianism—Sober tone of the Church—Duelling—Its character in America—Instance—Church resists duels—Canon—Instance—Unfavorable symptoms—Divorce—Marriage—Treatment of the colored race—The great sore of America—State of negroes in the south, religious, moral, physical—Slave-breeding states—Internal slave-trade—Duty of the Church to testify—Her silence—Participation—Palliation of these evils—State of the colored population in the north—Insults—Degradation—Caste—Duty of the Church—Her silence—Case of General Theological Seminary—Alexander Crummell—Estimate of her influence—Her small hold on the poor—Architecture and arrangement of churches—Pew-rent system—Prospects of the Church—Danger from indifference to formal truth—Chaplains to Congress—Thomas Jefferson—Romanism—Its schismatical rise in America—Spread in the West—Promises a refuge from the sects—Courts democracy—Main resistance from the Church—How she may be strong—Need of adhering to her own principles—Of a high moral tone—The slave-question—Favorable promise—Higher principles—More care of the poor—Colored race—Gains on the population—Conclusion.

In forming an estimate of the present state of the American Episcopal Church, there are several lines of inquiry which we may follow up. The first which naturally suggests itself is, its territorial and numerical hold upon the extent and population of the land. If, then, we compare the map of America with the fixed organization of the Church, we are at once struck with its rapid and universal extension. Bishoprics, as well as what in the looser language of the west are termed dioceses,* are well-nigh

* Districts in which a number of congregations are united together according to the rules of the American Church, and so termed " or-

co-extensive with the states of the Union. Through all that vast continent the living form of Church-polity has grown up as in a night, from the two bishops who landed at New-York on Easter Sunday, 1787. From puritan Massachusetts in the north, down to the slave-tilled bottoms of torrid Louisiana, and from the crowded harbor of New-York back to the unbroken forests and rolling prairies of Illinois, the successors of the Twelve administer in Christ's name the rule of His spiritual kingdom.

It is not so easy to estimate aright the proportion of the varied population of these wide tracts which have received this faith. The work of its leaven-like power and growing presence is noiseless and secret, and to obtain exact accuracy may be impossible ; but something may be done. It has been calculated, as the nearest approximation which can be obtained, that about 1,500,000 of the population of the United States belong to this communion ; its clergy amount to 1224.* Here, therefore, also, is abundant proof of a wide-spread and increasing growth of this fair plant of God amongst our western children ; since the hindrances imposed by our carelessness or fear were swept away, and it has been allowed to strike at will its roots among them.

But though there be goodly signs of life and growth in the extension of dioceses and the gathering in of souls, yet, on the other hand, when we see the vast extent over which diocesan authority is spread, it seems as if it must too often melt into a shadow: and when further we compare the number in the fold with the multitude without, we perceive that as yet the hold of this communion on the mass of living acting men can be but slight. It is too plain, that in many districts it consists only of a scattered handful here and there, and has not yet gathered in with a strong arm the ripe harvest of souls into the garner of the Lord. The annexed table will show at one view the number of the bishops and clergy in each state, and opposite to them the number of the square miles over which

ganized," and capable of sending delegates to convention, but which do not yet possess a bishop.

* Church Almanac for 1844: New-York.

their charge extends, and of the masses for whom they labor. As a general conclusion, we may see that these 22 bishops and 1202 clergy are ministering among a mass of human beings, of all colors of belief, or of no belief at all, amounting to above 17 millions, who are scattered over an extent of above one million of square miles.

Bishops.	Clergy.	States.	Population.	Square miles.
0*	6	Maine	501,793	32,000
0	10	New Hampshire	284,574	9,280
1	29	Vermont	291,948	10,200
1	58	Massachusetts	637,699	7,800
1	25	Rhode Island	108,830	1,095
1	102	Connecticut	310,015	4,800
1	202	New-York	1,293,783	21,751
1	105	Western New-York	1,135,138	21,463
1	47	New Jersey	373,306	6,600
1	115	Pennsylvania	1,724,022	46,000
1	11	Delaware	78,085	2,120
1	93	Maryland	469,232	10,930
2	98	Virginia	1,239,797	64,000
1	32	North Carolina	753,110	43,800
1	49	South Carolina	594,398	30,000
1	62	Ohio	1,519,467	50,000
1	14	Georgia	770,000	58,000
1	22	Kentucky	790,000	40,000
1	12	Tennessee	829,210	40,000
0†	11	Mississippi	375,651	48,000
1	7	Louisiana	351,176	48,220
1	24	Michigan	211,705	55,000
0‡	10	Alabama	650,000	46,000
1	14	Illinois	474,404	59,500
0	4	Florida	54,207	87,750
0§	15	Indiana	683,317	35,000
0§	10	Missouri	381,102	64,000
1	9	Wisconsin	30,852	
0§	4	Iowa	43,068	
0‖	2	Arkansas	95,642	58,000
22	1202		17,055,531	1,001,309

* Administered by the Bishop of Rhode Island.
† Administered by the Bishop of Tennessee.
‡ Administered by the Bishop of Louisiana.
§ These three administered by the missionary bishop residing in Wisconsin.
‖ Administered by the Bishop of Tennessee.

But another and a better measure of the influence of this body on the people of the west is afforded by its actual power over morals and opinions. Now, tried by this test, the conclusion does not differ greatly from that yielded by the last. Much, undoubtedly, it is doing, and has done. No where have the restless waters of the multitude of sects tossed themselves in wilder madness than in the new world. The line of this history forbids any minute examination of their state; but the general aspect they present towards the Episcopalian body must be noticed.* Between it and some of them there is as close an approximation as there can be without union. To many of the separation, Christ's truth has never been proposed in any other form than that in which they hold it. In them there has been no stubborn rejection of a higher teaching, but rather a diligent use of all which has been vouchsafed to them. On such men the blessing of God has visibly rested. No unprejudiced observer can doubt that His grace has wrought through them His blessed work for multitudes around them. As their light increases, many of these join openly the Church's ranks. So far, indeed, does this migration prevail, that no fewer than one-half of the existing clergy, and even of the bishops† themselves, have been won over from the sects. And this process seems still to be extending. At Boston there is now a striking revulsion of feeling towards the Church, of whose exclusively apostolical constitution many of the ministers amongst the sects are now convinced. Their present position seems to be one which honest men cannot long consent to occupy. They "admit the doctrine of the visible Church, and the apostolical succession, and consequently the schism of which the original founders of their sect were guilty;" but claim "prescription as effacing the flaw in the original deed." Thus it is their view, that sectarians, *as a body*, ought to reunite themselves to the Church, and that each individual ought to endeavor earnestly to bring about this reunion; whilst, without it, he would not be justified in straggling from his appointed place in the economy of Providence.‡ This position seems to imply much the same dishonesty of mind as would lead an English Churchman, whose affections had been unhappily seduced to Rome, to remain within

---

* See preface. † Caswall, p. 332.
‡ Letters from America, vol. ii. p. 160. The exact words are not given.

the English Church, seeking to bring her again under the bonds and corruption of the Papacy. Still, the effect on minds so disposed, of the institutions and doctrines after which they are reaching forth, cannot easily be overrated.

Greatly is such an influence needed by these bodies. Abundant as some of them have no doubt been in faith and good works, yet, taken as a whole, they signally illustrate the absurdities and degradation to which religious license, unlimited by fixed forms of belief, is ever prone to run. The rise and prevalence of Mormonism is a startling fact in the religious history of man; and the same features, though less broadly marked, may be traced in many other quarters. Religion has always exhibited a tendency to wear out within a few generations where it has not been kept fixed and permanent by the external framework at first appointed by the Lord. That such has been the case in America we have a striking testimony in the writings of Bishop Chase, himself, as has been seen,* sprung from a dissenting family which had maintained its early principles with unusual faithfulness. "When the Puritans," he says,† "by leaving the Church, broke the vessel, the oil was split upon the ground; and though some of it may be gathered in the sherds and burn brightly for a time, yet the flame soon expires, and all around is left in darkness." Such was the existing state of things he found in Vermont. Catechisms had been laid aside; to teach their children the fundamental principles of the Christian faith was deemed an infringement on their natural and inalienable rights; by far the greater part had not been baptised; and the general ignorance was turned to their own purposes by various classes of infidels.

Such has been too often, in the west, the unhappy progress of declining faith; and so the ground has been left open for increasing evil. Every fantastic opinion which has disturbed the peace of Christendom has been re-produced in stronger growth on the other side of the Atlantic. Division has grown up in all its rankness, and seeded freely on every side a new crop of errors. Even amongst those

* P. 239. † Reminiscences, p. 100.

sects which have retained the largest measure of original truth, the effects of this state of things are visible. The history of their "Revivals," as they are termed, with their "new measures," "anxious seats," "itinerant evangelists," and "protracted meetings," sometimes of forty days' continuance,* is little else than a record of the wildest extravagance,† which, in the judgment of the more sober even of their own body, "threatens to pour forth a host of ardent, inexperienced, imprudent young men, to obliterate civilization, and roll back the wheels of time to semi-barbarism, until New-England of the west shall be burnt over, and religion disgraced and trodden down, as in some parts of New-England it was done eighty years ago, when laymen and women, Indians and negroes, male and female, preached and prayed, and exhorted, until confusion itself became confounded." "This will unavoidably produce infidels, scoffers, unitarians, and universalists, on every side, increasing the resistance seven-fold to evangelical doctrine." ‡

This has been already the fruit of these fierce excitements. The children of "the pilgrims" have openly cast off their fathers' creed, and glory in doctrines which were marked out in the days of New-England's settlement for the direst anathema. In Massachusetts§ the Socinians

* Drs. Reed and Matheson's Visit, vol. ii. p. 40.

† The following extract from an unsuspected quarter will show the true nature of these artificial heats. "A revival-preacher, after delivering a sermon, called on 'the anxious' to meet him in the lecture-room. About 200 obeyed. He called on them to kneel in prayer; and he offered an alarming and terrific prayer. They arose. 'As many of you,' he said, 'as have given yourselves to God in that prayer, go into the new convert room.' Upwards of twenty went. 'Now,' he said to the remainder, 'let us pray.' He prayed again in like manner. He then challenged those who had given themselves to God in that prayer to go into the new convert room. Another set followed. This was repeated four times. The next morning he left the town, having previously sent a notice to the newspapers, stating that Mr. —— had preached there last night, and that 61 converts professed religion." Drs. Reed and Matheson's *Visit*. vol. ii. p. 29.

‡ Letters from Dr. Beecher,—Reed and Matheson, vol. ii. pp. 34, 35.
§ Reed and Matheson, vol. ii. p 60.

have 130 Societies and 110 ministers : in the town of Boston their congregations average from 600 to 1000. Theirs, "if not the religion of the numerical majority, is that of the opulent and official classes, who compose the aristocracy of the city. .... It is said, indeed, that with whatever religion men begin life, when they get very rich, and withdraw from active business, they"* join this party. In its tenets they find repose from the extravagant excitement of the other sects ; they are freely allowed such unlimited measures of infidelity or doubt as suit their own inclinations ; and they find themselves surrounded by those who take the lead in every walk of social life. This state of things has long been growing up: the Church was too weak around the Puritans to keep them by its indirect influence to the foundations of the faith ; and no sect that has ever yet arisen has possessed, within itself, the gift of permanence. Here the declension began early ; and so gradually did their deadly error overspread them, that Boston was not conscious of the change until it was incautiously disclosed by an English brother. It was then found, on inquiry, that "in Boston every thing was gone except the old South Meeting; and, within a radius of fifteen miles, not ten ministers could be found of the Congregational order holding the ' truth as it is in Jesus.' "†

Against such declensions the presence of the Church is, under the blessing of Almighty God, an appointed safeguard. From the excitements which sweep at times over the sects, burning all to-day with an intemperate heat, and leaving all behind them waste and bare, even those amongst her pastors have been free, who, from warmth of natural temper or doctrinal views, have most addressed themselves to the religious feelings of their flock.‡ And thus not only have they withheld from their own people these withering blights, but they have done much for all denominations round them. It was the remark of a Socinian gentleman, from Massachusetts, as floating down the Connecticut river (in 1834), he noticed the Episco-

Buckingham's America, vol. iii. p. 450.
† Reed and Matheson, ut sup.
‡ Life of Bp. Moore of Virginia, by Dr. Henshaw, p. 101.

pal churches on each side the stream. " If those churches had been in Massachusetts, there would have been few Unitarians."* The influence thus exercised can scarcely be over-rated. It breaks out visibly in smaller things,—as in the universal observance of Good Friday in Connecticut, from deference to Churchmen,†—and in greater matters is always in action. The fixed creed of the Church, its settled liturgy, its decent and reverent forms, its educated ministry, its tone of practical reality; these are felt continually as restraints to some, and patterns to others. Amidst the madness of the angry waves, one bark holds its anchorage, and becomes to those around it a witness for fixedness and truth.

On the general character of society it exerts continual influence. Throughout the states it ranks amongst its members those who, from position and superior education, must ultimately fix the standard of feeling: and against some of the great evils which infect American society it has raised its solemn and not wholly ineffectual protest.

Thus, to take one example : duels, such as barbarous times can scarcely parallel, are not uncommon in America. Utterly unchristian as are those we know in England, they are wholly of another character from these, of which vengeance and the thirst for blood are undisguised features. How little public opinion has as yet condemned them, a single narrative will show. It is a rule of Congress that when any member dies during the sitting of the houses, he shall be honored with a public funeral. During the winter session of 1838, two members of the house of representatives at Washington quarrelled, and met to fight a duel. Rifles were, as is usual, the selected weapons. At a distance of eighty yards they exchanged fire without effect. After an hour's pause they were placed again, and each taking deliberate aim, fired a second time with the same result. A longer pause than the preceding followed, during which it was arranged, that if at the next fire neither party were killed or wounded, the distance between them should be shortened. No such precaution, however, was needful

---

* Caswall's America, p. 149.   † Ib. p. 145.

to secure the necessary bloodshed, for at the next fire the receiver of the challenge fell, and died within five minutes. Three days later the senators and whole population of the town, male and female, " the ladies thronging the galleries," filled the hall of representatives, to honor the fallen duellist with a public funeral. At twelve o'clock the speaker of the house was seated in the chair, the bier before him, whilst the members, the judges of the supreme court, the heads of departments, the secretaries of state, and the president and vice-president of the United States, lined the hall around the coffin. Then came the mummery of religion, with " appropriate extemporaneous prayers from the chaplain of the senate," and then " a funeral address by the chaplain of the house of representatives."* Both the chaplains were Methodists of different kinds; and it was but a sorry sacrifice to violated principle, that the honor of the public funeral should be clouded by an unavoidable censure upon duelling, in the funeral address. Far different has been the conduct of the Church as to this system of detestable enormities. As early as 1808, convention had resolved, " That the ministers of this Church ought not to perform the funeral service in the case of any person who shall give or accept a challenge to a duel."† This raised a new standard, and from this we do not find them shrinking. Such an instance stands on record in Bishop Hobart's correspondence. " I have been severely tried"—one of his friends writes to him : " it has pleased the Almighty, in the order of His providence, to exact from me a proof of fidelity to His commands. Adversity has come on me in the hideous form of dishonor : it has struck me where I was most exposed. . . . . For one accustomed, as I have been, to the applause of the world, on whose ear the voice of censure has scarcely ever come in the slightest whisper, to be denounced by a man who has filled the second command in our Virginian army, and a seat in the senate of the United States, as a hypocrite and coward,

---

* J. S. Buckingham's America, vol. i. pp. 272, 273.

† Journals of Convention of 1816, p. 254. This was modified in the Convention, but only so far as to withdraw the application of the resolution from those who had since manifested penitence.

without being allowed to repel the latter charge but by confirming the former . . . . . to be thus persecuted, is a trial which has required all my piety to sustain without sinking beneath it. . . . . . I am justly though severely chastised : I bow submissively to the Cross, where my Saviour ignominiously expired. Blessed Jesus, inspire Thy poor follower with the humility which illustrated Thy life, Thy sufferings, and Thy death."*

One such testimony against this unchristian custom is beyond all price in a land so governed by opinion as the United States.

These, and many more, are the favorable features of the picture. There are others of a different character,— and they must not be withheld. And to touch first on a subject which has always been an especial charge of the Christian Church ; she has not in America maintained the outworks of domestic purity, by guarding carefully the sanctity of holy matrimony. Divorces are allowed on slight and insufficient grounds.† To divorce his wife, or even to fail in the attempt to obtain a divorce from the state, would not greatly impair the reputation, even of one in holy orders. On this point the Roman Catholics in America have maintained a Christian strictness on which the Protestant communion has never ventured. Allied to this are many kindred flaws ; marriages are publicly allowed within some at least of the prohibited degrees ; the divorced are speedily re-married ; and their second nuptials labor under no reproach. Again, amongst our western brethren,

---

* M'Vickar's Life of Bishop Hobart, pp. 457, 458.

† The facility with which divorces are obtained in some states is illustrated by a fact, mentioned to the author by a friend (the Rev. H. Caswall), which would be highly ludicrous, if it did not involve such serious considerations. An aged couple in Kentucky, remarkable for their long-continued domestic happiness, were marked out for a practical joke. A petition was sent into the state-legislature, praying, on some trivial ground for a divorce. The bill passed unopposed ; and in three weeks, to their horror, they found themselves divorced : they absolutely separated, the wife returning to her friends, and were afterwards solemnly re-married.—Perhaps it may not be safe to draw any very broad inference from such an incident as this.

the marriage ceremonial is rarely performed within the chnrch : a private room, and often a late hour in the day, are its usual place and time, to the grievous loss of reverential decency.

And now to turn to a subject less exclusively ecclesiastical. In forming an estimate of the moral influence of the Episcopalian body, we cannot fail to notice its bearing on the treatment of the colored race. This is in America the great question of the present generation : socially, politically, morally, religiously, there is none which can compare with it. Never in the history of any people was the righteous retribution of the holy and living God more distinctly marked than in the manifold evils which now trouble America for her treatment of the African race. Like all other sinful courses, it has brought in, day by day, confusion and entanglement into all the relations of those contaminated by it. It is the cause which threatens to disorganise the union; it is the cause which upholds the power of mobs and " Lynching;" it is the occasion of bloodshed and violated law; it is, throughout the south, the destroyer of family purity, the hindrance to the growth of civilization and refinement; it is the one weak point of America as a nation, exposing her to the deadliest internal strife, that of an internecine war, whenever a foreign enemy should find it suit his purpose to arm the blacks against their masters. Further, like all other great and established evils, it is most difficult to devise any escape out of the coils which it has already wound around every civil and social institution; whilst every day of its permitted continuance both aggravates the evil, and increases the difficulty of its ultimate removal. This, then, is exactly one of those sore evils of which the Church of Christ is the appointed healer. She must, in His name, rebuke this unclean Spirit: she who has been at all times the best adjuster of the balance between the rich and poor, between those who have and those who want; she who has redressed the wrongs of those who have no helper; she who, wherever she has settled, has changed slaves or serfs, by whatever title they are known, into freemen and peasants ;—she must do this in the west, or the salt of the earth hath lost its savor, and is given over, with all things around, to the wasting of that utter and extreme corruption which she should have arrested.

Now, to see how far the Church has fulfilled this her vocation, we must have distinctly before us the real posture of this question in America. Of the twenty-six states, thirteen are slave-states; admitting, that is, within their own borders, the institution of slavery as a part of their institutions; and of these, five—Maryland, Virginia, Kentucky, Missouri, and, in part, Tennessee—are slave-selling, whilst those south of them are slave-buying states.

It will, therefore, be seen at once, that in the various districts of the union widely different parts of the system are at work. But its curse is upon all. Chiefly does it rest upon the south. There, to his own, and little less to his master's degradation, the slave is held in direct personal bondage, and accounted merely as a chattel. Hence, at the caprice of his owner, he is treated not unfrequently with fearful cruelty: though these, it may be granted, are not the ordinary cases; since, except under the impulses of passion, no rational owner will misuse his own chattels. It is not, therefore, for these instances of cruelty, fearful as they occasionally are, that the system will be chiefly odious in the Christian's eyes.* Nor will

---

* Not to quote any of those occasional barbarities which may be turned in some measure aside as extreme cases, it is impossible to deny the ordinary cruelty of the system, when every southern newspaper abounds in such advertisements as these: "Ten dollars reward for my woman Siby, very much scarred about the neck and ears by whipping." *Mobile Commercial Advertiser.*—" Committed to jail, a negro slave; his back is very badly scarred." *Planters' Intelligencer,* Sept. 26, 1838.—" Runaway, negress Caroline; had on a collar with one prong turned down." *Bee, Oct.* 27, 1837.—" Detained at the police jail the negro wench Myra; has several marks of lashing, and has irons on her feet." *Bee, June* 9, 1838.—" Runaway, a negro woman and two children. A few days before she went off, I burnt her with a hot iron on the left side of her face; I tried to make the letter M." *Standard, July* 18, 1838.—" Brought to jail, John ———, left ear cropt." *Macon Telegraph, Dec.* 25. 1837.—" Runaway, a negro, name Humbledon; limps on his left foot, where he was shot a few weeks ago while a runaway." *Vicksburg Register,* Sept. 5, 1838.—" Runaway, a black woman; has a

it be from any notions of the abstract and inalienable rights of man. On these, in their common signification of the possession of political power, we do not touch; it is with the want of personal freedom we are concerned; nor is it needful to assert, that slavery is, under all circumstances, directly forbidden by the law of God. It is enough for our purpose, that as administered in America, it is a violation of the Christian precept, "Honor all men." That by its denial of all family life, its necessary irreligion, and its enforced ignorance, it deprives the slave of the privileges of redeemed humanity, and is directly opposed to the idea of the Christian revelation. To maintain this ground it is not necessary to assert that no slaves are happy in their servitude. For the happiest slave in American servitude is the greatest proof of the evil of the system. He is most utterly debased by it, who can be happy in such a state. What that state is is plain enough. The common language of the slave-states, which has given to all those who labor the title of "mean whites," is abundant proof of their own estimate of slavery. But, further, as a general rule, the slave is not happy. The advocates of the system confess this in a thousand ways. Their columns of advertisements for runaways, their severe laws against those who aid or harbor fugitives, their occasional gifts of liberty to slaves who have wrought some great act of public good, their fierce jealousy of all speech or action which threatens ever so remotely their property in man, all bespeak the same secret conviction:—they do know the misery of slavery. The testimony of the Canadian ferryman,* who described the leap of the escaped slave, when the boat reaches the British shore, as unlike any other, is not more directly to the point.

Accordingly, the master-evil of the south is, that the slaves are not treated as having souls; they are often petted, often treated like spoiled children, never as men. On this point there is no dispute. "Generally speaking they are a nation of heathen in the midst of the land. They are

scar on her back and right arm, caused by a rifle-ball. *Natchez Courier, June* 15, 1832.

* Retrospect of Western Travel, vol. i. p. 114.

without hope and without God in the world."* "They have no bible to read by their own firesides; they have no family-altars; and when in affliction, sickness, or death, they have no minister to address to them the consolations of the gospel."† They are destitute of the privileges of the gospel, and ever will be, under the present state of things. They may justly be considered the heathen of this country, and will bear a comparison with heathen in any country in the world."‡ "Throughout the bounds of the Charleston Synod there are at least one hundred thousand slaves, speaking the same language as the whites, who have never heard of the plan of salvation by a Redeemer."§ And this is the fruit of no accident,—it is inherent in the system. The black must be depressed below the level of humanity to be kept down to his condition. On this system his master dare not treat him as a man. To teach slaves to read is forbidden under the severest penalties in almost every slave-state. In North Carolina, to teach a slave to read or write, or give him any book (the Bible not excepted), is punished with thirty-nine lashes or imprisonment, if the offender be a free negro; with a fine of 200 dollars if he be a white. In Georgia this fine is 500 dollars; and the father is not suffered to teach his own half-caste child to read the Scriptures.‖

The moral state of such a population need not be depicted. The habit of despising the true redeemed humanity in those around them grows always upon the licentious and the covetous, as they allow themselves to use their fellows as the mere instruments of their gain or pleasure; and in the slave-states this evil habit reigns supreme. The quadroon¶ girls are educated in the south to live in bonds

---

* Sermon by Rev. C. C. Jones, preached in Georgia before two associations of planters, 1831.

† Report in Synod of South Carolina and Georgia, 1833.

‡ Report of the Synod of South Carolina and Georgia, to whom was referred the subject of the religious instruction of the colored population, 1834.

§ Charleston S. C. Observer.

‖ Caste and Slavery in the American Church, p. 27; a noble and heart-stirring protest.

¶ The mixed breed of the third generation.

of shame with their white masters. With the slave-population itself the licentiousness of the whites is utterly unbridled; and by this, all the ties of nature are dissolved. Family-life amongst the slaves cannot exist; its fountains are always liable to be poisoned by arbitrary power. White fathers view their own slave-born children as chattels. They work, they sell them. By law they cannot teach them, or set them free; for the jealousy of slave-state legislation lays it down as a first principle, that every slave must have a master " to see to him."

Here, then, in brief, is the curse of the southern-most or slave-buying states;—the holding property in man, keeping men in servile bondage, using persons as things, redeemed men as soulless chattels;—this is its essence. Here the testimony of the Church must be against this first vicious principle. This has been the example set to God's witnesses in this generation by their fathers in the faith. They protested against such dominant iniquities, and they delivered their own souls, and saved us their children from the eating canker of a blood-stained inheritance. "Let no man from henceforth," said the Christian Council of London, in 1102* " presume to carry on that wicked traffic, by which men in England have been hitherto sold like brute animals." This must be the Church's rule on the banks of the Mississippi, as it was on those of the Thames. So much for the extreme south.

As we come one degree northward, other features meet us. In the slave-selling states there is added to the evils of the south the execrable trade of breeding slaves for sale. By it " the 'Ancient Dominion' is converted into one grand menagerie, where men are reared for the market like oxen for the shambles."† This is no figure of speech. The number of slaves exported, from Virginia alone, for sale in the southern states, in one year, 1835-36, amounted to

---

* " Concilium Londinense, A. D. 1102, reg. Angliæ Hen. I. 3, statutum est: xxviii. Nequis illud nefarium negotium, quo hactenus homines in Anglia solebant velut bruta animalia venundari, deinceps ullatenus facere præsumat."—Wilkins, *Concilia*, vol. i. p. 383.

† Speech of Thomas Jefferson Randolph in the legislature of Virginia in 1832.

forty thousand;* whilst those imported from all quarters into the states of Louisiana, Mississippi, Alabama, and Arkansas, were reckoned in the year 1836 as not fewer than 25,000.† "Dealing in slaves," says a Baltimore newspaper‡ of 1829, "has become a large business; establishments are made in several places in Maryland and Virginia, at which they are sold like cattle: these places of deposit are strongly built, and well supplied with iron thumb-screws and gags."

The abominations of this trade must not pollute these pages. They may be readily conceived. But as a necessary part of such a traffic, an internal slave-trade, with its well-known horrors, re-commences. Here are slave-auctions, with all their instant degradation, and all their consequent destruction of family and social life.§ Here are

---

* Virginia Times. † Natchez Courier.
‡ The Baltimore (Maryland) Register.
§ One incident will tell this whole tale. "A gentleman of Virginia sold a female slave. The party professing to buy not being prepared to make the necessary payment, the slave was to be re-sold. A concealed agent of the trade bought her and her two children, as for his own service; where her husband, also a slave in the town, might visit her and them. Both the husband and wife suspected that she would be privately sent away. The husband, in their common agony, offered to be sold, that he might go with her. This was declined. He resolved on the last effort, of assisting her to escape. That he might lay suspicion asleep, he went to take leave of her and his children, and appeared to resign himself to the event. This movement had its desired effect; suspicion was withdrawn both from him and his wife, and he succeeded in emancipating them. Still, what was to be done with his treasure, now he had obtained it? Flight was impossible, and nothing remained but concealment; and concealment seemed hopeless, for no place would be left unsearched, and punishment would fall on the party who should give them shelter. However, they were missing; and they were sought for diligently, but not found. Some month's afterwards, it was casually observed that the floor under a slave's bed (the sister of the man) looked dirty and greasy. A board was taken up, and there lay the mother and her children on the clay, and in an excavation of three feet by five! It is averred that they had been there in a cold and enclosed space, hardly large enough for their coffin (buried alive there), for six months!

"This is not all. The agent was only provoked by this circumstance! He demanded the woman; and though every one was

droves of chained negroes marched under the whip, two and two, from the breeding district of Virginia to the labor-markets of Georgia and Alabama.

Here, then, as in the farther south, the testimony of the Church must be uncompromising and explicit. No motives of supposed expediency, no possible amount of danger, can justify her silence. She is set to bear a witness; a witness against the evils around her; a witness at all hazards; a witness to be at any time attested, if so it needs must be, by bearing any amount of persecution. She and she only can do this. The exceeding jealousy of the several states makes them resent with peculiar warmth any interference from without. The regulation of its internal concerns, and so the whole continuance and system of southern slavery, is solely under the jurisdiction of the several states. Congress cannot mitigate, much less abolish it. It can come before Congress only incidentally,—as, for instance, on the question of admitting a new slave-state into the union. Even moral influence from without is bitterly resented by the south. This is its ground of quarrel with the abolition-societies; with which the general government has so far sympathised as to leave unredressed the violation of the southern post-office, whereby abolition-papers are uniformly excluded from the south. Thus, at this moment, improvement can only arise from a higher standard of internal principle on this great question. This it is the business of the Church to create. She must assert her Catholic character on behalf of these unhappy cast-aways. In other respects, there is no country upon earth so fitted by pre-disposing elements for uniting in one visible body all the company of Christ's redeemed Gathered, as they are, from all countries, Americans are made partakers, even from natural causes, of a common political and social life. The strong lethargic common sense of the Dutch and the gay vivacity of the French, the phlegm of the German and the buoyant thoughtlessness of the Irish, the shrewd money-

clamorous to redeem her and return her to her husband, he would not sell! She was taken to his slave-pen, and has disappeared! The man—most miserable man!—still exists in the town." Drs. Reed and Matheson, ut supra, vol. ii. p. 188.

getting temper of the Yankee and the hospitable elegance of the southern gentleman,—are all here fused into one common mass. From this universal brotherhood the African alone is shut altogether out. Him the Church must take by the hand, and owning him as one of Christ's body, must lead him into the family of man. Not that she is bound to preach insurrection and rebellion. Far from it. It is quite easy to enforce upon the slave his duties, under a system, the unrighteousness of which is, at the same time, clearly stated. His bonds are illegal; but it is God's arm, and not his own violence, which must break them. Let the clergy of the south preach submission to the slave, if at the same time they declare to his master that these, for whom Christ died, are now no longer slaves, but brethren beloved;* and that a system which withholds from them their Christian birthright is utterly unlawful; that it is one which the master, not the slave, is bound to set himself honestly to sweep away. Above all should they, at any cost and by any sacrifice, protest in life and by act against this grievous wrong. The greater the cost, and the more painful the sacrifice, the clearer will be their testimony, and the more it will avail: to them it is given not only to believe in Christ, but also to suffer for His sake.

What witness, then, has as yet been borne by the Church in these slave-states against this almost universal sin? How has she fulfilled her vocation? She raises no voice against the predominant evil; she palliates it in theory; and in practice she shares in it. The mildest and most conscientious of the bishops of the south are slaveholders themselves. Bishop Moore of Virginia writes to Bishop Ravenscroft:† "The good and excellent girl presented to my daughter by Mrs. Ravenscroft paid the debt of nature on the 4th." She was treated, it is true, with all the indulgence which she could receive, but still, favorite as she was, she was a slave; and, after her death, was laid "in the colored burial-ground, which is not enclosed, and therefore much exposed, and where the grave was

---

* " Not now as a servant (lit. a slave, δοῦλος,) but above a servant a brother beloved." Philemon 16.

† Life of Bishop Moore, p. 282.

liable to be disturbed." This is no rare instance. The Bishop of Georgia has openly proposed to maintain "the Montpelier Institute" by the produce of slave-labor, and "The Spirit of Missions," edited with the sanction of the Church, and under the eye of the bishop (Onderdonk) of New-York, proposes to endow a mission-school in Louisiana, with a plantation to be worked by slaves, who should be encouraged to redeem themselves by extra hours of labor, before day in the morning and after night in the evening; and should, when thus redeemed, be transported to Liberia, and the price received for them laid out in "purchasing in Virginia or Carolina a gang of people who may be nearly double the number of those sent away."*

Nor are these merely evil practices into which, unawares and against their principles, these men have fallen. In a sermon preached before the Bishop of North Carolina in 1834, and published with his special commendation, it is openly asserted, that "no man or set of men are entitled to pronounce slavery wrong; and we may add, that as it exists in the present day it is agreeable to the order of Divine Providence;" whilst the Bishop of South Carolina,† in an address to the convention of his diocese, denounced "the malignant philanthropy of abolition."

Such are the fearful features of the life of Churchmen in the south. Nor is it any real lessening of this guilt to say that it is shared by all the Christian sects. The charge is, indeed, far too nearly true. There is no doubt that the evils of the system may be found still ranker and more gross amidst the prevailing sects of Baptists, Independents, Methodists, and Presbyterians.‡ But this is no excuse. It is the first duty of the Church to reprove the sins of others, not to adopt them into her own practice; to set, and not to take the tone. The cruelty of their tender mercies should lead her to speak out more plainly; it should force her zealously to cleanse herself from their stain, and then fearlessly leave the issue to her God. But she is silent here; and to her greater shame it must be added, that

---

* Caste and Slavery, p. 34. † Bishop Bowen.
‡ Vide Slavery and the Internal Slave-trade in America, pp. 133–145, for horrors with which these pages shall not be polluted.

there are sects* which do maintain the witness she has feared to bear.

But further: as has been already said, this clinging curse reaches even to the free states of the north, though it assumes in them another form. In them it leads to the treatment of the colored race with deep and continual indignity. They cannot be held in personal bondage, but they are of the servile class; they may be claimed as runaways, and thus dragged, if not kidnapped, to southern slavery.

A mingled scorn and hatred of the colored man pervades every usage of society. In the courts of law his testimony is not equally received with the white man's evidence ;† republican jealousy forgets its usual vigilance, in order to deny him his equal vote ; he may be expelled with insult from the public vehicle ; he must sit apart in the public assembly ; and though no tinge of remaining shade may darken his cheek, yet a traditional descent from colored blood will make it impossible for him to wed with any of the European race. Even in the fierce heat of the "revivals" this supreme law of separation is never for a moment overlooked. There are different "pens" for the white and colored subjects of this common enthusiasm. On all these points feeling runs higher in the free north than in the slave-states of the south. There the dominion of

---

* The Quakers, and four small sects, the Reformed Presbyterians, United Brethren, Primitive Methodists, and Emancipation Baptists. *Slavery and the Internal Slave-Trade in America*, p. 132.

The annual conference of the United Brethren in Maryland and Virginia passed, in 1839, the following resolution : " It appeared in evidence that Moses Michael was the owner of a female slave, which is contrary to the discipline of our Church. Conference therefore resolved, that unless brother Michael manumit or set free such slave in six months, he no longer be considered a member of our Church." *American Churches the Bulwark of Slavery*, p. 3.

† An American friend has made the following note on this statement: " The testimony of colored men is not excluded in all the free states. I am not sure that it is in any. In Massachusetts they have the civil and political rights of white men. There are three or four hundred colored voters in the city of Boston. The social prejudice, however, to which you allude, I am sorry to say, is very strong ; a mixed feeling of aristocracy, caste, and race.—*Note to second edition.*

the master is supreme, and he can venture, when it pleases him, to treat his slave with any degree of intimacy; for the beast of the field might with as high a probability as he, claim equal rights with man. But in the north, where the colored race are free and often rich, the galling insults of caste, are needful to keep up the separation between blood and blood; and here, therefore, more than any where, its conventional injustice is supreme; here, too, by an enforced silence as to the crimes of southern slavery, a guilty fellowship in its enormities is too commonly established.

Against these evils, then, the Church must here testify; she must proclaim that God hath made of one blood all nations of the earth; she must protest against this unchristian system of caste; her lips must be unsealed to denounce God's wrath against the guilty customs of the south. And what has been her conduct? If we seek to test her real power over men's hearts by asking what her influence has been, we shall rate it low indeed. No voice has come forth from her. The bishops of the north sit in open convention with their slave-holding brethren, and no canon proclaims it contrary to the discipline of their Church to hold property in man and treat him as a chattel. Nay, further, the worst evils of the world have found their way into the Church. The colored race must worship apart; they must not enter the white man's church; or if they do, they must be fenced off into a separate corner. In some cases their dust may not moulder in the same cemetery. Whilst " all classes of white children voluntarily attend the Sunday-schools on terms of perfect equality,"* any mixture of African blood will exclude the children of the wealthiest citizen. Recent events have shown that all this is not the evil fruit of an old custom slowly wearing itself out; but that it springs from a living principle which is daily finding for itself fresh and wider developments.

The General Theological Seminary, founded, as we have seen, at New-York, under the superintendence of the whole Church, was designed to secure a general training for all its presbyters. " Every person producing to the faculty," so ran its statutes, "satisfactory evidence of his

* Caswall, p. 297.

having been admitted a candidate for holy orders, with full qualifications, according to the canons of the Protestant Episcopal Church in the United States, shall be received as a student of the seminary."* Curiosity once prompted the question to Bishop Hobart, the founder of the seminary, " whether this wide rule embraced colored candidates?" " They would be admitted," was his answer, " as a matter of course and without doubt." Such, alas, is not the rule of his successor in the bishop's seat. In June, 1839, Alexander Crummell applied for admission; he came from three years' study at the Oneida Institute, from sharing equal rights with one hundred white students; he brought with him a character which, it was conceded, would warrant his admission if it could be right to admit a colored man at all; he was rejected for this single fault; one bishop (Doane) alone being found to protest against the step. Three years before, a similar injustice had been wrought.† Both remain to this day unredressed. The

---

* Statutes of the General Theological Seminary, chap. vii. sec. 1 See Act of Incorporation, 1836, p. 16.

† The diary of the young man then rejected tells so simply all the tale, that it is printed here from "Caste and Slavery," pp. 14, 15:—

"Oct. 10.—On Wednesday last I passed my examination before the faculty of the seminary, and was thereupon admitted a member of the school of the prophets.

"Oct. 11.—I called upon the bishop, and he was dissatisfied with the step I had taken in entering the seminary. Seems to apprehend difficulty from my joining the commons; and thinks that the south, from whence they receive much support, will object to my entering.

"Thus far I have met with no difficulty from the students, but have been kindly treated. I have thought it judicious, however, to leave the commons for the present.

"As far as in me lies I will, in my trouble, let all my actions be consistent with my Christian profession; and instead of giving loose to mortified feelings, will acquiesce in all things; but this acquiescence shall not in the least degree partake of the dogged submissiveness which is the characteristic of an inferior.

"My course shall be independent, and then, if a cruel prejudice will drive (me) from the holy threshold of the school of piety, I, the weaker, must submit and yield to the superior power. Into thy hands ever, O God, I commit my cause.

Church fears to lose the contributions of the south; she fears to raise the mobs of Philadelphia; she dare not stand

"Oct. 12.—At 9 A. M. I called on our spiritual father again, and sought advice in relation to my present embarrassing circumstances. He gave me plainly to understand that it would be advisable, in his opinion, for me not to apply for a regular admission into the seminary, and, although I had taken a room, and even become settled, yet to vacate the room, and silently withdraw myself from the seminary. He further said that I might recite with the classes, and avail myself of the privileges of the institution, but not consider myself in the light of a regular member. Never, never will I do so!

"The reasons of the bishop for this course are as follows:

"'That the seminary receives much support and many students from the south, and consequently if they admit colored men to equal privileges with the whites in the institution, the south will refuse to aid (it), and (will) use their influence to keep all from the seminary south of the Potomac. As head of the seminary, and knowing the feelings and prejudices of the south, he could not hazard my fuller admission at such an expense.

"'From the extreme excitability of public feeling on this delicate subject, and from my known and intimate connexion with the people of color, there would be a high probability not only of bringing the institution into disrepute, but of exciting opposing sentiment among the students, and thus causing many to abandon the school of the prophets.'

"I think these two form the reasons of the bishop against my being admitted. The course, however, he advises, viz. the being a 'hanger-on' in the seminary, is something so utterly repugnant to my feelings as a man, that I cannot consent to adopt it. If I cannot be admitted regularly, I leave the place; but in leaving I will ever hold the utmost good feeling towards the faculty and my friends. It is a cruel prejudice which drives me so reluctantly from the door, and makes even those who make high pretensions to piety and purity say to me, 'Stand thou there, for I am holier than thou.'

"In this matter, however, I shall acquiesce as a Christian, but shall preserve the independent feelings of a man. My most devoted thanks are due to my dear friends, the Rev. Drs. Berrian and Lyell, for the earnest solicitude which they manifest for my welfare. They seem heartily to regret that any difficulty has arisen on the present subject.

"Upon reflection, it is my present opinion that Bishop Onderdonk is wrong in yielding to the 'unrighteous prejudice' (his words) of the community. If the prejudice be wrong, I think he ought to oppose it without regard to consequences. If such men as he countenance it, they become partakers with the transgressors. He says, by and by Providence will open the way; but will Providence effect the change miraculously? We cannot expect it. He will, however,

between the dead and living: she cannot therefore stay the plague. Even when admitted to the sacred functions of the priesthood, the colored man is not the equal of his brethren. The Rev. Peter Williams, for years a New-York presbyter, of blameless reputation, was, for this one cause, allowed no seat in the convention of his Church. Thus, again, a special canon of the diocese of Pennsylvania forbids the representation of the African Church at Philadelphia, and excludes the rector from a seat.*

Tried, then, by this test, what can we esteem the present influence of this body? It plainly has not been conscious of possessing power to stand up in God's name and to rebuke the evil one; it has not healed this sore wound, which is wasting the true social life of America. It is a time for martyrdom; and the mother of the saints has scarcely brought forth even one confessor.

effect it by appointed means, and these means ought to be resorted to by His instruments—men. And what men more suitable than men high in office, high in public favor, high in talents? Particularly should men commissioned to preach the Gospel, which teaches mercy, righteousness, and truth, enter upon the work. What makes my case more aggravating and dreadful is, that the bishop says, that even admitting I have no African blood in me, yet my identity with the people of color will bar the door of the seminary against me. Horrid inconsistency!

"Oct. 13.—Called on the bishop yesterday, and had a final interview with him on this mortifying subject. His determination was settled and fixed, that from a sober consideration of all things, the interest of the seminary, the comfort of myself, and the ultimate good of my people, I had better silently withdraw, and, agreeably to my plan, study privately with a clergyman. He again, at this interview, suggested the plan of my embracing the privileges of the seminary without being regularly admitted; to which I would not consent, as it would be both a sacrifice of the feelings of a man, which I felt not disposed to offer, and, further, a sacrifice of principle, to which, I am confident, the noble-minded among my people would not allow me to submit.

"I cannot but conceive my case to be a very peculiar one, involving much difficulty, and one which will ultimately cause the guardians and controllers of this sacred institution to hang their heads for shame. This day I am driven, in the presence of all the students of the seminary, and the sight of high Heaven, from the school of the prophets."

* Caste and Slavery, p. 17.

To an Englishman this silence is the more eminently matter of the deepest pain, because he will at once admit that to his own people belongs the origin of that guilt in which the Church and nation of America are now entangled. So little has our colonial empire been administered on those principles for which our Church has witnessed,* that England forced upon her reluctant colonists the curse and crime of slave-holding institutions. Against remonstrance and resistance from the west, England thrust upon them this clinging evil. Freely do we take the shame of having first begun this course of crime; but the sense of this only makes us desire more earnestly that, through the blessing of that pure faith which also she received from us, this guilt and loss may be removed.

Other symptoms show that the mass of the population has not yet greatly felt the influence of the Episcopalian body. Few of the poor belong to it. It is the religion of the affluent and the respectable; but by it as yet the gospel is not largely preached to the poor. The very aspect of the churches bespeaks as much. These vary from the rude buildings constructed of unsawn logs, which first gem the solitude of the backwoods, up to the costly edifices of the city, of which the walls, "built of hammered bluestone trimmed with granite, rise forty feet above the ground, and in which the organ alone cost 1125*l.*"† In some of the new cities of the west they have been built at a cost of 12,600*l.* But they all bear one character. They are good specimens of what may be termed the modern Gothic. It would be difficult to find in the whole Episcopal communion throughout America one specimen of that glorious style of religious architecture which is to be found in our cathedrals, and below them in so many of our parish-churches here in England. The one predominant idea in the churches of America is to obtain the largest number of pews, which, from fronting the pulpit, shall let at remunerating prices. This regulates every arrangement. The pulpit occupies one end of the building, the communion table being thrust aside, and often consisting of no more

---

* Note p. 302.   † Caswall, p. 208.

than a narrow board which fronts the reading-desk. Instead of emulating the solemn grandeur of our ancient churches,* liberality here displays itself in the elegance and finish† of the internal decoration of the buildings. They are remarkable for the comfort of their cushioned pews, carpeted floors, warm stoves, and, in lieu of the small circular pulpit of England, their spacious platforms, well furnished with the requisite cushions, drapery, and lights." Some of these churches "rather resemble splendid drawing-rooms than houses of worship. Handsome carpets cover every part; the pews are luxuriously cushioned in a manner calculated to invite repose; while splendidly embroidered pulpit-hangings, superb services of communion-plate, and a profusion of silk and velvet, gilding and painting, excite the curiosity of the stranger more than his devotion. In these the poor man could hardly find himself at home."‡

The natural effects of such a state of things are plainly to be traced. "Intellectual sermons and elegant composition are held in high esteem," and these "frequently" degenerate into the dressing-up of ordinary sentiment in a florid style which approaches to bombast.§ Hence the stranger finds in the house of prayer "a large congregation of gay and fashionable visitors, engaged in cold, formal, and ostentatious worship."|| Hence such avowals as this by the venerable Bishop Griswold: "the evil most to be feared and most prevalent amongst us is lukewarmness. With shame must we acknowledge that we incline to be cold rather than hot. Enthusiasm is as rare in our churches as a scorching sun in a northern winter: the mercury of our zeal is constantly below the degree of temperature."¶ Hence, too, it follows, that the maintenance of a continual sacrifice of prayer and praise to God seems wholly foreign to the feelings of our brethren in the west. For whilst

---

* Caswall, p. 289.
† Buckingham's America, vol. iii. p. 472; vol. i. p. 190.
‡ Caswall, p. 289.   § Ibid. p. 296.
|| Buckingham's America, vol. i. p. 276.
¶ Bishop Griswold on Prayer-Meetings. See Life of Bishop Moore, p. 93.

"weekly lectures are very frequent," and the whole temper of the people favors frequent public meetings, there was, in 1839, "no place in America in which the service of the Church was performed daily, unless the General Theological Seminary at New-York may be regarded as an exception."*

This must be to a great extent the result of their position. As a general rule they possess no endowments. The building of a church is often a money-speculation; the sale of pews is to cover the expenses of the managing committee; the pew-holders are the parish, and they elect and pay the clergyman by an assessment on the pews. All this must exclude the poor. They cannot subscribe at first; they cannot pay pew-rents; they have no part therefore in the matter.† The clergyman has no parochial charge, the parish no territorial existence; the clergyman is the hired servant of the pew-owners to perform a certain work. Thus the poor are passed wholly by; they are the charge of no one.

In New-York, where the Episcopalian body is possessed of endowments, free churches have been opened for the poor. But these have not answered. The jealousy of poor republicans forbids their profiting by such distinctive benefits. This, moreover, is here exasperated to the utmost by the established custom of allotting to "negroes and other colored persons the privilege of occupying free seats by themselves, distinct from the rest of the congregation."‡ So does this curse of American society meet us anew at every turn.

* Caswall's America, p. 95.

† The practical effect of this may be gathered from the following supposed conversation between two of them, introduced into the "Lowell Offering," a miscellany composed by the "factory girls" at the Manchester of America:—

"*Dorcas.* The Gospel is an expensive luxury now, and those only who can afford to pay their four or six or more dollars a year can hear its truths. . . . .

"*Rosina.* Do not speak harshly, Dorcas . . . times have indeed changed . . . but circumstances also have changed. . . . It is true we cannot procure a year's seat in one of our most expensive churches for less than four present weeks' wages."—Knight's *Mind amongst the Spindles*, p. 123.

‡ Caswall's America, p. 282.

In another way, also, this system grievously impairs the Church's strength. It keeps the clergyman in a state of servile dependence on his congregation. " There is not a man in his flock, however mean and unworthy, whom he does not fear ; and if he happens to displease a man of importance, or a busy woman, there is an end of his peace."*
This makes his witness often feeble and uncertain ; for hence follows the temptation to truckle to popular opinion ; hence the Church's silence as to the treatment of the colored race. By this, again, the general standard of clerical character is depressed. "More commonly it is the lower order of talent which is found there ; and in a country where all depends on display and present popular effect, it is an unenviable doom to be attached to that profession."† This also has made a constant change of sphere almost a condition of clerical life in the west. " Popularity is the measure of a clergyman's comfort in America ; and he is generally most popular at first." Then his support begins to flag, his maintenance is reduced, or yielded in a manner painful to his feelings. He is forced to migrate : and thus there is everlasting change in the condition of the American clergy. They change ; the people change ; all is a round of change ; because all depends on the voluntary principle.‡

All of these evils are found in their full vigor amidst the various sects. Amongst them the instability of popular favor is bridled by no external influence. But the absence of endowment brings the Church itself to a fearful degree under the same influence, and to that extent impairs its character and moral weight.

That, under such a system, the clergy should be what they are in America is surely the fruit of God's especial mercy. In the midst of the busiest people upon earth, where all are getting or expecting to get money, there has

---

* Voice from America, p. 199. † Ibid. p. 194.
‡ Ibid. pp. 192, 193. It is well worth the most serious consideration of the American Church, whether the evil might not to a great extent be removed by the introduction of the principle of supporting their clergy by the collection of a common fund to be apportioned by the bishops.

been no want of young men ready to devote themselves to the service of their brethren, though they have no security of receiving even the necessary competence for ordinary domestic life, and are not led on by any possible expectation of obtaining one amongst some few great prizes, or allured by the expectation of learned leisure, or promised an opportunity of leading thereby a literary life. They choose their lot, knowing that in it their days must be spent in constant and exhausting labor, with the smallest earthly recompense. On such a ministry God's blessing must rest abundantly, and in its high character is, no doubt, found the practical escape from many evils inherent in the theory of the constitution of their Church.

Here, then, we may form some judgment of the present influence of this body in America; and if from this we may venture to anticipate its future progress, there is much ground for sanguine hope, not unmixed with reasonable fear.

Its dangers can hardly be mistaken. The great stream of religious opinion in America sets towards the chill decencies of Socinian error. This is the natural tendency of a busy, growing, wealthy, self-governing people, and this has been eminently the tendency of the West. The New-England states have already fallen into the snare; and from the revulsions which follow the extravagance of revivals, as well as from other causes, these tenets are generally spreading. "This doctrine," writes Jefferson in 1822, from Virginia, "has not yet been preached to us, but the breeze begins to be felt. . . . It will come and drive before it the foggy mists which have so long obscured our atmosphere."* "That this will ere long be the religion of the majority, from north to south, I have no doubt."† "I confidently expect that the present generation will see it become the general religion of the United States."‡

Exaggerated as were Jefferson's immediate expectations, there can be no doubt that they point towards the real danger. The mercantile turn, even of religion, inclines in this direc-

---

* Jefferson's Correspondence, vol. iv. p. 362.
† Ibid. vol. iv. p. 367. ‡ Ibid. vol. iv. p. 369.

tion. Where there is enough of a hovering tendency towards Chrisianity to lead to the erection of a new church in some newly-settled or increasing neighborhood, its fabric is divided out into a series of pews, on no other principle than how they will let to the greatest advantage. The minister is engaged on the same calculation. Even the doctrines to be preached are ruled by the same law. Hence we hear of such strange facts as that a Congregational population, having abandoned their old creed, hung long in doubt between electing a Socinian or Universalist teacher, and ended by addicting themselves to the Episcopal communion.* All of this is evidently highly unfavorable to the simple child-like fatih which Christ's gospel requires ; it is all injurious to that earnest personal faith in the blood of Jesus as the only hope of lost sinners, without which even the most orthodox creed becomes a set of barren and unmeaning dogmas.

And this tendency of the American temper is increased by the character of their political institutions. Absolute indifference to all religious distinction is the principle which lies at their root. They are full of a continual practical denial of the existence of any difference between truth and falsehood. It is not merely that all forms of worship and opinions are tolerated, although this is carried so far that even infidelity itself is treated with respect and deference as one peculiar " form of religious opinion, being certainly an opinion about religion ;"* but, beyond this, it appears to be the aim of the state to extend a just and equal measure of direct support and patronage to all sects and professions of belief. Thus, when a state-legislature assembles, it is the prevailing custom that the ministers of all such bodies should be invited to act by weekly rotation as their chaplains ; and this extends to every extreme of opinion. A professed Socinian is invited to officiate as chaplain before the descendants of those puritans who left their fathers' land to worship the Lord Jesus Christ in sincerity and truth ; and a Romanist offers up the public worship of

---

* Caswall, p. 136.
* Voice from America, p. 159.

states, from which a few generations back the priest was banished under the penalty of death.*

This custom is not confined to state assemblies. The congress, at the opening of every session, elects a chaplain for each of its two houses, with an understanding that both chaplains shall not be of the same sect. Thus every sect in the course of a few years receives in turn the compliment of this selection. The same rule applies to their army and navy chaplains, who are commonly elected merely for their personal attainments, and without the question being even asked to what sect or party they belong. So lax a system of entire indifference is, in truth, one development of infidelity; for in this common encouragement of all sects there is at one time or another a denial of every truth. This must leaven the whole mind of the nation with the persuasion that there is no such thing as objective truth,—and this is the first step towards professed unbelief. He who knows not whether any thing is true, begins to doubt of everything; and he who has once suffered doubt to dwell freely and at large within his breast, is already far advanced towards the positive disbelief of all things.

Against this, then, the Church has continually to strive and testify. It is the first principle of every Christian man, that God has revealed to us a knowledge of Himself, of His will, of ourselves, and of our duty; and that His word is true, that it is the truth. Of this truth the Church claims to be a "witness," and a "keeper" of this testimony. The points taught in the creeds are, therefore, no longer matter for doubt and speculation, but merely of faithful and willing reception, because they come from Him who is truth. On these matters it is not possible to enter into any compromise. It is not possible for the true believer to help forward the fearful blasphemies of the Socinian, who denies the honor due unto the Saviour, by putting him forward to act publicly as a minister of that Lord whom he dishonors.

Between, then, this fatal form of false religion and the

---

* Voice from America, p 161.

truth as it is in Jesus, there must be a hard struggle. But not between these only.

The sectarian principle itself must be successfully opposed. This is at once the ultimate occasion of Socinian increase, and the present mother of a monstrous and misshapen brood of heresies. With these the Church must do open battle for her Master's truth; whilst she must mildly open to others the truths after which they are seeking in their less perfect systems, and which perchance she may win them over to find fully in her own. Nor is this all: with the Roman communion, also, she has before her no common strife. True to the ordinary conduct of the papacy, the Roman pontiff founded the rival bishopric of Baltimore two years after the consecration of Bishops White and Provoost; and by the subsequent erection of the sees of New-York, Philadelphia, Boston, and Beardstown,* set up altar against altar through the West. Thus the Episcopal communion has always had to bear her protest against papal superstitions. But a severer strife is yet to be encountered. With the keen-eyed policy which has always distinguished the schemes of Rome, she has turned her main attention to the valley of the Mississippi. There a vast population is multiplying with unprecedented speed. The European emigrants to this quarter are, by a large majority, from popish countries; and if not already of the Romish faith, no pains are spared to make them so. There, on the outskirts of civilized life, the adventurous settler, having left behind him the forms and opportunities of Christian worship, seizes eagerly upon a soil of unbounded fertility, and devotes all his thoughts to making it his own; and there the enchantress meets him with her cup of sorcery, and wins him over, whilst there is no other near to whisper to him words of caution, or to shame the fallen Church with open rebuke. No expense is grudged in this

* "There are serious difficulties affecting the regularity, and even the validity, of the ordination of the above-mentioned Carroll, and all the Romish clergy of the United States derived from him, in consequenco of his ordination having been performed by only *one* titular bishop, who appears to have labored under a similar irregularity or deficiency himself." Palmer's *Treatise on the Church*, vol. i. p. 305, note.

peculiar work; funds are supplied, without any limit, from the Leopold Society of Austria, and from the Society for the Propagation of the Faith, the head-quarters of which are fixed at Lyons."* The population is becoming largely Romish; and this, beyond all doubt, is to be the future seat of empire. The best informed Americans expect that, after one more struggle, the west will command the elections of the union; and thus the centre of power will have been forestalled by Rome. But even now, and without waiting this accomplishment, her power is not to be contemned. Many peculiarities of life in America already tend to establish her dominion. The revulsion of feeling, which ever drives men from one extreme to another, naturally leads those who have been wearied out by the fierce excitements of the various sects to seek for shelter in her delusive quietness. Her claim of infallibility seems to be a blessing to spirits which are utterly hopeless of finding out any truth amidst the conflicting claims of ten thousand contesting teachers; whilst by her doctrine of the sacraments, her practical management of penances, and her perilous medicine of enforced auricular confession, with its attendant absolution, she heals slightly the wounds of many a morbid and diseased conscience. The Romanists, moreover, have always known how to modify their doctrines and discipline, so as to turn to the best advantage the political circumstances of the country and the times. Thus, whilst under an absolute monarchy they are the greatest enemies of rational and lawful liberty, in republican America they are the most thoroughly democratical of all sects. At first sight it may be difficult to conceive how the popish discipline can be made to harmonise with an equalising democracy; but upon looking more closely, it will be seen, as has been remarked by a keen oberver of American society,† that Romanism is really most favorable to

---

* "At St. Louis the Jesuits have lately erected, in addition to their cathedral, a spacious church and a university, with a library of ten thousand volumes, towards which only about eight thousand dollars were raised at St. Louis, the remainder of the funds coming chiefly from Lyons." *Private Letter of Rev. H. Caswall.*

† M. de Tocqueville.

democracy; for that under its system "the religious community is composed of only two elements, the priest and the people. The priest alone rises above the rank of his flock, and all are equal below him." None know better than the adherents of the papacy how to profit by such a state of society. Already they have tasted the sweets of political power "They have grown," we are told in 1839, "to an important political influence, by the acquisition of Louisiana and by emigration from Europe, so as to be capable of turning a vote for a national administration in whichever scale they cast their weight, in the present nearly equal balance of political parties. They are generally found on one side, namely, the most thoroughly democratical and radical; and as that is at present the dominant party, it may be said that they govern the country so far as that they are the means of keeping in power the party to which they are attached."*

Against the Episcopal communion the whole strength of the Romanists is bent. They fear no other body. In the multitude, variety, and extravagance of the sects is, they well know, the secret of their own strength, and the ground of their hope of one day reducing all to a common servitude. Their talisman of might is in the apparent shelter and visible unity of their church, and through it they hope to triumph; but these in their reality are possessed by the Episcopal communion, and with them the blessed truth of Christ's Gospel, free from those deep corruptions which throughout Christendom mar every where the countenance of Rome.

With Rome, therefore, in the new world as elsewhere, the pure Church of Christ must wrestle. But there is no doubt of the result, if only she be true to herself. If, indeed, forsaking this high ground, the Episcopalian puts himself upon a level with every unscriptural sect around him, then he may expect to find Rome too strong for him. But if he maintains his true position, he cannot but resist successfully her multiplied and fearful errors. And for this contest the Church in America has some peculiar advan-

* Voice from America, by an American Gentleman, p. 161.

tages. Her general convention enables her to meet the varying form of error, and to adjust internal grounds of difference, to an extent altogether unattainable where, as at home, the power of assembling lawfully in synod has been, for any cause, suspended or removed.

Such are the prospects of the Episcopal communion. There can be no doubt that a hard struggle is before her; that vast difficulties, social, moral, and religious, will impede her progress. The treatment of the negro race alone might amply occupy her energies; but besides this, she has the busiest people in the world to charm to Christian quietness. Peace must be breathed over their unresting eagerness; by cultivating college-life and the studies and devotions of a more learned clergy, still thoughts must be sheltered and fostered amidst those crowded haunts of men; and safe, quiet resting-places must be formed in streams madder and more troubled than the waters of her own turbulent Missouri. She must bridle or subdue the outstretching atheism of the backwoods population, the extravagance of the multitude of strange sects, as well as the decent unbelief of Socinian Boston; she must expose the subtle errors of the Romish Church. All this is no ordinary work; yet all this, and more than all of it, she may accomplish, if she is but true to her own principles. If she abandons these, she is indeed lost. Whether swallowed up by the sects, or engulfed by Rome, or sinking into the Socinian heresy, it were vain to prognosticate; but her fall is certain. The history of the King's Chapel* at Bos-

---

* Where the "King's Chapel" now stands, the first Episcopal church in New England was erected in 1689. It was built of wood, but was replaced in 1749 by a stone church, which cost little less than £10,000. It was distinguished by a succession of royal gifts. In 1697, communion-plate was given to it by King William and Queen Mary; and in 1772 arrived together gifts from Georges II. and III. Only eleven years after this, the first fatal step was openly taken, by the adoption of an altered liturgy, from which the Athanasian Creed and the opening sentences of the litany were formally excluded. From that time its descent has been rapid; and now, with a mutilated service and heretical creed, it is an avowedly Socinian congregation. Abridged from Dr. Greenwood's *History of King's Chapel*, as quoted by Buckingham, vol. iii. p. 447.

ton stands as a beacon-light to warn her from this dangerous course. Of the urgency of these dangers in times past, the absence of the Athanasian Creed from her public formularies is a painful record. It is still, no doubt, the abiding loss of one great safeguard against error. It is impossible to estimate too highly the value of those hymns of thanksgiving which associate with the emotions of our earliest worship the deep mysteries of revelation. Against all enticements therefore to adopt a lower tone, she needs specially to stand upon her guard. He who bears the vows of the Nazarite must not adopt as his rule the ordinary customs of society around him. If he slumbers in the lap of ease or worldly conformity, the Philistines will bind the champion of God's host; and he who should have delivered Israel will ere long grind sightless in the world's mill, or make rude merriment for God's enemies.

But if in the character of Christ's witness, loving and proclaiming His truth in its simplicity, ministering His sacraments faithfully and purely, she resists the evils around her, then in God's name will she surely triumph over all opposition. To do which there must be no dread of martyrdom when truth requires the sacrifice. At all costs she must bear the burden of the Lord, and bless the religious and social life of those given to her. This she can do in the strength God gives to His faithful witnesses, if that strength is called out and used for Him. But to be thus strong, she must bring out her own principles. There must be no faltering step swerving towards the sects around her, no secret coveting of the Babylonish garment which is stored within the tents of Rome. Her banner must be indeed "Evangelical truth with apostolical order,—the Gospel in the Church." There must be no paring down, on the one side, of the great doctrines of grace; no attempt, on the other, to win the good-will of men by changing, according to their wandering fancies, that form of Church-order which Christ has appointed. It is impossible by such a course to turn aside reproach and and opposition. This cannot be avoided by any sacrifice short of " the intercommunity of services;"* that is, of

* Reed and Matheson.

an entire abandonment of all claim to apostolic constitution. For this is the real question in dispute between herself and others: and the less are the ostensible reasons for separation from them, the greater is the irritation which inevitably awaits those who still insist on separation; for in them it seems to be founded on no great principle, and to be therefore causeless, which makes it injurious and insulting. They who have thought that the outcry sometimes heard against the Church at home is excited by its being established by the nation, and not by its bearing witness against the lawfulness of sectarian subdivision, may be surprised to find that, to an English dissenter, the claims of the Episcopal communion are more offensive in America than here, " where there is something of pomp, and privilege, and numbers to uphold these pretensions."* There it appears to him to be incredible exclusiveness Hence in that land it is doubly needful that the true grounds of those actions which provoke this judgment should be calmly but clearly stated. It must be felt that they who act thus do so because they believe that Christ having founded a fixed form of Church-life, it is not lawful for them at their own will to alter it, or to acquiesce in its re-construction, to please the taste of other men. This, and this only, can justify their separation: if the Episcopal Church of America, instead of being the witness against all sectarian division, is herself regarded as one of the sects, then is she indeed the most exclusive and overbearing of them all. Her sons must be felt not to be maintaining in a hostile spirit their own dogmas, but in the heartiest love to be bent on sharing with their less favored brethren the riches of their own inheritance; and this they cannot do unless they themselves believe in its reality. Nothing can more fatally deny their own true standing-ground than the unhappy custom, prevalent upon their days of solemn gathering, of publicly inviting, often by their bishop's voice, to the table of the Lord, not only their own members, but "all who consider themselves as in good standing with their own denomination."†

---

* Reed and Matheson, vol. ii. p. 75.
† No question is asked as to the great fundamentals of the faith;

But it is not enough that the distinctive features which mark this communion should thus be kept clear and plain. There must also be a high tone on those great moral and social questions which are rising daily, and on which mere politicians have no utterance of principle. There must be no timid silence as to great enormities. In those mighty issues which indeed try the spirits of men, her voice must be clear. Thus, for example, the treatment of the negro population must be her care; the equal worth of the colored race must be unequivocally held and asserted by her. It must no longer be the reproach of the Protestant Episcopal Church that it is only in the Romish Cathedral at New-Orleans that whites and blacks are seen to kneel together,* as those who were made of one blood by one Father, and redeemed from common death through the cross of one only Saviour. Timid, compromising conduct on these great subjects, safe as it may seem at present, will, more than any thing besides, weaken through the whole nation the moral weight of any religious body. By an universal law of God's providence, it is in doing battle for His truth that men exercise and train their own spirits, and subdue the herd of weaker minds to their rule and government. By its courage or unfaithfulness on this one question, the Church, as far as we can see, is fixing now for good or ill its true weight and standing in the coming generation.

Many favorable signs give hopeful promise of its rising to its true dignity of action. On all sides there is a growing disposition to act meekly and calmly, but yet steadily, upon its own principles. It is carrying throughout the Union its episcopacy and apostolic discipline. It is providing for clerical education and the formation of a clerical character amongst those who are to bear the ministry of Christ. On every side it is seeking to remove the irregularities and contradictions which, in its weak and uncertain beginning, were suffered in its constitution, as the fruits of ignorance within itself, or concessions to predjucice with-

but even Socinians may avail themselves of the promiscuous invitation.

* Retrospect of Western Travel, vol. i. p. 128.

out. Attempts are even now making to limit the elections of members of convention to those who are in regular communion. Conventions are increasingly commenced with the celebration of the sacrament of the Lord's Supper.* In its missionary organization the true and highest form of Church-societies is visibly developed. The whole body is thereby acknowledged the society, and its rule and government is placed in the same hands which have received from Christ's appointment the administration of His Church. On other points, at the same time, the tone of thought and action is manifestly rising. The poor are, far more than they were, the care of this communion. The institution of free churches, although not yet wholly successful, is a practical avowal of their sense of this obligation. Even on the slave-question the Church is not wholly silent. She has turned away from the baits held out by the Colinization Society.† One bishop, and not the

---

* Before the general convention of 1841, nearly 1500 communicants met together at the Lord's table in St. John's church, New-York.

† In the convention of 1823 the bishops declined the proposal of sending a delegate to an intended meeting of that body, but expressed approbation of their object. *Bishop White's Memoirs* p. 51. This was a charitable construction of the purposes of that society. No doubt many truly humane men have joined it with the hope of colonising Africa with free blacks, and thereby introducing into that unhappy continent, and amidst its estimated 30,000,000 of the negro race, civilization and Christianity. And to a certain extent, this, we may hope, will be the result of their colony of Liberia on the African coast. But the great effect of the scheme, if it succeeded, would be to remove from America all the free colored population who are the natural guardians of their brethren in slavery, and so to rivet for ever the fetters of the slave. It is, in fact, the safety-valve of that system, and therefore is in favor amongst all the advocates of slavery in the northern as well as the southern states. For whilst it promises to the south the secure possession of their slave-labor, it falls in with northern prejudice by being a practical declaration, that the two races cannot co-exist together in a state of freedom, and that deportation must be a condition of the black man's liberty. The statements of one of its ablest advocates,‡ carefully prepared, too, to fall in, as far as possible, with the prejudices of England on this

---

‡ Letter to the Hon. Henry Clay, &c., by R. R. Gurley.

least distinguished of his order, has been scarcely held back by the full force of official forms from recording his solemn protest against the exclusion from the General Theological Seminary of the candidate of negro blood; and in two at least of the churches of the north the African has been acknowledged to be, as much as his white brother in the priesthood, the witness of Christ's resurrection, and the stewart of His mysteries.* Even in Virginia, from the bishop's seat, a whisper may be heard. Bishop Meade has put into his Manual of Devotion this prayer for the use of a master of a family in the slave district :—" O heavenly Master, hear me whilst I lift my heart in prayer for those unfortunate beings who call me master. O God, make known unto me my whole duty towards them and their oppressed race; give me courage and grace to do it at all events; convince me of sin if I be wrong in retaining them another moment in bondage." In the freedom of this happy land we cannot without effort, easily beleive how much true Christian daring was required to put forth even this gentle rebuke. God grant that it may soon be spoken in accents like those of the faithful prophet whose righteous soul would not endure that the people of the Lord should continue halting between two opinions.

For if on this, and on other kindred subjects, her wit-

subject, scarcely veil this view. Their tone cannot be mistaken. They are a plausible apology for the " peculiar social institutions of the south." They would justify perpetual bondage amidst the sugar-canes and cotton-plants of Georgia and Alabama, and the perpetual trampling on the free negro in the streets of Philadelphia and New-York.

* It is due to those who, in this day of trial, have not shrunk from their principles, to record the names of those who have borne this witness. Bishop Doane of New Jersey, in June, 1839, opposed and sought leave to enter his protest against the decision of the trustees as to Alex. Crummell; and he having since been ordained by the late Bishop Griswold, has been invited to share in the public services of the Church, "in the presence of large and fashionable congregations, as an equal brother, without a syllable of disapprobation disturbing the harmony of the scene," by the Rev. George Burgess, rector of Christ Church, the Rev. Arthur Coxe, (author of Athanasion, &c,) minister of St. Gabriel's, Windsor, and rector of St. John's Church, Hartford, Connecticut. *Caste and Slavery*, p. 22.

ness for God were clear and explicit, what could we fear for the Church in America? It has already even gained on the rapidly increasing population of the United States.* Between 1814 and 1838, whilst the population of the Union has little more than doubled, it has quadrupled itself. Should its increase continue at this rate, it would in fifty years outnumber the mother Church, and before the end of a century would embrace a majority of all the people of the West. What is there but want of faith to limit this progress, or to prevent its dispensing every spiritual and social blessing to the busy people round it? To say that it is beset by peculiar dangers, is only to assert of it that which may be said of the Church Catholic at every period since her first foundation. Never has she been free from danger; never has it seemed less than imminent and menacing. At one time, persecution from without has threatened to beat down and root it out; at another, heresy has raised against her its parti-colored banner, and seemed ready to swallow up the faithful. Schism has sometimes divided her; and sometimes the friendship of the world and the fair speech of men has almost robbed her of her jealous love for truth, and sullied her virgin holiness. Yet in all trials, and through all opposition, God has ever held her up. And so it must be; ever ready to fail, but never failing; leaving, it may be, one land, to rise with new splendor on another; out of weakness waxing strong: this has been, and this must be, her course. This was foretold of her when it pleased our Lord to show to His first Twelve the shadow which her long-after history cast forward: "Then shall many be offended, and shall betray one another, and hate one another: and many false prophets shall rise, and shall deceive many. And because iniquity shall abound, the love of many shall wax cold. But he that shall endure unto the end, the same shall be saved. And this gospel of the kingdom shall be preached in all the world for a witness unto all nations, and then shall the end come."

So it has been, and so it must be to the end. Always

---

* Caswall's America, p. 386.

is there trial enough to betray the ungodly and the insincere; always is the danger enough in following Christ to lead the half-hearted to go over to the world's side: but ever is there in Christ's presence and in Christ's promises strength enough to hold up them that will cleave to Him. And so it will be until He come again : for He has founded His Church upon a rock ; and the gates of hell shall not prevail against her.

APPENDIX.

The editor of this American edition of Bishop Wilberforce's History of the Church in these United States, published the annexed sermon on "Communion of Saints," more than a year since. He had never seen the bishop's book nor knew any thing of its contents. He has carefully looked over the statements made by him on the subject of slavery, and cannot find a single error in any particular. Within the last year the sin and evils of slavery have been most ably set forth in resolutions and addresses to the public of the slaveholding States themselves. I have before me the resolutions of a convention of delegates in Kentucky, assembled in Frankfort, the capital of the State, on the 25th of April, 1849. The first resolution is as follows: "1. Believing that hereditary slavery, as it exists by the laws of Kentucky, is injurious to the commonwealth, inconsistent with the fundamental principles of a free government, *and opposed to the rights of mankind,* it therefore ought not to be perpetuated." This is speaking quite as plainly on the subject of slavery, as Bishop W. does in any expression of his, or, as does the author of the sermon annexed. This convention was attended by many distinguished persons of all parties and sects; some preachers made very able exposition of the sin and evils of slavery. Where was the testimony of either branch of the Church, holding "par excellence," *the* doctrine of "the Communion of Saints." Where was the Bishop of Bardstown, or the Bishop of Kentucky? Their voices are not heard in defence of "the rights of mankind," to say nothing of "the liberty wherewith Christ has made us free."

"The Communion of Saints."

DISCOURSE

DELIVERED IN

ST. MICHAEL'S CHURCH,

BROOKLYN, N. Y.

ON SUNDAY, THE 26th OF MARCH, A. D. 1848.

BY

EVAN M. JOHNSON,

RECTOR.

THE author of this discourse is not a member of any Colonization, or Anti-Slavery, or Abolition Society whatever, and fully believes all these would be unnecessary, if the Catholic Church would do as she ought. It is with the humble hope of calling the attention of Her members to what he esteems a neglected duty that he is induced to publish this.

DISCOURSE.

1 COR.. XII., 13 AND 14, 25, 26 AND 27 VERSES.

"For by one Spirit are we *all* baptized into *one body*, whether we be Jews or Gentiles, whether we be *bond* or *free*, and have been all made to drink into one Spirit; for the body is not one member, but many; that the members should have the same care one for another and whether *one member* suffer, all the members *suffer* with it. Now ye are the body of Christ, and members in particular."

In the Apostle's Creed, Christians are taught to believe in "The Holy Catholic Church; The Communion of Saints." Every one, who pretends to be a member of the one Catholic Church in the world, receives each and every article of this Creed as containing a truth not to be disputed—one article may be excepted. He that rejects one, denies in fact the whole. For instance, if a person believe every other Article of the Creed and deny the existence of 'The Holy Ghost,' he is an heretic; so, if he deny the existence of "the Holy Catholic Church: the Communion of Saints;" he is an heretic. The doctrine taught by these clauses in the Creed and as more fully explained in other Creeds and the teaching of the Church is this, that the Church which is holy, is also Catholic; that is, universal, as it exists in the whole world. It is one. However separated as to locality, however high or low the station in life, of its members, or however they may differ as to their ideas of the supremacy of its *earthly* Head; it is One, as it is the body of Christ. All are united in the belief, that Christ is its Divine Head; and the Holy Ghost its animating, living principle. Individuals have been and are made, and will continue to be made members of this one body of Christ by Baptism. "For by one Spirit we are all baptised into one body." The Head of the Church instituted the Holy Sacrament of Baptism, in which He implants (without reference to the fitness of His earthly agent,) through *His* Ministry the seed of Divine life in the soul of man. He has also made provision for the nurture of the "plant of renown." He gives His Holy Spirit, in answer to the sincere prayers of the members of His Body. He enables them to confess and forsake their sins—to become more and more holy and blameless. He feeds their souls with angel's food, "the manna that came down from heaven." His Body is to them "meat indeed and His blood drink indeed." Thus, in communion with Him the Head, any member of this one Church may thro' the grace given by the Holy Ghost, become one of the number of the Saints—any member of this one Church may by neglect, or thoughtlessness, or sin, or waywardness, drive away the Holy Spirit and never enter into the joy of his Lord. It was the great object of our adorable Saviour by His humiliation to raise our fallen humanity, that any of our race may be enabled to become "Sons of God." Those, who in this one Catholic Church, do cultivate the graces of the Spirit and through obedience and self mortification and "fasting" and "praying" and "alms-giving" and "serving God day and night" with sincerity and humble obedience, thus showing that the righteousness of Christ is in them, are called SAINTS. They are Holy, in a very peculiar sense, because Christ is Holy and they are one with Him. "He in them and they in Him." All such, wherever they may be, whatever may be their condition in life, bond or free, stand in a special relation to one another as members of the great Body of which He is Head. This relation is called "the Communion of Saints." It is through the Spirit of "the Father and the Son," animating the whole body and enlivening every member of it, that Christ communicates His grace, through His Sacraments; and it is by the same Spirit that believers have "access by one Spirit to the father." As the Spirit of a man enlivens the body of a man, so does the Holy Spirit enliven the whole body of the Church. Thus, the faithful have communion one with another and with Christ the Head. Whether then Christians believe that the Bishop of Rome or the Bishop of Constantinople is the head of the whole Church, or that there is but one Head and that is Christ in Heaven, and that each Bishop is Head of the subordinate branch committed to his charge, and that each individual Christian holds his communion with the great Head through his own Bishop, they are substantially agreed in believing this doctrine of "Communion of Saints." If we look into the Scriptures we find that this doctrine is most distinctly brought to view, as enforcing various duties of an highly practical character. Our Saviour himself said to his disciples, " A new commandment give I unto you that ye love one another ; as I have loved you, that ye also love one another ; by this shall all men know that ye are my disciples, if ye have love one to another." Says the Apostle, " We being many are one body in Christ, and every one members one of another. Let love be without dissimulation. Be kindly affectioned one to another, with brotherly love ; in honor preferring one another." The same Apostle exhorts the members of Christ's body to " bear ye one another's burdens, and so fulfil the law of Christ"—again, " we are members one of another, be ye kind to one another, tender hearted." I will not quote farther from the Scriptures on this point. Saints in all ages of the Church have considered these and such like parts of Holy Writ, as enforcing upon them the discharge of these duties and the exercise of these affections thus prominently brought to notice. It has been and it always will be the most decided test of Christian character, the best evidence both to one's self and to others, of the existence and growth of the divine life or of its decay, that, when a Christian examines himself, he finds he discharges these duties and exercises these affections, or that he neglects the one and does not cultivate the other. A person may profess to believe in the doctrine of " the Communion of Saints"—that all Christians are one in Christ and made partakers of His nature ; if he do not discharge the *duty* which is imposed on him, by the Word of God, as an individual member of this one body of Christ, his is nothing else than profession—he does not really believe the doctrine—he deceives himself.

In all ages of the Church, this doctrine, taught by the Saviour Himself and enforced by so many and so striking passages of God's word, has powerfully influenced the members of the true Church of Christ and inspired them with feelings of deep commiseration for the oppressed, and with determined exertions for their relief. In the first centuries a community of suffering among Christians produced also a community of commiseration, and whenever any were released from their persecution, or oppression, or bondage, they immediately sought to obtain the relief of others, who with them were one in Christ. I have time only to state a few historical facts to confirm this statement. About the year 340 after Christ, a canon had been passed strictly prohibiting the appropriation of the sacred vessels of the sanctuary to any secular purpose. St. Ambrose of Milan, *to redeem captives*, when no other means could be obtained, sold the sacred vessels and utensils of the Church, to make provision for what he called "the living temples of God." He speaks in his own defence, and personifying the Saviour, he says, "the ornament of my Sacraments is the redemption of captives." St. Austin disposed of the plate of his Church for "the redemption of captives." In an after age, when the Northern herds overran the Roman Empire, making slaves of those they captured, the power of the Church was soon brought to bear upon these ferocious barbarians. As soon as they became Christians they were compelled to release their slaves. See too, in the contests of the Bishops and the Church of England, with the Norman Kings; they held in abject slavery almost the whole population of England. The Bishops were the friends of the oppressed, and some even sacrificed their lives in behalf of oppressed humanity. We have an eminent instance in the modern history of the Church, where, really believing the doctrine of "Communion of Saints," and acting under the influence of its truth, St. Vincent of Paul *permitted himself to be made a slave*, that he might go and carry the consolations of the Gospel to those who had been made slaves for their crimes. For many centuries it continued to be the Church's rule, that whenever a slave became converted and was baptized, he became a free man.* From these few facts, selected from many hundreds of the like kind, we are sure, that many of the most eminent Saints, of all ages of the Church, have been the friends of the oppressed—have done what they could to mitigate the evils of slavery, and, whenever it was possible, to release men from bondage. We see not how they could have done otherwise, if they really believed that every individual, whether bond or free, that had been renewed after the image of Christ and been received into his Church, had become a part of himself; of the body of which He is Head. "If one member suffered, the other members suffered with it."

There are in these United States about three millions of persons of African extraction. The ancestors of these people were brought here from Africa, as slaves. In these northern States slavery has gradually been abolished; in some of the western States it has never existed. These descendants of Africans with us are all said to be free. In the southern States, slavery exists, as it ever has, in all its rigor. Some few colored persons are free, so called; but so great are the difficulties, created by the law, of liberating slaves, that the number of free persons of color diminishes rather than increases.† It is computed that there are two and a half millions of slaves and four hundred thousand of free persons of color in these United States. In these, there are twenty-seven Prelates of the Roman Communion and twenty-nine of the Anglican Communion; the one holding their Apostolical succession through the Roman branch of the Church; the other through the Anglican. There are subject to the former eight hundred and ninety-two Priests, and to the latter about fourteen

---

* In some of the Southern States this humane provision of the Christian law has been expressly repealed by Statute.

† In many Slave States it is unlawful to manumit a slave unless he consent to go out of the state; or, I believe in some cases, he must go to Liberia.

hundred and twenty-seven, making in all fifty-six Prelates and two thousand three hundred and nineteen clergy in these United States.

Many thousands of our most distinguished public men, men of influence and character, belong to one or other of these communions and attend upon the public ministry or service of these prelates and clergy. These all, both clergy and laity, in their daily or weekly religious service, before God's holy altar, in his Church, renew their oaths of fidelity to Him and the Church, by repeating the Apostle's Creed and say, "I believe in the Holy Catholic Church; the Communion of Saints."

Now, I would ask, how have those, who profess this faith, discharged the duties which we have seen are required by the Holy Scriptures, towards this class of their fellow christians and fellow men? Here, in these northern States, free States, so called, what is the actual and true state of the case, as regards the colored people. I will not speak of their deprivation of many civil rights, which all others enjoy, but I shall speak of their religious privileges. Here, in many of our cities, we have established *colored* churches with *colored* persons in Holy Orders to serve in them. Now, why was this separation of Christians made, and why continued on account of color? Is it not purposely to keep these latter in a separate external communion? Is it not on purpose to perpetuate caste in the Christian Church? Indeed, this is all but openly avowed in the report of the committee of the convention of the Episcopal Church in New-York, upon the application of one of these Churches to be admitted to the convention.*

Who would say that the colored Churches enjoy the same privileges as Churches, or that the individuals composing them take the same rank as Christians, as the members of white Churches, or of those individuals belonging to white Churches? Then, what shall we say of those persons of color admitted to Holy Orders? We have a Theological Seminary, where it is thought the Students enjoy peculiar advantages of a literary and theological

---

* Appendix A.

nature, and where some think their religious and pious habits are improved and strengthened. To this Seminary, a young man of color, though he be baptized with the baptism of the blessed Jesus, both with water and the Spirit—though he have received grace and strength by the imposition of the chief pastor's hands—though he have received the body and blood of his once sacrificed Saviour and Lord—though thus his humanity is exalted to a participation of the Divine Nature, and though he be hereby enabled to live godly, righteously and soberly, yet he cannot be admitted because his skin is not as clear and his complexion as bright as others, who are permitted to enjoy these opportunities for intellectual, moral and religious improvement? What a comment this upon the doctrine of "Communion of Saints!" Such are compelled to seek their education where best they can obtain it.—When such have received Holy Orders, they are empowered to admit members into this Holy Fellowship of which we have spoken; to "remit or retain sins;" to offer the Holy Sacrifice on God's Altar, and to distribute to penitent sinners the bread of life. They are to stand in the immediate presence of Christ at His Altar, to intercede for the people. This is their high calling in the Church of Christ. But they can only do this in the presence of colored persons; to permit such to minister in white congregations would, even now by many, be considered an outrage upon decency.* How is this feeling and this practice at variance with the doctrine of "Communion of Saints." How earnest should be our prelates and clergy to enforce upon their hearers the importance of carrying out the principles involved in the belief of this doctrine. The Church with us should take the lead in abolishing all those remaining distinctions on account of color, which interfere with a cordial reception of this doctrine and the full enjoyment of every Chris-

---

* In one of our northern Churches, the priest happened accidentally, on administering the Holy Elements at the Communion, to deliver them to a colored communicant when one white woman had not received—she rejected the offered bread, because it had not first been given her. This produced such a prejudice against the pastor that he was obliged to leave the place.

tian and Spiritual privilege by each member of the Body of Christ. If the laity are brought to see their duty as *Christians*, they will soon be convinced of it as *Statesmen;* then, all those laws which tend to continue caste, and all those customs which pepetuate it, will soon, with us, be done away. Of the whole number of prelates and clergy in both branches of the Catholic Church, eight hundred and twenty-eight are now exercising their holy functions and preaching the gospel of "peace and good will" among men in the southern part of this Union. Their congregations are composed, for the most part, of persons of influence and intelligence. Indeed, I think we may say that if we consider the Anglican Church as it exists in most of these states, and the Roman Church as it exists in Maryland, Louisiana and Missouri, it may be affirmed with confidence, that the persons who attend on the congregations connected with these Churches exercise a great influence, and if united on this one subject, would exercise a controlling power over the civil and religious institutions there existing. Let it be remembered that it is professed by all these persons, "I believe in the Holy Catholic Church; the Communion of Saints." Within the part of the country where this doctrine is or ought to be proclaimed are, as we have said, two and a half millions of slaves. I am willing to admit that many of these clergy do labor for the spiritual good of this colored race—all thanks and all praise be to them for this. Let us consider under what disadvantages these labor in prosecuting their "labor of love." I am compelled to bring into view the state of the slave laws as they exist, to show that so long as these laws remain in force, but little hope need be entertained of any success in extending the Catholic Church among those who are subjected to them. God forbid that I should refer to them for the sake of exciting hostility or hatred towards those who permit them to remain, but rather, should this discourse ever reach such as these, to exhort them to labor day and night for their amelioration or repeal. From a work written by a lawyer condensing the laws by which slaves and people of color are governed, (for there is one set of laws for whites and another for blacks, even though they be free,) I make extract of the following propositions, which bring prominently to view the general character of these laws.

I. "The master may determine the kind and degree of labor to which the slave shall be subjected.

II. The master may supply the slave with such food and clothing only, both as to quantity and quality, as he may think proper or find convenient.

III. The master may, at his discretion, inflict any punishment upon the person of his slave.

IV. All the power of the master over his slave may be exercised, not by himself only in person, but by any one whom he may depute as his agent.

V. Slaves have no legal right of property in things, real or personal; but whatever they may acquire belongs, in point of law, to their masters.

VI. The slave, being a personal chattel, is at all times liable to be sold absolutely, or mortgaged, or leased, at the will of his master.

VII. He may be sold, by process of law, for the satisfaction of the debts of a living, or the debts and bequests of a deceased master, at the suit of creditors or legatees.

VIII. A slave cannot be a party before a judicial tribunal, in any species of action, against his master, no matter how atrocious may have been the injury received from him.

IX. Slaves cannot redeem themselves nor obtain a change of master, though cruel treatment may have rendered such a change necessary for their personal safety.

X. Slaves, being objects of property, if injured by third persons, their owners may bring suit for the injury.

XI. Slaves can make no contract.

XII. Slavery is hereditary and perpetual."

All the laws to regulate the intercourse between slaves and their masters are based upon these propositions. These laws are exceedingly severe in the penalties which they inflict. They recognize the unlimited right of the master over the person of his slaves, or his creditor, or assignee, or executor to sell them in any way, young or old, married or unmarried, to be transported, if the purchaser will, to any part of these United States where slavery is established. Hence, it often happens that such sales are made solely with reference to the greatest amount of money to be realized. If this can be effected by the separation of father and mother from their children or from one another, it is done without scruple.* In most of the principal cities from Baltimore to the extreme south, there are slave marts, where hundreds and thousands, young and old, are exposed for sale by those who have purchased them on speculation. I will mention no other of the many, many hardships and sufferings which slaves are called to endure under the operation of these laws. Those who are called free persons of color, though they may not be sold as others are, yet are under the most rigid restraints, and are governed by laws almost as severe. To all persons of color, either slaves or free, it is unlawful to communicate the elements of learning. The individual who instructs such to read or write, is liable to conviction as a public offender.—But, my hearers, I will go no farther into detail; it is a subject on which I delight not to dwell; I have said enough to show you what is the real condition of colored people in our southern States. Recollect, then, that some of these very persons have been baptized into the Body of Christ, have received His Body and His Blood and are one with Him and one with us, as the members of His one Body. He died to redeem them as well as us—to raise their fallen humanity, that they may become Saints here and heirs of His kingdom hereafter. Such, no doubt, some of them are.

In view of all this, let us look at the practical operation

---

* An acquaintance was travelling in Virginia—he met a large number of youths of both sexes, from ten to fourteen years of age. They were under the charge of DRIVERS. He said, "where bound?" "To Alabama." "These slaves are all young," said our friend. "O, yes! we find it most profitable to buy young negroes and take advantage of their growth." Some of these children perhaps, had Christian parents, and had been, by Christ's ministers, "baptised into His Body," made His "children and inheritors of the Kingdom of Heaven." They were torn from their parents and consigned over to the drivers, to be sold on speculation. What an awful thought, to sell and make merchandize of parts of the Body of Christ!!!

of what are called efforts to extend the Church in this quarter, among these people. Bishops and Clergy have not been found in any great number, who defend this system. Many are the number of those who are doing what they can to instruct these oppressed human beings. Some of our Bishops have framed catechisms, to be taught them orally. Many of our Clergy labor among these people, by teaching them to repeat their catechisms, to join *memoriter* in parts of the Church service, and they read and explain to them the Scriptures. According to their reports, they succeed frequently in adding numbers of such to the communion of the Church, and we hope to the Communion of Saints. They tell them, that it is the duty of every truly penitent sinner to be baptised with water and the Spirit, and to give his children to God, that in Holy Baptism they may receive the gift of the Holy Ghost, and be grafted into the Body of Christ. Those who are fit to be confirmed, he presents to the Bishop for confirmation. Such young persons as come to him desiring to be united in Holy Matrimony, he marries. Those that give evidence that "Christ is in them," and who lead holy and godly lives, he admits to partake of the ever blessed Sacrament of His Body and Blood.

Trace now the progress of a single individual through this training of the Church. In infancy, he is baptized; his parents or sponsors were made to promise that he shall be taught the Creed, the Lord's Prayer and the Ten Commandments; that he shall, at a suitable age, be brought to the Bishop to be confirmed by him. When he comes to confirmation, the Bishop says: "Defend this thy servant with thy heavenly grace; may he continue thine for ever, and daily increase in thy Holy Spirit more and more, until he come to thine everlasting kingdom." He comes to his Pastor to be united in Holy Matrimony, and he is made to promise to live with his partner till *death do them part*. I ask, how can a minister of the Church require these promises of his Christian brethren, when he knows that the children do not belong to the parent, nor wives to their husbands, and that at the will of the master, or in consequence of his embarrassment, or debt, these ties may at once be rent asunder; the father sold to one, the mother to another, the children to others, and all perhaps to go to Texas or other parts, where they can never enjoy the small Christian privileges which they have have had?

How discouraging this to a minister if he have a real and firm belief in this doctrine of Communiou of Saints. What a damper must this thought, that all these promises and all these exhortations may have been made or given for nought, cast over all his efforts.*

_{* I wish to enforce this idea with a few examples. Bishop Meade of Virginia, one of our Evangelical Bishops, was once a slaveholder. He has given his slaves freedom on condition, of course, that they leave the state; some have gone to Liberia. Now I do not know whether Bishop M. believes the Catholic doctrine, but I suppose he holds a doctrine of "Communion of Saints." Suppose one of his brethren in Christ, when he offered to him the alternative of perpetual banishment from his home, his family and his friends, or else continued slavery, had said "my dear pastor, you taught me that as a Christian I must do to others as I would have them do to me. Now, how would you like to have banishment or slavery offered to you, and you be compelled to choose either one or the other?" Says the Bishop, "But you know that the law is such, I cannot give you freedom except on this condition." Says the slave, "But who makes and alters laws? what have you said or done to try to procure the repeal of such a law?" What could the Bishop say?}

Go a little farther South. Here resides our Evangelical brother Barnwell of Charleston, S. C. He established a paper to disseminate the blessed doctrine of God's sovereign grace. Would not his paper have been more useful, had it inculcated the doctrine of "Communion of Saints?" He and his congregation, which is composed of some of the most distinguished and influential laymen in the State, have contributed one thousand dollars per annum, to support Bishop Boone in China. Suppose an intelligent Chinaman were to say to Bishop B.: "Is it true, that in the country from which you came to convert us to your religion, millions of men, women and children are slaves—have no rights as men and are bought and sold like beasts of burden?" He would be compelled to say "yes." He might be asked, "Did you raise your voice against this evil? Do those who send you here, strive to procure the repeal of those laws, which, heathens as we are, we should reject with horror?" What could Bishop B. say to this?

Go a little farther South. We find that Bishop Elliott established a literary institution where young men were to be educated for the ministry, to be supported by slave labor. Suppose Bishop E. to have succeeded in the conversion of some of these slave laborers, might not one have said, "Bishop E. is it not hard for one, whom

What then is to be done when such a state of things exists in the Catholic Church? We apprehend the mission of these Prelates and these Clergy is first of all to the whites; to those who wield the power of making and altering the laws.. The excuse, usually made by the Clergy to justify those practices which seem to be, and really are, inconsistent with the divine precept of " doing unto others as we would wish they would do unto us," is, that they must submit to the civil law. Granted—but who makes the law? Do not the members of the Catholic Church constitute a large proportion of law makers? The Clergy should constantly, unitedly, and perseveringly, insist upon the repeal of every law, *which imposes a burden on their Christian slave brethren, that they would not willingly submit to, if they were slaves themselves.*

The painful question now comes up, how has this duty, in our whole country been discharged? Where have you call a brother in Christ, to work hard with no pay, to be exposed to all the hardships of the slave law, not to be even the owner of his wife and children, that these young men may be educated to preach the gospel of peace and good will?" He would say, "It is so indeed, but the law is so and I cannot help it." He might say, "What have you done or said in opposition to this law, where have you protested against this injustice done to your fellow Christians?"

Go farther South. Bishop Polk, who is said to be a most amiable person, is the owner (so reported) of three hundred and fifty slaves. We have no reason to think that he does not attend to their spiritual and temporal interest as a kind master should. Suppose one of these of the number of his own communicants, one whom he himself had baptized and confirmed and admitted to the Holy Eucharist, should say, " My dear master, I feel my situation to be very insecure, at present; I am happy under your care; I have the company of my wife and children; but suppose death were to remove you or misfortune to overtake you, then, what is to become of me and mine? Where, then, will be the Christian privileges which I now enjoy as a member of the Body of Christ?" The Bishop might say, " I know the laws which prevail here, are severe and seem to be at variance with the teaching and practice of the Church, but I did not make them " " But who sits still and permits these laws to remain in all their severity? What have you even said or done to call the attention of Christian people to their enormity and effect their repeal?"

15*

been the Prelates, where the Clergy, of either branch of the Church, that have had the Christian fortitude and boldness, fearlessly to preach the doctrine of Communion of Saints, and insist upon the discharge, by the members of their flocks, of the duties required by its belief? There have not been wanting those who have palliated and excused these customs and these laws in the United States, by which one class of Christian brethren in *the North* are purposely kept as a distinct, separate and neglected people; in *the South* are oppressed with bondage "grievous to be borne," and are compelled to submit to laws and injuries a parallel to which cannot be found upon earth.*

But where have been the exhortations, the counsel, and the instructions of the Clergy of the Church? In the Pastoral Letters of our House of Bishops, which ought to have great influence in this land, we look in vain for an allusion to this subject.†

These laws and these uncatholic practices have existed since our country called itself free and independent. When and where has any portion of the Church, through its accredited organs, the Bishops and the conventions within its boundaries, entered its solemn protest against this oppression and degradation of some portion of her own members, even the members of the Body of Christ? It is not to be desired that the Church, as a Church, should enter upon a crusade against slavery, and should denounce all those, who, perhaps not by their own consent, are owners of slaves. But she ought, where slavery does exist, to insist that the laws should be so altered, as to give to her colored members the privileges to which they are entitled as co-members with themselves of the "Body of Christ," and where it does not exist, that all those practices, and customs, and exclusions, be abolished, which tend to separate one Christian flock from communion, as Christians, with another.

If the united voice of the Church were put forth it would be heard, it would be regarded. If the exertions of

---

* Even in Cuba the laws are far less severe.
† Appendix B.

every Catholic in this land were directed to ameliorate the condition of the slave and to elevate the character of the colored people—if their prayers were unitedly to ascend before His throne in whose hand are the hearts of all men, that He would dispose all Christian Rulers to " do justly, and to love mercy," then might we hepe to see this all important doctrine of " the Communion of Saints" held, not as a speculative theory, but as a living, acting, and influential principle. God grant that we may live to see this '

APPENDIX TO DISCOURSE.

THE CASE OF ST. PHILIP'S CHURCH, N. Y.

A.—St. Philip's Church in the year A. D. 1846, made application to be admitted into the Convention of the Episcopal Church of New York. It was moved by the Hon. John C. Spencer to lay the *subject on the table.* This was not carried, the vote stood: Clergy, ayes 54 noes 88—Laity, Ayes 70 noes 54. The application was referred to a select committee to report to the convention, consisting of Wm. H. Harison, Esq., Rev. E. M. Johnson, Rev. Dr. Sherwood, the Hon. J. C. Spencer and John A. King, Esq. The following was the report of a majority of the committee.

REPORT: COMMITTEE ON ST. PHILIP'S CHURCH.

The Committee to which was referred the subject of the admission of St. Philip's, and other colored congregations, into representation in the Convention of this Diocese, report:

That in their view, the question referred to them is one exclusively relating to the temporal government of the Diocese, and is wholly unconnected with the religious rights or duties of the applicants. The Convention is but a part of what may be called the civil machinery, instituted by human wisdom, for the purpose of regulating the Society, by which, and for whose benefit, it was established. It is no more a part of our Church in this country, in a religious view, than are the civil establishments and the connection with the government in England, part of the Church there. In both countries the arrangements for the administration of the government of the Church are the result of experience and adaptation to circumstances. Among the considerations of expediency, which any body of men, uniting together for a common purpose, would deem the most important, must be that of determining with whom they would associate, and who should be permitted to participate in the government of the Society. Thus, for reasons of expediency, females, however worthy, are by our canons excluded from being representatives in our Convention, and are, by law, incapable of being incorporated as members of Churches. Candidates for orders, are, by a canon of the General Convention, prohibited from being members of that body. These instances are sufficient to illustrate the principle on which our Church organizations are founded, and to show that they are entirely distinct from the religious rights and spiritual privileges of those, who, in a spiritual view, are members of our Churches. If it be an incident to Church membership to be represented in the councils of the Church, then have we, in common with all Christian denominations, from the time of the Apostles, unjustly and tyrannically deprived female members of sacred rights.

When society is unfortunately divided into classes—when some are intelligent, refined, and elevated, in tone and character, and others are ignorant, coarse, and debased, however unjustly, and when such prejudices exist between them, as to prevent social intercourse on equal terms, it would seem inexpedient to encounter such prejudices, unnecessarily, and endeavor to compel the one class to associate on equal terms in the consultations on the affairs of the Diocese, with those whom they would not admit to their tables, or into their family circles—nay, whom they would not admit into their pews, during public worship. If Christian duty require that we should in all respects, treat equally, all persons, without reference to their social condition, should we not commence the discharge of that duty in our individual and social relations? And is it not the fact that we have never so regarded our duty or have wilfully violated it, sufficient evidence of the existence of a state of society among us that renders an amalgamation of such discordant materials, impracticable, if not hazardous to our unity and harmony? We deeply sympathize with the colored race in our country, we feel acutely their wrongs, and, not the least among them, their social degradation. But this cannot prevent our seeing the fact, that they *are* socially degraded, and are not regarded as proper associates for the class of persons who attend our Convention. We object not to the color of the skin, but we question their possession of those qualities which would render their intercourse with the members of a Church Convention useful or agreeable, even to themselves. We should make the same objections to persons of the same social class, however pure may be their blood, or however transparent their skin. It is impossible, in the nature of things, that such opposites should commingle with any pleasure or satisfaction to either. The colored people have themselves shown their conviction of this truth, by separating themselves from the whites, and forming distinct congregations where they are not continually humbled by being treated as inferiors. Why should not the principle on which they have separated themselves be carried out in the other branches of our Church organization?

Striking instances are furnished in the early, and indeed in every period of the history of the Christian Church, of conformity in outward things, and in matters not essential, to the customs, usages, and even prejudices of the age. We have in our own country inveterate customs and prejudices, on the subject under consideration, which cannot be overcome. Is it not the part of wisdom to submit to them until, by a change of circumstances, the occasion for them shall cease to exist? Would not our present duty to this unfortunate race, be fully performed by extended and liberal efforts to improve their mind and their condition by intellectual culture, by religious instruction, and as they advance in intelligence and refinement, by relaxing the severities of *caste*, which now separate us, until by degrees they become fitted for the duties and enjoyments of a higher social condition; and then admit them, in our public and private intercourse, to free and equal communion.

The efforts of zealous philanthropists to break down the barriers which custom has interposed, and which have so long existed between the colored and other races, and against the laws of society, and the sentiments and feelings of the community, to compel an unnatural and forced equality, have hitherto been attended with results equally unfortunate to the peculiar objects of their solicitude, and to the great interests and beneficient institutions, in connection with which such efforts have been made. They have been directed to our common schools; and not satisfied with the abundant provision which has, in many places, been made for the education of colored children, their special friends and advocates have insisted that they should be admitted to the schools of white children, and have thus caused dissensions and conflict to the great injury of those institutions, while fee'ings of sympathy and commiseration have been too frequently converted into disgust and anger.

Efforts of a similar character, and for the same purpose, have been made to give position in our Churches to colored people, which would compel association and intercourse with them. It is obvious that such movements are but incipient steps to ulterior objects in relation to the vexed and irritating subject of slavery. Beginning with simple and apparently just propositions respecting the abstract rights of this portion of our population, their professed friends and advocates have advanced, step by step, until they have prepared the way to agitate the bold question of the Christian character of those whose sentiments do not accord with their own. The rending asunder of Churches—the disruption of societies—bitter animosities, and all manner of uncharitableness, have been the invariable results.

By the wise and prudent counsels of the Fathers of our Church, *our denomination!!* has been hitherto happily free from the agitation of these and kindred questions—such as temperance, or abstinence from liquors and wine—and the consequences have been peace and quiet among ourselves, and the respect of others. An instance of this caution is furnished in the case of St Philip's Church, whose application to be represented in the Convention is now under consideration. It appears from the minutes of the Standing Committee of this diocese, that in March, 1819, on the application of the lamented Bishop Hobart to that committee for advice in relation to the admission of a colored person as a candidate for Holy Orders, they unanimously advised his admission, upon the distinct understanding, that in the event of his being admitted to Orders, he should not "be entitled to a seat in the convention, nor the congregation of which he may have charge, to a representation therein." It is understood that these conditions were approved by the bishop, and were assented to by the applicant and the congregation. And although that church has been organized, and in existence for more than a quarter of a century, it has, until now, abided by the terms thus settled. The present applicants, it is presumed, were not aware of these arrangements, as it is not to be supposed that they would intentionally be guilty of a violation of good faith. Thus, for this long period, has this question been actually and peaceably settled, and remained undisturbed.

The legal, moral, and equitable right of the convention to determine what churches it will admit into union, so as to entitle them to a representation in this body, seems to your committee unquestionable. The fourth canon provides certain indispensable conditions to entitle any church to admission—but no where is it declared that these are the only conditions—and the invariable practice of the convention in taking the vote upon the admission of any church, shows that it has reserved to itself the right of judging of the expediency of the measure, after all the former requisites are complied with. Otherwise the report of the committee, certifying to the fact of such compliance, would be in itself conclusive. The provision in the same canon, requiring the preliminary approbation of the bishop or of the standing committee "of the incorporation of such church," relates only to the separate and independent existence of the congregation as a corporate body, and not to its union with or representation in this convention.

Besides, the very requirements of the canon,—that churches shall be politically incorporated, before admission into union with the Convention, shows conclusively that the right of admission is subject to regulation, and therefore that such question is one purely of expediency, and not one of Christian privilege or right.

Cases may easily be conceived, and such have actually occurred, where it would not only be highly inexpedient, but grossly unjust to existing churches, to admit into union new applicants. Various circumstances, more or less important, will necessarily enter into the consideration of the convention in determining such a question.

In the short time allowed the committee to consider the subject, and to express their views, they have been unable to give such a full exhibition of all the considerations which present themselves as they would have desired. They think, however, that they have said enough to cause reflection, and to show how full of difficulty would be the adoption of the principle in relation to St. Philip's Church, or any other colored congregation, of admitting their representatives to seats in this Convention. If once here they would be entitled to all the consideration, and to participate in all the duties and stations to which members may be assigned, or we shall practically repudiate the principle which admitted them. It is not believed that this convention, for instance, would send one of them as a deputy to the General Convention, on account of the offence it would occasion to our brethren of other dioceses. Thus, their condition would be practically and continually one of inferiority and humiliation—more painfully aggravated by the expectation induced by an act which apparently promised their perfect equality. Your committee do not believe that such an equality can be produced—that in the nature of things it can exist in this community—great and palpable inequality must prevail to the extent of preventing the colored race from any active participation in our Church government—and they believe that an attempt to correct it, contrary to the feelings and customs of our country, would not only be abortive, but would be attended with the worst consequences to our unity, our harmony, and our efficiency. They, therefore, recommend that neither St. Philip's, nor any other colored congregation, be admitted into union with this Convention, so as to entitle them to a representation therein. The consequence of such a determination probably will be, that such Churches and congregations will not be responsible to, or under the government or control of this convention, but will remain subject to the ordinary jurisdiction of their bishop—and when their members become adequate, may have church councils of their own for their own peculiar government.

All which is respectfully submitted,
WM. H. HARISON,
REUBEN SHERWOOD,
J. C. SPENCER.

New-York, Oct. 2, 1846.

This report was *never submitted to the Committee at all.* The minority report was drawn up without a knowledge of what the majority report would contain. Its author hardly need say that this is entirely opposed to the doctrine of "Communion of Saints," and to the exercise of those Christian graces which a belief of it imposes upon the members of the Catholic Church. The following is the minority report.

MINORITY REPORT: ST. PHILIP'S CHURCH.

The undersigned, a minority of the Committee appointed by this Convention of the Protestant Episcopal Church in the Diocese of New-York, to consider the application of St. Philip's Church in this city, to be admitted into communion with this Convention, do hereby Report:

That they regret exceedingly to be obliged to differ from the majority of said Committee. They do not make this report with a view of exciting or encouraging any discussion in this Convention of topics, in no way connected with the subject of this application. About thirty years ago, a congregation of colored people was organized in this city as an Episcopal Church, with the approbation of the Episcopal Authority of this Diocese. It has continued since to conform to the doctrines, worship, and usages of this Church most uniformly and constantly. It now asks to be admitted to enjoy what its members consider to be the privileges which other Churches have, of being received into the full fellowship of their Christian brethren, by admission to this Convention. The minority of your Committee do not hesitate to say, that, although at the time of the organizing of this congregation, it was thought to be a wise and salutary measure, yet in their opinion, subsequent events should lead us to doubt the propriety or expediency of such organization.

It is now too late to undo, in this particular, what has been done. The minority of your Committee can see no reason why this application should not be granted, and think there are special reasons why it should.

It is said that it was stipulated on the part of individuals of that congregation at the time of its organization, or before the ordination of the late pious and reverend Mr. Williams, that they would not apply for admission into this Convention. This we believe *they* did not do; but we cannot conceive how the present generation, belonging to that Church, can be bound by any stipulation of that kind, made by those who, we trust, have long since departed hence in the Lord, and been received into communion with the saints in Paradise. The present members of that Church do not think as their fathers did on that subject. It may be said that if this Church be admitted, others will be organized and apply for admission. However much this is to be regretted, yet we suppose such will be the fact, and on this very account, this subject merits the very serious consideration of this Convention. Suppose Churches, now to be composed of colored people exclusively, are organized in our principal cities—suppose they are refused equal Christian privileges with other Episcopal Churches—that the Conventions of our Dioceses refuse to take them under their charge, and into their fellowship—will not these Churches unite and form a Convention of their own? Will they not choose a Bishop or Bishops of their own? And *under such circumstances*, would they find any difficulty in obtaining Apostolical succession? We fear the refusal of our Convention to admit into their fellowship this portion of their Christian brethren, will inevitably lead to a schism in the Church, by the establishment of another Episcopal Church in these United States. All must admit this would be a sore evil.

The minority of your Committee beg the Convention to pause before they take a step which may lead to such a disastrous result.

It may well be asked, Can it be that because those who seek admission here are of a different race and complexion from ourselves, that doubts are entertained of the expediency of admitting them to union with this Convention? Have they not the Bible for their guide? Do they read in it that its divine precepts, its universal charity, its promised rewards, are limited to any race or nation? Was not the Gospel vouchsafed to all men, to be proclaimed to all nations?

The minority of your Committee expressly disavow any other motive in thus recommending the admission of this Church, than that of promoting peace and harmony, and carrying out into practice the great Catholic doctrine of intercommunion of saints, as taught in the Bible, the word of God. These persons who apply for this fellowship have been made, in Holy Baptism, "members of Christ, children of God, and inheritors of the kingdom of heaven"— they "eat his flesh and drink his blood," and thus are incorporated into Him; with us, they are one with Him, and He is one with them. However just and proper distinctions in society may be in other respects, yet as members of one Holy Catholic Church, there ought to be no other distinction than that made by superior self-denial, holiness and virtue.

The minority of your Committee would deprecate most earnestly any prolonged or excited discussions of this subject, or the introduction of questions not necessarily connected with it, and recommend that this Church be admitted into union with this Convention.

All of which is respectfully submitted,
EVAN M. JOHNSON,
JOHN A. KING.

New-York, Oct. 2, 1846.

Had the author of this last report been permitted to know the contents of the former, he would have corrected some of its *misstatements* and called special attention to some of its *strange positions*. He will endeavor to do this now. It is not true, that this question "is wholly unconnected with the religious rights or duties of the applicants," or that our Conventions are "civil machinery." I ask, who elects our Bishop? Who elects the delegates to our General Convention? All the rites of the Church and its liturgy may be changed, or modified by this body—doctrines set forth and duties prescribed by these, the Bishops and Conventions; and yet we are told, in this report, that our Convention is only to regulate "the Society" and is like the *Parliament* in England in respect to the Church in England. Had it been said that our State Conventions were like the Provincial Synods of Great Britain, this would have been true. I ask if the Bishops, in the West Indies, were to call a meeting of a Provincial Synod, is it probable that they would call only the *white* clergymen of their Dioceses?

One would, from this report, think that this application for admission was from the *females* of St. Philip's Church. This is not true. I suppose the females of that congregation wish to be represented as other females are, by their fathers, and husbands, and brothers.

We hardly know what to say to this. "We object not *to the color of the skin*, but we question their possession of those *qualities* which would render their intercourse with the members of *a* Church Convention useful or agreeable, even to themselves." What qualities are here meant? Do none of them possess those "qualities" which our Saviour recognizes in them as all sufficient to make them members of His body? They may have these, but these are not the qualities which they must have to belong to *a* Church Convention. I am glad it is said *a* Church and not *the* Church Convention.

I have striven in vain to reconcile the following passage with other parts of this report and with the rejection of this Church which it recommends, " Would not our present duty to this unfortunate race be fully performed by extended and liberal efforts to improve their mind and condition, by intellectual culture, by religious instruction, and, as they advance in intelligence and refinement, by relaxing the severities of *caste*, which now separate us, until, by degrees, they become fitted for the duties and enjoyments of a higher social condition, and then, admit them in our public and private intercourse, to free and equal communion?" I answer to this question, yes, it would be—and the best time to begin to discharge this duty is, now: and by rejecting the recommendation of this majority report, convince our brethren that our intention is sincere and not a mere profession of words.

When the author of the minority report wrote of the possibility, if this Church were rejected, of the establishment of another Church, he did not know that the very thing itself would be recommended by the majority.

"The consequence of such a determination (to refuse admittance) probably will be, that such Churches and congregations will not be responsible to, or under the government or control of this Convention, but will remain subject to the ordinary jurisdiction of *their* Bishop—and when their members become adequate, may have *Church Councils* of their own for their own peculiar government," (and of course Bishops.) Here is a positive and direct recommendation to destroy the unity of the Church, rather, than to adopt the *training process* recommended in the former extract. I can only say that if the Convention of New-York adopt, as their own, the sentiments advocated in this report and the measure recommended by it, they may boast themselves as much as they please, of their adherence to Catholic truth, and speak of the sacrifices they are called to make for their defence of it; the whole Catholic Church will give them little credit for their consistency or orthodoxy. Some time during the last year, in the State of Indiana, a newspaper controversy was carried on in opposition to and in defence of the Church. It was argued by the Church opponents, that by this very report which was quoted, the Episcopal Church did not desire or expect *common people* to belong to it—that it was for those who thought themselves *select members* of Society. Let us hope and pray that our brethren of the Laity, will not be alarmed at the cry of "Abolitionism," or any other "ism;" but will strive to disarm themselves of prejudice and will pray the great Head of the Church, to preserve them from giving just cause of complaint to any, even the *weakest*, the *most oppressed*, or the most *despised* of their fellow Christians, who are, with them, members of the one Catholic and Apostolic Church in the world, which is, and which is to come.

B. SLAVERY EXTENSION.—The Christian Philanthropist will rejoice that public attention is now distinctly turned to this subject. It must be remembered that the Mexican States, when they threw off the Spanish yoke and declared themselves free and independent, did, with far more consistency than these States, abolish slavery absolutely and wholly. When the adventurers, mostly from the slave States of this Union, took possession of the State of Texas, they re-established slavery where it had for many years ceased to exist. It was admitted to this Union as slave territory. The operation of this, politically, is, that in Texas two white votes are as good as five in New-York, and the same laws by which slavery is enforced in our slave States are in operation there. Indeed it was openly declared to be one principal object in receiving Texas into this Union, to obtain a market for human beings and to extend the area of slave territory. We have now in effect conquered New Mexico and California. At present there are, in these States, no slaves. The questions now are, shall slavery be again established there, or shall it not? Shall this great region be settled by freemen wholly or by slaves and their masters? Shall those severe and cruel laws under which so many millions of men, and women, and children now suffer, be extended over this territory, or shall it be subjected to but one system of laws and those for freemen? As a political question, would any one suppose, that a *single individual* in these northern States, who calls himself a Republican, in any sense of the term, would either advocate this extension or fail to do every thing in his power, by his influence, by his vote, by his voice, and by his pen to hinder such a lasting evil and disgrace from being brought upon his country? Thank God, as a party, the pro-slavery party are few in number and becoming still fewer in influence. If worldly-minded politicians at the North are found who oppose this extension simply from political motives, I ask where are the Christian clergy at the South? What are they doing? Has one of them raised a voice against the extension of slavery? Suppose St. Vincent de Paul were, at this time, Bishop of New Orleans, would he see thousands and thousands of his fellow men and Christians, marched in chains to perpetual slavery in Texas, and not raise his voice in opposition? Would he see an immense addition to this country in his immediate neighborhood, acquired on purpose to plant the worst of slavery and to establish the severest slave laws that ever existed, and remain silent? Oh! may a spirit like his be stirred up in the breast of every Prelate and every Clergyman, that whether it cause them to be persecuted even unto death or not, they may fearlessly proclaim their opposition to every law, and every practice, and every custom, inconsistent with the cordial reception of the doctrine of "Communion of Saints" and the discharge of those duties which it enjoins.

CPSIA information can be obtained
at www.ICGtesting.com
Printed in the USA
BVOW05s1819040117
472634BV00015B/169/P